HUSTON SMITH

ESSAYS ON WORLD RELIGION

EDITED BY
M. DARROL BRYANT

PARAGON HOUSE
New York

First edition, 1992
Published in the United States by
Paragon House
90 Fifth Avenue
New York, N.Y. 10011

Copyright © 1992 by Paragon House

Library of Congress Cataloging-in-Publication Data

Smith, Huston.
    Essays on world religion / Huston Smith; edited by M. Darrol Bryant.
    — 1st ed.
          p.   cm.
    Includes bibliographical references.
    ISBN 1-55778-447-7
        1. Religions. I. Bryant, M. Darrol. II. Title
    BL87.S59 1992
                                          291—dc20
                                        91-29536
                                            CIP

Manufactured in the United States of America

HUSTON SMITH

ESSAYS ON
WORLD RELIGION

Contents

Foreword

HUSTON SMITH

The editor of this volume has asked me to precede his Introduction with a brief Foreword that situates these essays in the historical currents of our time. Since it is a personal assessment he asks for, my mind goes back to a moment on the *Today* show the morning after Irving Berlin died—at the age of one hundred, as I recall.

I was surprised to find that to reflect on the lifework of this tune-smith, *Today* had invited a world-class musician, Isaac Stern; the host of the program wanted to learn from him the secret of Irving Berlin's success. As a musician, Berlin was so mediocre that he could play only in the key of C and to move to other keys had to build a piano that could transpose by pulling levers. Yet this run-of-the-mill musician became the most successful songwriter of our time, composing over one hundred hits, many of which will outlive our century. How did Stern account for the discrepancy between Irving Berlin's achievement and his modest native talent?

Isaac Stern's answer was so direct that it was breathtaking: "To him," he said, "it was obvious."

Irving Berlin's philosophy of life, Stern went on to explain, was simple. He saw life as composed of a few basic elements: life and death, loneliness and love, hope and defeat, not many more. In making our way through these givens, affirmation is better than complaint, hope more viable than despair, kindness nobler than its opposite. That was about it. But because Berlin believed these platitudes implicitly, without reservation, he helped people cut through the ambiguities and complexities of our bewildering century.

I relate this anecdote because, on the disparity between talent and achievement together with Stern's explanation for it, my case parallels Irving Berlin's. My mind and writing ability are no more remarkable than his musical talents were, and yet, *mirabile dictu*, my essays get salvaged and reprinted—this book is here for proof. Why? The enigma needs explaining, and Stern's formula is at hand. For me in my domain, as much as for Irving Berlin's in his, things seem obvious.

What seems obvious? Some of the things relate to the human condition, and others (apropos these essays) to the study of religion.

On the human condition, it seems obvious that the finitude of mundane existence cannot satisfy the human heart completely. Built into the human makeup is a tropism for a "more" that the world of everyday experience cannot requite. This outreach implies the existence of something that life reaches *for.* Plants reach for light and bend in its direction because light exists. Comparably, people seek food because food exists; given individuals may starve, but bodies would not experience hunger if food did not exist to assuage it. The same holds for spiritual hunger.

The object that excites and fulfills the soul's longing is God, by whatsoever name. Because the human mind cannot come within light years of comprehending God's nature, we do well to follow Rainer Maria Rilke's suggestion and think of God as a direction rather than an object. The direction is always upward, toward the more, the best that we can possibly conceive. In the formula of theology's principle of analogical predication: In using objects and concepts from the natural world to symbolize God, the first step is to affirm what is positive in them, the second to deny to God what is limiting in them; and the third to elevate their positive features to supereminent degree—which is to say to the highest point that our imaginings can carry us.

With God and the world—the Absolute and the relative—categorically distinguished but nowhere disjoined, other things fall into place in ways these essays ponder. One of these ways deserves mention for running like a leit motif through the first two parts of this book; in a way (as the Editor suggests in his Introduction) it ties them together. God's unity does not require uniformity of expression; in theological terms, it does not require that God's revelations be carbon copies of one another. If it is appropriate for human beings to reveal different sides of themselves in different contexts, God must be equally versatile and considerate.

As for the study of religion, it seems obvious, first, that it suffers from the fragmentation of modern life and knowledge. Students are treated to the history of religion, the sociology of religion, the psychology of religion, and the philosophy of religion; or alternatively to courses on religious ritual, religious art, and religious language. Where are they exposed to the living reality before it is thus dismembered? Second, the study of religion suffers from the academic shibboleth that knowledge should be objective. In the natural sciences this does no harm, and even in the social sciences it doesn't twist things out of shape completely. But in the humanities, where sensibilities and meanings count for more than facts and figures, it is (if unrelieved) disastrous. Finally, religion suffers from the naturalistic ideology that the university works under. It was the displacement of revelation by science that brought the modern university into being, and to this day the university remains the stronghold of the naturalistic outlook. So teaching about religion *as a human enterprise* is countenanced, but to take seriously (as vital religion always does) a transcendent reality that relativizes the entire natural world, the university included, is academic heresy. How else are we to account for facts such as the one that came to me in a letter just this week? It reports that my correspondent's son has discontinued his religious studies major at Harvard University because it was teaching him everything about religion except why anyone would ever believe it.

To revert to the anecdote with which I began, if my writings have a certain edge, a bit of a bite to them, the reason (as far as I can make out) is the one Isaac Stern gave me words for. The features of human existence, and the failings of higher education that I have mentioned, strike me as obvious. The first are to be grasped and worked with wisely. The second should be countered with as much forthrightness and ingenuity as we can manage.

Finally, a word about the essays that Darrol Bryant has brought together here. The ones that I myself assembled in *Beyond the Post-Modern Mind* (Crossroad, 1982; revised in its 1989 Quest Book edition) centered on Transcendence: its decisiveness for religion (or any adequate view of things, for that matter) and the recent conceptual strategies that challenge its existence. I was prepared to leave matters there, but my friend, Darrol Bryant, saw what I did not see: namely, the need for a complementing set of essays that highlight the divine immanence. And highlight it in a distinctive way: by focusing on the way Transcendence has disclosed itself distinctively, in complementing modes, in history's three enduring civilizations—East Asian, South Asian, and Western. I don't in these essays stress the revealed character of these civilizations' guiding orientations, but readers who are inclined to do so will have no difficulty seeing, as I do, the divine initiative at work. Archeologists have discovered no founding city of a civilization that does not have a sacred center.

If the central thesis of these essays is correct, it marks a step toward global historical understanding; if it is mistaken, it invites criticism and correction. In either case I am deeply grateful to Darrol Bryant for showing me that the Divine Transcendence and its major historical variations have been the twin emphases in my work, and for molding my chief essays in the latter vein into the pages of this book.

Acknowledgments

This collection of essays by Huston Smith could not have been completed without the assistance and cooperation of a number of persons and institutions. From first to last, there was the unstinting cooperation and generosity of Huston Smith. He not only encouraged the project but was unfailingly helpful as he answered my many questions about his intellectual journey and about the essays included here. I want to express my gratitude to him not only for his assistance, but also for what I have learned from him and his friendship. Furthermore, as this project unfolded, I discovered that Kendra Smith was an insightful commentator on Huston's work, and I profited from her comments and her friendship as well.

At Renison College I was assisted in this project by Gill Stephens, who looked up addresses for me; by Dawn Bailey, who entered the bibliography into the computer; and by Freda Walker, who made seemingly endless copies of material for me. I am also grateful to Debbie Gollnick for her suggestions about the Introduction; to Sherryl Roth for her reminders about gender issues; and to Susan Bryant for her editorial magic in transforming some vague ideas into grammatical clarity. At Paragon, Jo Glorie was consistently helpful and understanding of the delays that slowed the completion of this project.

Finally, I wish to thank the author and the publishers for their permission to include in this volume the work of Huston Smith that first appeared in their journals and publications: The Eastern Buddhist Society for permission to include "Spiritual Discipline in Zen and Comparative Perspective" and "Four Theological Negotiables: Gleanings for Daisetz Suzuki's Posthumous Volumes on Shin Buddhism," which appeared in the *Eastern Buddhist*; the American Anthropological Association for permission to include "Unique Vocal

Abilities of Certain Tibetan Lamas," which appeared in *American Anthropologist*; The Bhaktivedanta Institute for permission to include "The Conceptual Crisis in the Modern West," which appeared in T. D. Singh and R. Gomatam, *Synthesis of Science and Religion: Critical Essays and Dialogues*; Cambridge University Press for permission to include "Transcendence in Traditional China," which appeared in the journal *Religious Studies; Religious Studies and Theology* for permission to include "Another World to Live In, or How I Teach the Introductory Course"; Scholars Press for permission to include "Wasson's Soma: A Review Article" and "Postmodernism's Impact on the Study of Religion," which appeared in the *Journal of the American Academy of Religion*; Kluwer Academic Publishers for permission to include "The Relevance of the Great Religions for the Modern World," which appeared as the introduction to F. P. Dunne (ed.) *The World Religions Speak*; Schenkman Books Inc. for permission to include the Introduction to G. Marshall, *Buddha: The Quest for Serenity*; Prentice-Hall Inc. for permission to include "Tao Now: An Ecological Testament," which appeared in Ian Barbour (ed.) *Earth Might Be Fair*; *Philosophy East and West* for gracious permission to include "Accents of the World's Philosophies," "Western and Comparative Perspectives on Truth," and "Man's Western Way: Essay on Reason and the Given"; the NCC Center for the Study of Japanese Religion for permission to include "This Ecumenical Moment: What Are We Seeking?" from their journal *Japanese Religions*; the University of Notre Dame Press for permission to include "Western Philosophy as a Great Religion," which appeared in A. Olson and L. Rouner (eds.) *Transcendence and the Sacred*; and Vedanta Press for permission to include the Foreword to *Spiritual Heritage of India*. I am grateful to them all. More information on the original place of publication of each essay is provided in the editorial note at the beginning of each entry.

Introduction

The essays collected in this volume were written by Huston Smith over more than three decades: the earliest in 1957, the latest in 1989. Collectively they bear witness to a lifetime of scholarly activity devoted to the analysis and interpretation of the religious life of humankind. Since the beginning of Huston Smith's scholarly life, it has been the religious life of humankind as a whole—rather than any particular tradition—that has attracted his attention. Smith remarked as early as 1958 (in *The Religions of Man*) that "authentic religion is the clearest opening through which the inexhaustible energies of the cosmos can pour into human existence."[1] Thus he has always looked at religion with special emphasis on the outlooks, worldviews, and patterns of thought that emerge among the many religious traditions. This attention follows, Smith observes, from a deep intuitive sympathy that is warranted by the nature of the subject.

> Religion alive confronts the individual with the most momentous option this world can present. It calls the soul to the highest venture it can undertake, a proposed journey across the jungles, peaks, and deserts of the human spirit. The call is to confront reality; to master the self. Those who dare to hear and follow this secret call soon learn the dangers and difficulties of its lonely journey.[2]

Over a lifetime of scholarship, Huston Smith has turned time and again to the religious life of humankind to explore its many and varied insights into reality. In the religious traditions, he has found challenging patterns of thought and life that enliven perception and give rise to the experience of meaning.

Trained in the philosophy of religion and comparative methods,

Huston Smith has explored the religions of humankind with an eye to their truth. This stance goes against the dominant tendencies of the modern academy. The modern study of religion has insisted that our study of religion should be descriptive alone and that the question of truth should be bracketed. Smith, as these essays reveal, does not share this pervasive assumption. Instead, he assumes that the religious traditions are attempting to speak truthfully, in the varied meanings of that term, about their perception of life's meanings and about the Ultimate itself.

Thus Smith seeks to discern the particular contributions of the diverse traditions to universal issues and to the human quest for meaning. These sustained endeavors resulted in some remarkable books—most notably *The Religions of Man* (now *The World's Religions*) and *Forgotten Truth: The Primordial Tradition*—and a host of essays that appeared throughout the 1960s, 1970s, and 1980s. While we have ready access to Smith's books, his articles are less accessible.

The nineteen essays collected here reveal the range of Huston Smith's contributions to the hermeneutical or interpretive science of comparative religion and philosophy. They also provide an intellectual archeology for understanding the process that led from *The Religions of Man* in 1958 to *Forgotten Truth* in 1973 and then to *Beyond the Post-Modern Mind* in 1982. For students of Huston Smith and for those who have read his books, this collection will be immensely valuable as a further insight into his study of diverse traditions. Students of comparative religion and philosophy will find here something of Smith's contribution to this difficult area of study. The volume also includes the most comprehensive bibliography of Huston Smith's writings currently available.

Huston Smith's classic study *The Religions of Man* deserves a special word. First published in 1958, it has been widely used in colleges and universities throughout the United States and Canada and widely read by the general public. It has been continuously in print since it was first published and has been translated into Swedish, Korean, Danish, Pakistani; and Indonesian. Its current edition, retitled *The World's Religions* contains significant additions.[3] The work's sympathetic and insightful presentation of the spiritual heart of seven great traditions—Hinduism, Buddhism, Confucianism, Taoism, Islam, Judaism, Christianity, and in the new edition the primal, oral traditions—has made it a popular success as well as an academic benchmark for the empathetic portrayal of the great traditions of religious life. *The World's Religions* is largely responsible for making Huston Smith one of the most widely read scholars of the world's religious traditions.

Although no other of his publications has the widespread readership of *The World's Religions,* it is important to underscore the importance of his later work, *Forgotten Truth: The Primordial Tradition.* Smith himself saw this as the companion work to his earlier study. He writes as follows in the preface to *Forgotten Truth:*

> Twenty years ago I wrote a book, *The Religions of Man,* which presented the world's enduring traditions in their individuality and variety. It has taken me until now to see how they converge. The outlooks of individual men and women... are too varied even to classify, but when they gather in collectivities— the outlooks of tribes, societies, civilizations, and at deepest level the world's great religions—these collective outlooks admit of overview. What then emerges is a remarkable unity underlying the surface variety."[4]

The World's Religions and *Forgotten Truth,* therefore, provide the bookends for this current collection of his papers. The twofold principle reflected in these two works is the unity and diversity of the spiritual life of humankind.

What is the nature of the unity of the diverse religious traditions of humankind? Is there unity or is there simply sheer multiplicity? These are vital but difficult questions, ones that Huston Smith allows us to see in new ways—at least new in relation to the currently dominant views of the academy. The argument that emerges in Smith's work is that unity and diversity are not two opposing principles but rather two aspects of a single truth. For Smith, the spiritual life of humankind simultaneously bears witness to the unity of Transcendence as it is manifest in the very diversity of the spiritual traditions of humankind.

This understanding of the relationship of unity and diversity is, I believe, one of Smith's crucial contributions to the methodology of comparative studies. Unity and diversity are not, as most assume, alternatives. Rather, in relation to the spiritual life of humankind, they are complementary. This insight has important methodological implications for the study of religion, for it challenges the more relativistic and reductionist assumptions characteristic of comparative study. The relativist assumption sees the diversity of the religious traditions of humankind as evidence of sheer multiplicity. The reductionist assumption explains this diversity by an appeal to psychological, sociological, economic, or cultural factors rather than to any transcendental factor. Smith's study of religions and their philosophical assumptions, on the other hand, moves us beyond these prevalent assumptions. The insight that gradually emerges in Smith's work is that the variety in religions does not contradict a singular Transcendence. Instead, it witnesses the richness of Transcendence—its plenitude that allows for an endless number of complementary finite expressions.

What brought Smith to this insight? Had he always held such a conviction? Smith's route to this insight is, we shall see, partly unfolded in the essays found here and partly in the story of his own intellectual journey from his Chinese origins to the present. Thus, this collection of his writings clarifies his contributions to comparative studies, allowing us to chart his intellectual journey from *Religions of Man* to *Forgotten Truth* and beyond.

II

Born on May 31, 1919, in Soochow, China, the son of missionaries, Huston Smith grew up in China and learned its language during the turbulent years of the 1920s and 1930s. China was then in the throes of a transition from centuries-old traditional values rooted in the Confucian/Taoist and Buddhist heritage to more modern and secular values. His immediate family was part of the Christian mission to China, so Huston himself was deeply entrenched in that tradition. But the traditional culture of China and its religious underpinnings also had a strong impact on the young Smith. Completely fluent in spoken Chinese, he remembers being taught when eleven and twelve the traditional wisdom and the written Chinese language by an elderly Confucian scholar. The dominant ethos for his life was, nevertheless, provided by his devout and gentle missionary family.[5]

As China was being convulsed by the events that were to culminate years later in the epic march of the Chinese Communist forces from western to northern China, Huston Smith was completing four years at the Shanghai American School, together with other sons and daughters of missionary parents. At seventeen, Smith made the voyage across the Pacific from a China he would always remember with great love to the United States to study at Central Methodist College in Fayette, Missouri, a college with roots deep in the Methodist tradition, at a time when America was just beginning to recover from the worst of the Depression.

At Central Methodist College Smith encountered the world of philosophy and the thrill and challenge of ideas:

My junior year in college brought another surprise: ideas jumped to life and began to take over. To a certain extent they must have slipped up on me gradually, but there was a night when, with the force of a conversion experience, I watched them preempt my life. Returning from a meeting of a small honor society, which met monthly for dessert and discussion in the home of its faculty sponsor, several of us lingered in our dormitory to continue arguments the evening had provoked— as unlikely a knot of peripatetics as ever assembled. My excitement had been mounting all evening, and around midnight it exploded, shattering mental stockades. It was as if a fourth dimension of space had opened, and ideas—now palpable— were unrolling like carpets before me. And I had an entire life to explore those endless, awesome, portentous corridors![6]

Such events were to shape his life and career. It is obvious that, for Smith, it is inappropriate to speak of "mere ideas" as if they were unimportant or unworthy of our most serious attention. Later, Smith would discover a longer tradition in which his experience would make more sense and for which there is a language more fitting than that of the current academy. The tradition I refer to is the primordial tradition, and the language is that of intuition and the intellect rather than sense data and reason. Huston Smith never lost his love for the world of ideas; to this day, a conversation with Huston Smith will be filled with sparkle and verve as he explores with you the contours of an idea, its implications, and meanings. He shares the ancient conviction that one can be led to truth through the interplay of ideas in discussion, dialectic, and dialogue. But he never confuses the ideas with the truth to which they seek to bring you.

Following graduation from Central Methodist College, Huston Smith went to the divinity school of the University of Chicago to study with Henry Nelson Wieman, a distinguished theologian and philosopher. Smith's vocational plans had shifted from the Christian ministry to teaching, an option that would give him the opportunity to pursue his love of ideas. Smith has written of his time at the Divinity School of the University of Chicago that, despite World War II, "the early 1940s were a heady time for me."[7] What captured his enthusiasm was the "theistic naturalism" of his mentor Wieman and the prospect of a new reconciliation of modern science and traditional theism. Eventually, his energies were poured into a dissertation on "The Metaphysical Foundations of Contextualistic Philosophy of Religion" that sought to provide a philosophical rationale for

Wieman's theistic naturalism, using insights gained from Stephen Pepper's book *World Hypotheses*.

Smith went off to the University of California at Berkeley to write his dissertation. He chose Berkeley because Stephen Pepper was teaching there and had agreed to direct the work on his dissertation. There Smith encountered the writings of Gerald Heard, a friend of Aldous Huxley and author of several books on the spiritual crises of the modern era. Reading one night Head's book with the unlikely title *Pain, Sex, and Time*, Smith encountered the worldview of mysticism. An encounter with this grand tradition and intellectual option had been missing in both his undergraduate and graduate education, but it immediately won Smith's assent:

> What "grasped" me that night, as Tillich would say, was the worldview of mysticism. Never before—not during my four years as an undergraduate religion major, nor during the four subsequent years as a graduate student of philosophy and theology—had mysticism been sympathetically presented to me, and when it was, I instantly cathected. The naturalistic world I had loved and lived in since my mind's arousal was, with a single stroke relativized. It was but part of the whole. An island— lush to be sure, but rimmed round about by an endless shining sea.[8]

Smith realized that the mystic vision would move him beyond the theistic naturalism that had enthralled him. But, for now, he prudently put Heard aside, finished his dissertation, and moved on to teach philosophy, first at the University of Denver and then at the University of Colorado.

The insight he had encountered in Heard was to have a deep and abiding impact on Smith's life and thinking. For Smith, the mystic vision is not a flight into fancy and the obscure. It is rather a worldview, demanding in its discipline and intellectual rigor. Within its vision, the intellectual task now took on a new orientation and challenge. The orientation was toward the Whole grounded in the Divine; the challenge was to discern this vision in the religious life of humankind and to articulate that vision in the language of the academy.

But those tasks still lay ahead. Before moving to St. Louis and Washington University in 1947, Smith went to California to meet Gerald Heard, who was then living a monastic life on the edge of the desert. Smith tells us that he went with a copy of Aldous Huxley's *Perennial Philosophy* tucked under his arm. When he met Heard, whose writings he had devoured during the past several years, he found he had nothing to ask him. He was content just to sit with him on the brown hills that surrounded his monastic retreat. It was significant for his own future that Heard wrote him a letter of introduction to Huxley on that trip. Huxley's *Perennial Philosophy,* a volume that gathered together wisdom and teachings from several traditions under topical headings, had impressed Smith and provided a counterweight to the dominant preoccupations of the philosophical academy of the day.

At Washington University, Smith was assigned the task of teaching an introductory course in the world's great religious traditions. He had not taught such a course before, and he found himself cramming to prepare for the task. He also felt it was imperative that he have some feel for the particular traditions. This conviction, coupled with the advice of Heard and Huxley, led Smith to Swami Satprakashananda in St. Louis. Thus it was in St. Louis that Huston Smith came in contact with the Vedantic tradition in Indian philosophy. His search for a more existential sense of the Hindu tradition, one of the areas in which he was expected to instruct his students at the university, led him to encounter the Upanishads. This was another decisive step on Smith's intellectual journey, as he immediately found himself at home in the soaring world of the Upanishads. As he has remarked, it was from the Upanishads that he learned about the capacities of intuitive thought to plumb the Absolute while at the same time recognizing the limits of reason to fully grasp that which always lies beyond its reach. Study of the Vedantic tradition was to be at the heart of Huston Smith's efforts for more than a decade.

These events in Huston Smith's life illustrate another principle he was to follow in his study of the religious traditions of humankind: existential immersion in the practices and life of the different traditions was essential to a deeper grasp of their principles and dynamics. For Smith, the academic study of religion did not preclude familiarity with its practice or a personal awareness of the power of a tradition to shape people's lives. Indeed, to the contrary, he saw such familiarity as essential to a fuller grasp of the tradition one is trying to understand. Thus when one reads in *The World's Religions* that "it is a book that takes religion seriously,"[9] that statement should be heard, in part, as precisely what Smith was attempting to do in his own life.

It was in St. Louis that Huston Smith wrote his famous introduction to the great traditions of religious life, *The Religions of Man*, now *The World's Religions*. The book makes clear the depth of his commitment both to the sympathetic exposition of the diverse paths of the spiritual life and to the communication of his understanding of these traditions to his readers. After eleven years in St. Louis, Huston Smith accepted an invitation to join the faculty at the Massachusetts Institute of Technology in Cambridge in 1958. This move put him at an important center for scientific and technological work and had a lasting impact on Smith's development. At MIT, he came gradually to reverse his earlier optimistic belief in the reconciliation of science and religion. He came to see that scientism, not to be confused with authentic science, was inherently hostile to the great religious and spiritual traditions. Scientism, Smith was later to argue, denied that there was anything beyond the spatio-temporal reality that was uncovered by the methods of the experimental sciences.

During his years at MIT, Smith also deepened his understanding of Buddhism as he explored the spiritual practices of Zen. He spent one summer in Japan, living in a monastery under the direction of a Zen Roshi. That summer of meditation in Kyoto at Myoshinji monastery led Smith to adopt Zen as his contemplative practice for several years. It is worth noting his remark about his shift from Vedanta to Zen:

> In switching, I did not feel as if I was deserting Vedanta. Sunyata seemed similar to Nirguna Brahman and the Buddha-nature similar to Atman—so much so that I felt I was encountering the same truth in different idiom.[10]

This sense of the variety of languages or idioms to explore a common truth was important to Huston Smith's study and exploration of the religious life of humankind.

While in Cambridge, Huston Smith was also touched by the excitement that surrounded the research of Timothy Leary at Harvard with hallucinogenic drugs and their parallels to religious experience. Smith took the research in this area quite seriously, as evidenced in the appendix on "The Psychedelic Evidence" in *Forgotten Truth,* where he explores the possible religious import of psychedelics.[11]

While these developments extended the range of Smith's interests and competencies, it was the encounter with the writings of Frithjof Schuon in the early 1970s that proved decisive for his intellectual journey. Schuon was the intellectual heir of a group of thinkers who represented the perennial tradition in philosophy. René Guenon in France and Ananda Coomaraswamy in Sri Lanka and Boston had been important exponents of the tradition that championed the intuitive intellect rather than the technical reason of the Enlightenment.

Schuon had continued that tradition in his many writings, and Smith's encounter with those writings proved to be especially important. Their significance for him did not lie so much in their content as in their categories for the analysis and understanding of the religious and intellectual life of humankind. These categories and insights gave Smith a way to formulate the cumulative consequences of his own deep involvement in the religious and spiritual heritage of humankind. As Smith remarks about the significance of Schuon's writings,

> I discovered that he situated the world's religious traditions in a framework that enabled me to honor their significant differences unreservedly while at the same time seeing them as expressions of a truth that, because it was single, I could affirm. In a single stroke, I was handed a way of honoring the world's diversity without falling prey to relativism, a resolution I had been seeking for more than thirty years.[12]

Thus Huston Smith was now armed with categories for articulating the unity of the religious traditions while acknowledging their diversity. The result was his *Forgotten Truth.*

In *Forgotten Truth: The Primordial Tradition,* Smith unfolds the structural similarities that underlie the surface diversity of the religious life of humankind. Evident in this book is his capacity to communicate those insights to his readers, a capacity not as evident in some authors who have been influenced by the perennialist tradition. In the years following *Forgotten Truth,* a volume produced after he moved to Syracuse University in 1973, Smith turned his attention to the implications of the primordial tradition for the analysis of this current moment in Western culture, especially the phenomenon that Smith had come to call "scientism." This exploration involved a considerable departure from where his journey had begun nearly forty years earlier when he had hoped to bring about a new reconciliation of science and religion. He now realized that such a reconciliation was not possible on the basis of the scientism that seemed to permeate our cultural moment. For Smith, the primordial tradition could make room for the empirical sciences, but scientism could not make room for Transcendence, the basis of the primordial tradition.

Thus in the late 1970s and through the 1980s, Smith sought to bring his insights to bear on contemporary philosophy and religious studies in article after article bearing witness to his intellectual journey and to the stance he had come to adopt. His important volume *Beyond the Post-Modern Mind* reflects this engagement with the implications of the primordial tradition for analysis of the modern era. In this volume, as well as in the numerous other articles he wrote, the life of the spirit as mediated by the great religious traditions become the guides, as Smith argued they had always been, to the truth.

Smith's story is also important to the student of religion in showing that existential exploration of a tradition is not necessarily opposed to an objective study of that tradition. As we see in Smith's own intellectual journey, objective study is deepened by one's immersion in the disciplines and cultures to which particular traditions have given rise. It is part of the process of gaining insight into the patterns of religious, spiritual, and intellectual life.

What one sees in this brief review of the intellectual development of Smith's outlook is his movement from a naive supernaturalism to theistic naturalism, and on to the mystical primordialism of the traditionalist outlook. While Smith speaks of his late-1940s encounter with the mystic vision as decisive, it took him a while to see its full implications. His essays in the 1950s and 1960s carry traces of his earlier naturalism, which suggest that their relation to his newfound mysticism had yet to be worked out. It was only after his encounter with Frithjof Schuon that Smith seems to have achieved the clarity of vision—and the categories—that could resolve those interim ambiguities. Throughout the journey, however, there was a remarkable consistency in the respect he accorded the religious traditions of humankind. Far from seeing them as reflecting an outlook that the great new age of reason and science would replace, they always remained for him the house of the spirit in which the mind could retire for inspiration, renewal, and succor.

III

In the opening section of this collection, Foundations, the essays focus on the religious and philosophical foundations of three of the world's great cultural traditions: the Western, the Indian, and the Chinese. Smith's work here involves a philosophical hermeneutics, an attempt to identify the integrating beliefs and ideas that are fundamental to these cultural traditions. Unlike many of his contemporaries in the field of philosophy, Smith sees that the comparative philosophical task is, in part, the explication of the religious and philosophical foundations of culture. For Smith, it is the religious traditions that largely underpin cultures and give them their primary orientations. They do so, as the reader will note in these essays, by providing the culture with its *fundamental self-understanding of and orientation toward what is.* Thus the religious traditions are not, as the Marxists argue, the superstructure of culture. They are its base.

In his comparative investigation of the foundations of the great cultural traditions, Smith looks for the convergence of these traditions in the coming "world civilization" or planetary society. In his earlier essays from the late 1950s and early 1960s, Smith was more optimistic than we find in his later essays, especially those that appear after *Forgotten Truth.* Later, Smith sees, in ways he did not earlier, that "Modern culture" was the great dissenter from the primordial traditions that had sustained cultural life East and West (and North and South, we could add) in the preceding millennia. But now Smith sees a negative side to "modernity" that amounts to a full-scale no to the primordial traditions of the past. Thus in the later essays and in *Beyond the Post-Modern Mind,* Smith indicts "scientism," the view that *all-there-is* is disclosed through the methods of the empirical sciences, in ways that he did not in his earlier essays.

But looking ahead to the later essays somewhat deflects our attention from the essential point—Smith's contribution to the comparative study of civilization. This contribution is found in the essays in the first section of this collection. Here we can see Smith striving to identify and articulate those core orientations that integrate the life of a culture. For Smith, again unlike the positivist schools that championed the work of A. J. Ayer and increasingly dominated departments of philosophy in the West from the 1940s into the 1960s, philosophy is the perennial quest for and love of wisdom. Thus Smith seeks to use his philosophical skills and insights to pursue wisdom by probing the insights that have been imbedded in the great cultural streams of the West, India, and China.

These studies of the great cultural streams of life and thought have led Smith to recognize the diverse—though not necessarily contradictory, perhaps even complementary—understandings of truth found in different cultures. In his essay on "Truth in Comparative Perspective," Smith argues that truth is not to be understood only as propositional, as it is in the dominant Western tradition. Truth is also person-centered, as is recognized in the Chinese tradition, and tied to things, as is clear in the Indian tradition. The West's exclusive preoccupation with propositions is a development that is not altogether a happy one, in Smith's view. This development leads to a narrowing of the quest for truth. Strikingly, Smith's analysis of the Western tradition is congenial to recent feminist critiques of the dominant Western tradition which see the propositional fixation as reflective of male projections rather than the inclu-

xxvi Essays on World Religion

sively human quest for truth. Comparative studies, as one can see here, can lead to a reopening of the fullness of the question of truth, leading us beyond our cultural or philosophical or gender provincialism.

The second section of this collection, The Splendid Prism, is the longest. It contains essays on particular traditions in East Asia, South Asia, and the West. These essays were all written after the publication of Smith's *The Religions of Man* and testify to his continuing efforts to understand both the discrete traditions and their comparative dimensions. The essays here range broadly: from studies on Taoism and Shinto to the unique vocal abilities of Tibetan lamas to the interpretation of Western philosophy as a great religion.

The title for this section implies a view of religious diversity that is fundamental to Smith's work. With humanity and culture acting as a prism refracting and reflecting the light of the Ultimate, the many traditions create a splendid rainbow of light and insight.

Smith's sensitivity to the land of his birth is evident in several of the essays in this section. The essay on "Transcendence in Traditional China" tackles the controversial issue of transcendence in relation to the Chinese traditions. An almost standard or textbook view of the Chinese traditions tends to emphasize the humanistic orientation of the religions of China, even questioning the appropriateness of the category of religion for the Chinese phenomenon. Is it religion or philosophy? But in this important essay Smith argues that the noumenal dimension is equally important for the Chinese traditions, even though it does not get the degree of attention that is generally focused on the human realm. His essay "Tao Now, An Ecological Testament" is a sympathetic portrayal of the Taoist tradition and its relevance to the current ecological crisis. Written in the early 1970s, long before ecology had become the front-page issue it is today, this essay is indicative of Smith's sense of the continuing significance of the great traditions for contemporary life.

Smith's brief "Note on Shinto," written as the foreword to a forthcoming Japanese edition of *The World's Religions,* evokes the contribution of this little-known tradition of Japan. His essays on "Spiritual Discipline" and "Celestial Mirages" draw on his familiarity with Buddhism, especially in its Zen form, to explore issues of the life of the spirit and the relation of thought to reality.

In the second part of this section of the collection, Smith turns his attention to India. The brief essay "India and the Infinite" was written as a foreword to Swami Probhavananda's *The Spiritual Heritage of India,* reflecting the respect members of particular traditions have for Smith's work. It also gives Smith the opportunity to acknowledge his debt to the Hindu tradition. The essay "Vedic Religion and Soma" is a very careful essay-review of R. Gordon Wasson's *Soma, Divine Mushroom of Immortality.* In Wasson's controversial study, he claims to have discovered the true identity of soma, long the subject of speculation among specialists in the Indian traditions. According to Wasson, soma was a psychedelic mushroom, *amantia muscaria.* Smith carefully reviews the book and its critics before pronouncing his own, largely affirmative, view of Wasson's argument.

In "The Importance of the Buddha," Smith gives his response to a perennial question. For Smith, the importance of the Buddha lies in the fact that "he founded a civilization"; that is, "a total view of the world and man's place in it." This fact, Smith argues, is often over-looked in accounts of the Buddha that focus only on his "spiritual contributions." The last essay in this part of the volume focuses on Tibetan chanting. This Huston Smith once laughingly remarked to me, is his "only contribution to the empirical study of religion." Smith collaborated with an MIT colleague for the study that appeared in *American Anthropologist.* It offers a technical and acoustical analysis of what is going on in the astonishing sounds produced by the Tibetan chanter as well as a hermeneutical assessment of the meaning of chanting within the Tibetan context.

In the third part of this section of the collection, Smith turns his attention to the West. In "Man's Western Way: An Essay on Reason and the Given," Smith explores again a theme he raised earlier: the way the West focused on nature and reason in its orientation toward what is. In this essay from the early 1960s, Smith continued to be optimistic about science. But that view had shifted by the time he wrote "The Conceptual Crisis in the Modern West" in the 1980s.[13] At some point in the 1970s Smith abandoned his optimism that an immanent or easy reconciliation of science and religion was about to take place. This shift coincides with his recognition of the depth to which scientism has penetrated our age. Part of that transition is probably related to the new view of Western philosophy he outlines in "Western Philosophy as a Great Religion." In this striking essay, Smith argues that the basic dynamics of Western philosophy, from the Greeks on, are better grasped if we see it as a great religion, one funded by a thrust toward transcendence.

In the final part of this collection, Consequences: Social, Educational, and Ecumenical, are four essays in which Huston Smith outlines his understanding of the social relevance of religion to the modern world, describes his own way of teaching an introductory course in world religions, offers his view of the current ecumenical situation, and argues for a change of direction in the discipline of religious studies. In these essays his voice shifts from the more analytic and theoretical to the practical and immediate. We see Smith communicating his views to audiences concerned about social relevance, education, the dialogue between men and women of different faiths, and the future of the discipline of religious studies.

In "The Relevance of the Great Religions for the Modern World," Smith focuses on the contribution of religion to society. This, he believes, is the distinctive religion/world relationship in the modern era, in contrast with the different kinds of relationship that dominated the archaic and axial eras. Smith warns that the focus on society should not become the sole focus of religion since "society is important, but not all important." The fullness of religion requires attention to the metaphysical and interpersonal dimensions as well as to the social.

The wisdom acquired through a lifelong study of the religious life of humankind is also evident in Smith's essays on teaching the introductory course in religious studies and his analysis of the ecumenical scene. In his account of how he teaches an introductory course, Smith again urges attention to the truth of religion. For Smith, truth here means the way in which religions give us, using Evelyn Underhill's phrase, "another world to live in." This is the essential point for the scholar or student of religion to grasp. And it is equally essential for the teacher to try to make these alternative "worlds" available to the student. Smith's originality is evident in this essay, as is his passion as a teacher.

In "This Ecumenical Moment," an address given in Berkeley in 1987 at a major conference on Buddhism and Christianity, Smith asks his audience to consider what we are seeking in the wider ecumenism that embraces persons of many different faiths. Surely, Smith argues, we are all diminished if the impact of the wider ecumenism is a lessening of commitment to our respective traditions. Instead, Smith argues that what we are seeking is always a deepening understanding of one another and a greater respect for the integrity of each tradition. This surprising advice is worth attending to.

In his plenary address to the 1989 meeting of the American Academy of Religion, Smith offers a penetrating analysis of the impact of postmodernism on the study of religion. Defining *postmodernism* as the view that abandons modernism's scientistic worldview without replacing it with an alternative because it doubts the existence of such deep structures, Smith argues that it is doubtful that we will find in postmodernism what we need to adequately understand the religious phenomenon. Rather, he argues that the way ahead for the discipline involves a return to what is given in the religious traditions themselves.

This final essay in the collection brings us, in one sense, full circle. We are once again confronted by the phenomenon of religion in all its splendid diversity and mystery as well as its less majestic moments. And we are left again with the perplexing question of how we approach and seek to understand what is given in the patterns and structures of life and insight found in the great traditions. Huston Smith's advice is the same here as it was at the outset: that we "return to the truth claims of our field as impounded in the world's great traditions." That return should be undertaken with the same respect for the religious traditions of humankind that has all along characterized Huston Smith's work in the field of religion.

Smith's approach to the great religious traditions of humankind has been marked out in his *The World's Religions*. This approach seeks to focus on the crucial elements of each tradition, those points where the human being is transformed by an encounter with a Beyond. The same sensitivity to the life of the spirit is present in *Forgotten Truth*. Huston Smith is not content with mere description of religious phenomena. Rather, he seeks to uncover the meaning of these phenomena, in the life of humanity. Isn't that still the way to proceed?

NOTES

1. Huston Smith, *The Religions of Man* (New York: Harper & Row, Colophon edition, 1964), p. 10

2. *Ibid.,* p. 10.

3. The new edition of *The Religions of Man,* with its new title and additional material, will be welcomed. Huston Smith has written of the motives for the revision and some of the major changes in "Turning *The Religions of Man* into *The World's Religions:* Reflections on the New Edition," in *Anima,* Summer 1991. I have mainly used the newer title for this introduction. It should also be noted that the language of Huston Smith's essays in this collection has been made more inclusive, but that quoted material, has been left in its earlier form.

4. Huston Smith, *Forgotten Truth: The Primordial Tradition* (New York: Harper & Row, Colophon edition, 1977), p. ix.

5. Information about the life of Huston Smith is drawn from David Griffin and Huston Smith, *Primordial Truth and Postmodern*

Theology (Albany, N.Y.: SUNY, 1989), pp. 8–13, and conversations with Huston Smith in August 1989 when we were together in my home in Elmira and at a conference together at Jackson Point, Ontario.

6. D. Griffin and Huston Smith, *Primordial Truth and Postmodern Theology,* p. 9.
7. Ibid., p. 9.
8. Ibid., p. 10.
9. Huston Smith, *The World's Religions*, p. 9.
10. D. Griffin and Huston Smith, *Primordial Truth and Postmodern Theology,* p. 13.
11. Huston Smith, *Forgotten Truth,* pp. 155–173.
12. D. Griffin and Huston Smith, *Primordial Truth and Postmodern Theology,* p. 13.
13. The issues surrounding science and religion are more fully discussed in Huston Smith, *Beyond the Post-Modern Mind* (Wheaton, Ill.: Quest Books, 1982, revised ed. 1989).

PART I

FOUNDATIONS

Accents of the World's Philosophies

When a Belgian newspaper called the 1955 Asian-African Bandung Conference "a conference of children without their fathers," it was merely voicing in straightforward language the superiority over other peoples which most Westerners have long assumed. But when the Indonesian Foreign Ministry came back in kind, declaring that "such a comment could come only from an underdeveloped mind," the retort was evidence of a new day. East and West are no longer meeting; they are being hurled at each other. But what is really new is that for the first time in the modern world they face each other as equals. Compared with this double fact—East-West depth encounter on the basis of full equality—everything else about the twentieth century is likely in time to appear episodic.

The primary problem world-encounter poses for philosophy is that of synthesis, for philosophy is never happy about unintegrated perspectives. This essay, working in broad strokes and risking over-simplification to keep the outlines clear, takes its place among other recent attempts to see the philosophies of East and West in relation. It differs in tone as well as solution from Arthur Schopenhauer's attempt to subordinate Western thought to that of the East and from Schweitzer's effort to do the reverse. As to the existing non-invidious schemes, of which F. S. C. Northrop's is the most thorough and best known, the purpose of the present statement is not to challenge these but to supplement them by suggesting a somewhat different

This essay, the earliest of Smith's writings to appear in this volume, originally appeared in Philosophy East and West *VII, 1 and 2 (1957). A revised version appeared in 1961 from the Department of Humanities, Massachusetts Institute of Technology, in "Publications in the Humanities Number 50."*

approach.[1] In this matter of intercultural understanding we are at the beginning where exclusive claims are presumptuous. What the times demand is a variety of hypotheses that can provide fruitful leads for further explorations.

I

In *New Hopes for a Changing World*[2] Bertrand Russell points out that people are perennially engaged in three basic conflicts: (1) against Nature, (2) against others, and (3) against themselves. Roughly these may be identified as humanity's natural, social, and psychological problems. The great surviving cultural traditions are also three—the Chinese, the Indian, and the Western. It helps us to understand and relate the unique perspectives of these three traditions if we think of each as accenting one of the three basic human problems. Generally speaking, the West has accented the natural problem, China the social, and India the psychological.

If this is true, the question immediately arises: What gave these cultures their distinctive slants? If we reject the racist theory that different peoples are innately endowed with different capacities and temperaments, we should expect to find the answer in environmental differences, both geographical and social. This is the lead I shall follow.

The Western tradition's preoccupation with Nature seems traceable, at least in part, to the hospitality of its cradle environment, significantly christened the "Fertile Crescent." Here Nature almost coaxes inquiry and certainly rewards advances. The Nile Valley is conspicuous in this respect. To begin with, it furnishes two invaluable assets: a self-operating transportation system and abundant alluvium. The reliable currents of this amazing river will float one its full length down, while a strong and countering wind, blowing from the comparatively cool Mediterranean into the intense heat of the deserts, will carry one back up if one just lifts the sail. From the beginning, it was possible for the population to be in continuous, almost effortless, circulation. To this blessing the Nile added free fertilizer. Regularly as the monsoon floods broke upon the Abyssinian mountains the river rose, spreading freshly irrigated mud over the fields. After the first cataclysmic floods, caused by the breaking of the moraines in the Armenian mountains, much the same circumstances were found in Iraq—the land of the Tigris and Euphrates. In both cases Nature was in it's most favorable mood—rich and joyous and treating humanity as a friend.

Western culture accepted Nature's overtures. From the first, the West's primary curiosity was directed outward, toward Nature. It was in Mesopotamia that humanity wrung its first pattern from the stars, the signs of the zodiac.[3] It was the Kingdom of Sumer that first divided the year into months and the day into hours, launching that measuremental approach to things which was in the end to prove so triumphant.[4] Before long even the virtues were being conceived quantitatively: Michael, judge of humanity's destiny, is pictured blindfolded holding scales in which the soul is weighed against the feather of truth. The growing feeling is that everything is orderly, exact, measurable, impartial.

How this intuition became conviction for the Greeks and issued in Western science needs no retelling here.[5] What is less obvious is the way this basic interest in Nature colors the rest of Western culture including philosophy and religion. There are, of course, many anti-Nature eddies in the stream—Gnosticism, Neo-Platonism, the Mystery religions, Plotinus, and others. But these never take over, and—what is equally instructive for our thesis—their inspiration usually comes from the East, often from India itself. For India, matter is a barbarian spoiling everything it touches. Western philosophy in its indigenous orientation respects matter and takes it seriously, meshing thought with things wherever possible. As a consequence it is, in the main:

1. Realistic in ontology. On the whole, it rejects the Platonic identification of being with intelligible and stable ideas or forms and joins Aristotle in giving purchase to matter.

2. Hylomorphic in anthropology. Humanity is composite in nature, constituted of soul and body. Both are real and ultimate aspects of human nature.

3. Sense-involved in epistemology. Knowledge originates in sensible things and is, in the main, about sensible things.

Even in its religion—the aspect of culture which always tends to be most otherworldly—the West fits in with Nature as the others do not. "God so loved the world" involves a totally different theology than "God so loved the souls of the world." "Christianity", as Archbishop Temple used to contend, "is the most avowedly materialistic of all the great religions."[6] I would add Judaism and Islam to the list, but with this enlargement, the statement stands as true. Time and again the West seems on the verge of slipping into the view that spirit is good and matter bad, but the West always recovers. "In the beginning God created the heavens and the earth.... And behold, it was very good." Its goodness lies not only in beholding it but in working with it: humanity is commissioned to "have dominion...

over all the earth." The incarnation pays matter its highest conceivable compliment—it can become divine. The Kingdom of Heaven, from Jewish and early Christian apocalypticism down to the social gospel, is to come on earth. Even in death, the West will not desert the body. If there is to be life after death it, too, must be in some sense physical: "I believe... in the resurrection of the body." Throughout the entire sequence runs the effort to maintain a sense of kinship between humanity and Nature which totemism had earlier pointed up. All creation is in travail as it waits for the decisive moment in history. An earthquake forms the backdrop for the crucifixion: "Nature also mourns for a lost good."

Thus the entire arc of Western thought, from its science through its philosophy to its religion, remains firmly and affirmatively oriented toward Nature. In specialization, Western humanity has been, *par excellence,* the natural philosopher.

II

China, on the other hand, became the social philosopher. Here, too, the environment seems to offer some clue. Chinese culture, like that of the West, is riverine in origin; it was founded on the Yellow River and the Yangtze. But these rivers are not playthings. Mixed blessing and scourge, the northern one particularly has an incurable passion for changing its bed at infinite cost in life and labor to those who must live by it and on it. Not without reason has it been called "China's Sorrow." The superstitious dread embedded in its other title, "The Lord of the Rivers," bears witness to the terror felt by the riverside dwellers of primitive times for this untamed neighbour. In order to propitiate the "The Lord of the Rivers" they used to offer periodic sacrifices of youths and maidens. In these great tracts of low-lying ground, defenceless against flood or drought because of the lack of forestation, the peasant was more narrowly dependent on the soil than in any other part of the world."[7] Very early in China the rivers came to be symbolized by the unmanageable dragon, which was also for centuries the national emblem. We should be prepared to find in China, then, a certain deference toward Nature. There is a naturalism in Chinese thought, but it is the naturalism of the artist and the romanticist instead of the scientist, the naturalism of Thoreau and Wordsworth rather than Galileo or Bacon.[8] Nature is something to be appreciated, intuited, communed with, and reverenced; there is no sustained thought of using it, or suggestion that it might be mastered.

Those who would take over the earth
And shape it to their will
Never, I notice, succeed.
The earth is like a vessel so sacred
That at the mere approach of the profane
It is marred
And when they reach out their fingers it is gone.[9]

Chinese science, as a consequence, does not develop. For a field of constructive experimentation and action the Chinese turned instead to society. Chinese philosophy was forged in the social furnace of the "Time of Troubles," those five convulsive centuries between 700 and 200 B.C. culminating in the terrible epoch of the "Warring Kingdoms," a period of endemic warfare in which anarchy was the order of the day. In this context the burning question facing every philosopher was: How can we live together without destroying one another? As Waley has said, "All Chinese philosophy is essentially the study of how men can best be helped to live together in harmony and good order."[10] The answers differed, but the problem was always the same. The solution finally reached gathered together many strands but bears the distinctive stamp of Confucius' genius. It centers in a number of key and related concepts, chief among which is *jên,* the ideal human relationship usually translated as benevolence, or simply goodness. Practice of *jên* produces the *chün-tzŭ,* or gentleman in the best sense of the term; the one who is completely poised, competent, confident, and adequate to every social occasion, the one of perfect address, who is always at ease within and therefore can put others at their ease, whose approach to others is always the perfect courtesy and openness of "What may I do for you?" Under this constant gentlemanliness, the appropriate approaches to persons of different stations are indicated in the Five Great Relationships—father and son, elder brother and younger brother, husband and wife, friend and friend, ruler and subject. In the end, all these fitting responses are summarized in the concept of *li,* meaning propriety or ritual, since it amounts to a complete ordering and ritualization of all life-processes, from the offering of sacrifices to heaven to the way one entertains the humblest guest and serves tea. Politically this adds up to a society being held together internally by *tê,* the power of moral example. It is the responsibility of the rulers, acting with cultivated wisdom, benevolence, and *savoir faire,* to establish a pattern of prestige which holds the community together by inspiring the populace to want to live together decently and in harmony. A society which is thus ordered has a *tê* or prestige factor which leavens the culture as a whole and renders it secure against destruction from without. Outsiders may knock one down, but, if one really has a more polished, adequate, satisfying way of life, in the end it will of necessity commend itself to those who are less assured, less self-sufficient, and less wise in the ways of living. In the long run the invisible but invincible factor in imperial success is not military force but cultural and moral prestige *(wên)*.

How successful this social solution was seems amply evidenced by history. Chinese culture has a flavor all its own. It is a compound of subtlety, brilliance, and reticence that produces an effect that can be described only as good taste. The Chinese have exalted the life of reasonable enjoyment and despised the destructive. As a consequence they have been able to unite an immense area of fertility and to create—if we multiply duration by size of population included— the most extensive civilization humankind has ever achieved, one which at its height included one-third of the human race. The political structure of this civilization alone, the Chinese Empire, lasted under various dynasties for 2133 years (from 221 B.C. to A.D. 1912)— a period that makes the empires of Alexander the Great and Caesar look insignificant. Its power of assimilation was equally impressive. Having the most open frontier of all great civilizations, China was subject to wave after wave of invasions by cavalried barbarians who were always ready to fall on the earthbound agriculturalists. Always at their gates were the very Tartars whose one long-range raid inflicted a mortal wound on the Roman Empire. But what the Chinese could not exclude they absorbed. Each wave of invasion tends quickly to lose its identity. As the great Sinologist Arthur Waley has remarked, there is scarcely a barbarian conqueror who came in purely for profit who within twenty years was not attempting to write a copy of Chinese verse which his master, who is also his conquered slave, might say was not wholly unworthy of a gentleman. And already the conqueror is hoping to be mistaken for Chinese. Kublai Khan, of course, is the most striking instance. He conquered China, but was "himself conquered by Chinese civilization. His victory enabled him to realize his lasting ambition: to become a real Son of Heaven."[11] Here is a cultural furnace with enough heat to effect a real melting pot. There is no evidence that these barbarians were ever as impressed with what they found in Europe. When the entire stretch of Chinese civilization is remembered, one is tempted to say that China has been the world's social philosopher.

III

Turning last to the third great tradition—the Indian—we find neither the natural nor the social environment looking promising to her. India's natural environment is different but no more friendly than China's. The tropical region of the Ganges with its thick vegetation, unbearable humidity, and burning heat; the parching dryness of other regions, where for ten months of the year there is nothing but the nightly dew to quench the thirst of the ground—the Indian environment is one of fierce extremes. Humbled by the overpowering forces of Nature. Indians surrendered their initiative and turned away from Nature. Their outlook becomes unrealistic in the technical sense. The desert, particularly, must have been discouraging.[12] Facing Nature in this form, gaunt, bleak, desiccated, dangling its haunting mirages—no wonder the Indian began to think: Nature is ungovernable and, in some strange way, unreal.[13] Nature is shadowy, ever-shifting, mysterious, horrible if you will, but what is the use of trying to find out its laws.[14] It is all *māyā.* It is all magic; a trick, the play of a mysterious cosmic illusion.

Faced with a seemingly intractable Nature, China (as we have seen) turned its attention to society. But here India found itself facing the most devilish of social problems—a color-culture barrier. The distinction between Aryan and Dravidian was clear, and to this day—3500 years later—the line persists.[15] No Indian ingenuity was adequate to break this curse. Caste tried to do so, but, instead of caste's remedying the evil, in the end the evil took over caste, turning it into a device for perpetuating social distance. Relatively early, India abandoned hope of solving life's problem on the social plane. Instead, India turned inward, centering her attention on the psychological problem. Nature? No, there is no hope of governing the physical world. Society? As long as humanity is what it is there will always be hopeless social inequities and blockage. But the individual looks promising.[16] If we could only understand who we truly are we might win an inner freedom beyond the opposites which block both Nature and society. The following lines from the *Katha Upaniṣad* will be recognized at once as typical of the Indian theme: "...The senses turn outward. Accordingly, man looks toward what is without, and sees not what is within. [The wise man] shuts his eyes to what is without and beholds the Self."[17] For the Indian, the senses are false witnesses. "The world is not what it appears to be. Behind this surface life, where we experience the play of life and death, there is a deeper life which knows no death; behind our apparent consciousness, which gives us the knowledge of objects and things... there is... pure...

consciousness.... Truth... is experienced only by those who turn their gaze inward."[18] As this conviction spreads, "such intellectual energy as had formerly been devoted to the study and development of a machinery for the mastery of the... forces of the cosmos... was... diverted inward.... The cosmic energy was being taken at its fountain head... all secondary, merely derivative streams of energy... being left behind. In Indian thought... the whole outer world was dwindling in importance."[19]

India, then, became the introspective, psychological philosopher.[20] One evidence of India's preoccupation in this area is found in the elaborateness of its psychological vocabulary. Coomaraswamy, while he was curator of the Oriental Museum in Boston, used to say that for every psychological term in English there are four in Greek and forty in Sanskrit. Mrs. Rhys Davids lists twenty Pāli words whose subtle distinctions of meaning are obscured by single, indiscriminate English rendition as "desire" or "desires."[21] Proliferated terminology in itself is no test of acumen. That Bakairi (an idiom of Central Brazil), for example, has individual names for each species of parrot and palm tree but no name to express the genus "parrot" or "palm" may indicate low powers of abstraction as readily as high powers of discrimination. The same might be claimed of Arabic with its five to six thousand terms for describing camels but none that provides a general biological concept.[22] But, granting this general point, two observations must be added: (1) Proliferated vocabulary is at least a sign of interest in the area to which the vocabulary refers. (2) When, as in Indian psychology, it is developed in addition to general concepts, not in lieu of them, language pushing simultaneously in the directions of both the idiosyncratic and the universal, the result escapes the charge implied by examples such as those just cited.

What India actually developed of continuing worth in psychology is, of course, a moot question. Leaving the more controversial topics aside, I should like to suggest that at least the following insights are remarkably contemporary to have been discovered and explored in detail over two thousand years ago:

1. That our consciousness lies not entirely on the surface but includes layers of subconsciousness. (Compare Freud, the whole psychoanalytic movement, and age regression under hypnosis.)

2. That the human being is a psycho-physical whole with interaction between its two aspects far more subtle than most people suppose. (Compare the startling mind-body connections which have come to light in hypnosis and psychosomatic medicine.)

3. That in addition to the obvious gross body *(sthūla śarīra)* there

is a sheath of vital force *(prāna-maya-kośa)* which, while still physical, is much more subtle and is invisible. (Compare contemporary discoveries about the electrical field of the body and brain waves.)

4. That with respect to the mind we must distinguish between *manas* and *buddhi,* i.e., between rational, critical, analytic thought and what Radhakrishnan calls integral thought. (Compare the distinctiveness of the hypothecating faculty as described, e.g., by Descartes, by Hamilton, and by Poincaré in his essay on "Mathematical Creation."[23])

5. That the basic emotions are controlled not by the surface mind but by a deeper part. (Compare Freud; also the discovery that the seat of the emotions is in the thalamus.)

6. That human temperaments are different and not indefinitely malleable. (Compare the theory of personality types in the philosophical conception of caste and the four *yogas* with the work of William Sheldon, Charles Morris, and other workers in contemporary characterology.)

7. That what we see is not a simple mirroring of the external world but in part a function or projection of the perceiving organism. (Compare the doctrine of *māyā*—defined not as illusion but as psychological construct—with most contemporary theories of perception, including most emphatically constructivism.)

8. That most life is dislocated or out of joint *(dukkha)* and that the cause of this is *tanhā,* the will for private existence or individual fulfillment. (Compare the Buddha's Four Noble Truths with contemporary psychotherapy generally.)

Neither China nor the West has given a fraction of India's attention to the mind. Historically, then, India rightly deserves the title I have proposed of the world's Psychological Philosopher.

IV

We have suggested that each of the three great living civilizations shows a unique specialization on the cultural level—the West in natural wisdom, China in social wisdom, India in psychological wisdom. It remains to point out the inevitable price of specialization: ineptness in the subjects neglected. "Nothing fails like success"—in the end all three cultures are brought to disaster or its brink because each succeeded so well on one front that it felt safe in neglecting the other two.

China and India have both neglected the natural problem; consequently science has not developed, and the standard of living remains impossibly low. In China, the problem periodically proved too much for even social genius. Between dynasties there was regularly a long period of civil strife, which, as Shu-Ching Lee points out, can always be correlated with "population pressure on cultivated land" which failed to increase in productivity because "improvement of agricultural technique was negligible."[24] At the beginning of the Ming Dynasty (1368) China and the West were on generally the same level with respect to technical and mechanical skill. At the end of that dynasty (1644), Europe was in possession of modern science and China was still in its Middle Ages. As for India, its only scientific contributions to the world at large have been in pure mathematics, where India was dealing not with the outer world but with the resources of the mind.[25] In addition to this ineptness toward Nature,[26] India adds social clumsiness (vividly illustrated by the present state of the caste system) and China adds psychological naïveté. Occasionally we catch a glimpse in China of an interest in the mind as such and what it can do, as in the quietistic movement in the Chou Dynasty, the *Tao Tê Ching*'s esoteric rendering of the idea of *tê*, Mencius' passage on "the dawn breath," and Chu Hsi's discussion of "silent sitting." But these are never systematically pursued, and the interest in them usually takes a social turn; the mind is being inspected not for itself but for what it can contribute to social stability. One gets the impression that when China does concern itself with psychology it is only social psychology that really interests her. China's deficiencies in this field are seen most clearly in the failure to recognize the dangers of repression. The Chinese scheme had no place for emotional catharsis, spontaneity, and unrepression. Consequently, negative emotions got dammed up until eventually the dam gave way and the emotions came forth in terrifying form. Examples of this are found in the Mongolian capacity for torture and the frequency of those homicidal outbursts known as "running amok" which, as Sorokin points out, mark the East Asian tradition more than others. It carried over to Japan, where, as Robert Guillain has pointed out, a youth "received a Spartan training which developed his aggressive instincts and, at the same time, screwed down over his violent nature a sort of lid of blind obedience and perfect politeness. This made him an explosive creature, ready to burst like a bomb."[27]

The deficiencies of the West have been in psychology and sociology. Psychologically the West has been merely inconspicuous, but in sociology the West's record has been deplorable. At least four facts must be faced as evidences of the West's ineptitude in social relations and lack of perceptiveness as to the forces which make for social cohesion and group harmony.

1. Whereas Chinese civilization had the power to expand, uniting more and more people in a common heritage, and whereas Indian civilization could at least hold its own, the record of the West has been one of continuous secession. After the union of the Northern and Southern Kingdoms in Egypt, there is no further fusion in the Fertile Crescent. Instead, fission sets in. The Hebrews divide into Israel and Judah. "The fatal danger of Greece," writes Gilbert Murray in *The Five Stages of Greek Religion,* "was disunion as many see it in Europe now."[28] The church splits into East and West, and the Western Church into Protestant and Catholic. The Medieval Empire shatters into nations, and the process continues. Norway, Denmark, and Sweden, originally a homogeneous unity, have split. Belgium and Holland, originally a single viable unit, are apart, and Belgium in danger of splitting again. The British Isles have been in constant fission with separatist movements still in evidence. The United States has its Civil War and continuing North-South animosity. What has enfeebled and discredited us in our own day, writes Arnold Toynbee, "is the atrocious fratricidal warfare, within the bosom of our Western Society, since 1914.... We Westerners have fought among ourselves another bout of wars that have been as savage, destructive and discreditable as our earlier wars of religion."[29] Western history since the Middle Ages is one long story of inability to inspire embracing loyalties strong enough to outweigh provincial attachments.

2. Western religion, sharing its culture's interest in Nature, shares its social ineptitude as well. The only large-scale persecuting religions have been those of the West—Judaism, Christianity, and Islam. Since the Middle Ages, Christianity has been divisive by itself. To continue with Toynbee: "For 400 years and more, from the outbreak of the struggle between the Papacy and Frederick II in the thirteenth century down to the end of the Catholic-Protestant Western wars of religion in the seventeenth century, the Christian Church in the Western World was a force that made not for gentleness and peace and concord, but for violence and war and dissension.... Before the end of the seventeenth century, the hatred, strife and atrocities inflicted on the Western World by Christian *odium theologicum* had become a scandal and menace to the Western Civilization."

3. The West has conceived the problem of intercultural relations in physical rather than in anthropological terms. Time after time, nations of the West seem to behave as if the only attitude to take toward strangers is one of belligerency and domination. The Eastern idea of *tê,* of the ultimate victory's being decided in terms not of

physical might but of moral and cultural prestige, seems lacking.

4. Eventually (one almost says inevitably) there emerges in Europe a social theory that pushes the Western emphasis to its logical extreme. Paralleling the West's inclination to reduce psychology to physiology, Marx reduces sociology to economics. In the end, there *is* no social problem. Once the material problem is solved, the social problem will take care of itself.

We have suggested that each of the world's three civilizations has achieved notable results with one of humanity's basic problems, but has been brought to the brink of ruin by not attending sufficiently to the other two. The obvious conclusion is that an adequate culture must strike all three notes as a chord. In developing this chord of an adequate world-culture the three traditions come as equals. Each has something to contribute, and something to learn as well.

NOTES

1. It may be helpful as a background for the present discussion to summarize the main lines of several familiar theses. Northrop holds that the West has stressed the theoretical component of knowing, the East the intuitive component *(The Meeting of East and West,* New York: The Macmillan Co., 1946). Conger sees Indian culture as basically idealistic, Chinese as naturalistic, and Western as dualistic *(Toward the Unification of the Faiths,* Calcutta: Calcutta University Press, 1957). Burtt sees India as most interested in the self and its growth toward cosmic maturity, China as preoccupied with society and harmonious interpersonal relations, the West absorbed with individualism, analysis, and the external world ("How Can the Philosophies of East and West Meet?," *The Philosophical Review,* LVII, No. 6, Nov. 1948). It will become apparent that the present statement is closer to Burtt's thesis than to the other two. I am also indebted to Gerald Heard, whose lecture series at Washington University during the autumn of 1951 first suggested to the writer a number of ideas here elaborated. *Cf. The Human Venture* (New York: Harper and Brothers, 1955), chap. 5, coauthored by Heard and myself.
2. B. Russell, *New Hopes for a Changing World* (London: George Allen & Unwin Ltd., 1951), p. 18.
3. *Cf.* Ernst Cassirer, *An Essay on Man* (Garden City: Doubleday and Co., 1944, 1953), p. 68: "The Babylonians were not only the first to observe the celestial phenomena but the first to lay the foundations

for a scientific astronomy and cosmology."

4. "The Euphratean valley ...bequeathed to us a system of weights and measures and the sexagesimal system by which time is still measured." Philip K. Hitt, *The Arabs: A Short History* (Princeton: Princeton University Press, 1949), p. 6.

5. John Burnet's *Early Greek Philosophy* (London: A. & C. Black, Ltd., 1930) is still the best single treatment of this theme.

6. William Temple, *Nature, Man and God* (London: Macmillan and Co., 1953), p. 478.

7. René Grousset, *The Rise and Splendour of the Chinese Empire* (Berkeley: University of California Press, 1953), pp. 12–13.

8. The major exception here was *Hsün Tzŭ,* but his contention—that everything of value is the result of human effort—did not prevail. "The Chinese people," as Chiang Mon-lin has said, "are devoted to nature, not in the sense of finding the natural laws but in the sense of cultivating the poetic, artistic, or moral sense of lovers of nature." From Chiang Mon-lin, *Tides from the West* (New Haven: Yale University Press, 1947), p. 257.

9. *Tao Tê Ching,* chap. 29; Witter Bynner, trans., *The Way of Life According to Laotzu* (New York: John Day Co., 1944), p. 43.

10. *The Way and Its Power* (London: George Allen & Unwin Ltd., 1934), p. 64. *Cf.* also Fung Yulan, *A Short History of Chinese Philosophy* (New York: The Macmillan Co., 1948), pp. 7, 9: "Chinese philosophy... regardless of its different schools of thought, is directly or indirectly concerned with government and ethics.... [It is] inseparable from political thought.... Metaphysics... ethics... logic... all... are connected with political thought in one way or another."

11. Even the invasions China does not formally absorb, like Islam, she transforms in spirit. "The most noticeable thing is that, compared with the adherents of Islam in other countries, the Mohammedans of China seem always to have been content to be a community apart, living among the Chinese, and marrying Chinese women... without apparently any urge to extend their faith and political influence by the warlike methods usually associated with their creed. Can it have been that the original Arab temperament was affected by the prevailing Confucianist atmosphere of peace-loving compromise?" (E. R. and K. Hughes, *Religion in China,* London: Hutchison House, 1950) p. 98.

12. "Two-thirds of India is either semi-desert or for months in the year parched land." Horace Alexander, *New Citizens of India* (Oxford: Oxford University Press, 1952), p. 118.

13. "There are, assuredly, two forms of *Brahman,* the formed and the formless. Now that which is formed is unreal (asatyam); that which

is formless is the real (satyam)...." *Maitrī Upaniṣad* VII. 3, in S. Radhakrishnan, *The Principal Upaniṣads* (New York: Harper and Brothers, 1953), p. 817. Also the *Dhammapada* XIII: "Look upon this world as you would on a bubble, look upon it as you would on a mirage"; F. Max Müller, trans., *The Dhamma-Pada: A Collection of Verses,* The Sacred Books of the East, Vol. X, Pt. 1.

14. *Cf.* Heinrich Zimmer, *The Philosophies of India,* Joseph Campbell, ed. (New York: Pantheon Books, 1951): "Here is no bending of cosmic forces to the will of man, but on the contrary, a relentless shelling off of cosmic forces."

15. Note, e.g., the rise of the Dravidian party in South India today.

16. Cf. Heinrich Zimmer, *op. cit.,* p. 356. "They turned their backs on the external universe... because they were discovering something more interesting. They had found the interior world, the inward universe of man himself, and within that the mystery of the Self."

17. II.i.1. Swami Prabhavananda and Frederick Manchester, trans., *The Upaniṣhads* (Hollywood: Vedanta Press, 1947), pp. 30–31.

18. Swami Prabhavananda, "Religion and Other-Worldliness," in Christopher Isherwood, ed., *Vedanta for Modern Man* (New York: Harper and Brothers, 1951), p. 200.

19. Heinrich Zimmer, *op. cit.,* p. 357.

20. *Cf.* S. Radhakrishnan: "In India the interest of philosophy is in the self of man.... The life of mind is depicted in all its mobile variety and subtle play of light and shade.... Metaphysical schemes are based on the data of the psychological science." *Indian Philosophy* (London: George Allen & Unwin Ltd., 1923), Vol. I, p. 28.

21. Rhys Davids, *The Birth of Indian Psychology and Its Development in Buddhism* (London: Luzac and Co., 1936), p. 279.

22. *Cf.* Hammer-Purgstall and Karl von den Steinen's studies on language as described by Ernst Cassirer, *op. cit.,* pp. 174–175.

23. *In Foundations of Science* (Lancaster, Pa.: Science Press, 1913).

24. "Administrators and Bureaucracy: The Power Structure in Chinese Society," in *Transactions of the Second World Congress of Sociology* (London: International Sociological Association, 1954), p. 12.

25. *Cf.* Laplace's tribute: "It is India that gave us the ingenious method of expressing all numbers by means of ten symbols, each symbol receiving a value of position as well as an absolute value.... We shall appreciate the grandeur of this achievement the more when we remember that it escaped the genius of Archimedes and Appolonius, two of the greatest men produced by antiquity." Quoted in Tobian Dantzig, *Number: The Language of Science* (New York: The Macmillan Co., 1930), p. 19. To this Dantzig adds: "The achievement of the unknown Hindu who sometime in the first centuries of

our era discovered the principle of position assumes the proportions of a world-event.... In the history of culture the discovery of zero will always stand out as one of the greatest single achievements of the human race."

26. *Cf.* Zimmer, *op. cit.,* p. 31: "Nothing in Hindu physics, biology or zoology can compare with the mature achievements of Aristotle, Theophrastus, Eratosthenes, and the scientists in Hellenistic Alexandria.... The Indian natural sciences cannot be said ever to have equaled those known to Europe."

27. Werner Bishoff, *Japan* (New York: Simon & Schuster, 1955), p. 7. *Cf.* also Frank Gibney, *Five Gentlemen of Japan* (Tokyo: Chas. E. Tuttle, 1954), p. 33: "It has so often been Japan's tragedy that cruelty and atrocities have formed the one escape valve for the freer human feelings which a ruthlessly tight society did its unconscious best to inhibit or suppress."

28. London: Watts & Co., 1935, p. 81.

29. "Man Owes his Freedom to God," *Colliers,* 137, No. 7 (March 30, 1956), 78.

Accents of the World's Religions

Nearly a hundred years ago, in the syllabus of The Religious Science Club of The Australian Church, Dr. Charles Strong wrote:

> "The use of studying other religions than our own is that our sympathy becomes thereby widened. We learn to think more charitably of those outside our religion and more worthily of God as not our God only, but a God who cares for all and whose spirit has always been working in the world. And we thus learn to understand our own religion, and see what it is in our own religion that has to be emphasized, and what the higher truth is that is wrapped up in it, and that we must try to communicate to mankind."[1]

An earlier version of this essay was given as the first Charles Strong Memorial Lecture to selected university and adult education audiences in Australia during 1961. It then appeared in Milla wa-Milla: The Australian Bulletin of Comparative Religion 1 *(Spring 1961) : 6–21. There is a certain overlap between this essay and the earlier "Accents of the World's Philosophies." That overlap has been allowed to remain as it indicates how intertwined Huston Smith understood the religious and philosophical traditions to be. Moveover, it allows us to see the development of Huston Smith's thinking. As he noted in a letter to me: "When I was asked to deliver the Charles Strong Memorial Lecture in Australia, I used the occasion to move into the world's religions the thesis that I had previously directed to philosophy. As the essays were for different audiences, I did not change my account of the underlying thesis where I was satisfied with the original wording. This explains the occasional overlap in these first two essays."*

It is in the spirit of these words that this first Charles Strong Memorial Lecture is offered.

I

Inescapably, human beings are involved in three basic encounters: with nature, with other people, and with themselves. Roughly these may be identified as humankind's natural, social, and psychological problems.

The great surviving cultural traditions are also three: the East Asian, the Indian, and the Western. It is the thesis of this lecture that it helps us to understand and relate the unique perspectives of these three traditions in their religious as well as other dimensions if we think of each as having attended to one problem more diligently than to the other two. The decision to do so represents each tradition's fundamental option, the main direction each has chosen in its ceaseless pursuit of salvation and the real. Thus, though in one sense the language of the human spirit can be regarded as a universal language in that wherever it is spoken it must attend to some extent to all three human problems, it is equally the case that this language has been spoken in different accents, each bespeaking a unique symphony of emphases and orientations which has constituted its culture's religious self-identity.

Specifically, the religions of the West (Judaism, Christianity, and Islam) have accented the problem of humanity's relation to nature; those of East Asia (Confucianism, Taoism, and Shinto) have stressed the social problem; and those of India (Hinduism, Buddhism, and Jainism) have attended primarily to the psychological issue.

That is my thesis. Now for the supporting evidence.

II

I begin with the West: with Judaism, Christianity, and Islam, which, despite their important differences, can be grouped together on grounds of their family resemblances.[2] All were semitically originated, all share a common theological vocabulary (while using it to say different things at times), and all stand in a single historical tradition inasmuch as Christianity claims to be the fulfillment of Judaism and Islam the fulfillment of Judaism and Christianity.

It may sound surprising to suggest that these religions are notable for their interest in nature, for we have been more conscious of their supernatural than of their naturalistic components. This, though, is because we tend to compare them with other strands of Western culture, rather than with other religions. Compared with Western science, Western philosophy, or even Western art, Western religions *are* more otherworldly. But when they are compared with other religions, their distinguishing feature is seen to lie in their higher regard for nature and the greater extent to which they have come to grips with it.

Initial evidence for this appears in the principal discoveries that the West came up with, the three most important of which are modern science, the idea of progress, and the concept of the individual and its rights. On examination, each of these turns out to be directly related to one of nature's matrices: space, time, and matter. Science obviously focuses on matter. Scrutinize the material world and one notices invariant sequences which, abstracted from, become the laws of nature. The idea of progress, for its part, is obviously related to time. Ponder the mystery of time long enough and one becomes aware, first, of the novelty that it can introduce into experience, and from there it is but a step to the realization that the new might be better than the old. Finally, the individual relates to space. What ultimately distinguished human beings from one another is the fact that they occupy different bodies, which is to say, different regions of space. The connection also turns up in the adage that the frontier (with its wide open spaces) is the breeding ground of individualism.

That the West's great discoveries mesh with nature in these ways seems clear, but if we push on to ask what inclined the West toward nature in the first place, we are on trickier ground. This may not be due only to the fact that questions of origins root back into the twilight zone of protohistory where evidence is too scanty to allow for confident conclusions. Such questions may have no final, empirical answers. That this is consonant with theories that trace religious differences to divine revelation—theories which, though this is not commonly recognized, are as prominent in Hinduism as in the West—does not displease me; but the inherent mystery of origins, if such it be, may have a human explanation as well. For if freedom is real, the innovators who first pressed their faiths in different directions may simply have chosen differently, in which case the differences would have no empirical cause. What I am reaching for is a balance between total explanation and none. I shall cite influences that may have encouraged early Westerners to look expectantly toward nature without presuming that they dissolve the mystery that resides in all great historical, as in all great personal, happenings.

(a) *Matter.* "Christianity," as Archbishop Temple used to contend, "is the most avowedly materialistic of all the great religions."[3] Denis de Rougemont concurs: "Compared with the religions of the East, Christianity might be called materialism."[4] Judaism and Islam should be ranked beside Christianity in these judgments, but thus enlarged they stand.

Obviously there have been anti-matter eddies in the Western stream—Manichaeanism, Gnosticism, Docetism, Neo-Platonism, Plotinus, and others. But they never take over. The first three are explicitly condemned as heretical, and Plotinus and the Neo-Platonists are by passed in favor of Aristotle and Aquinas' acceptance of matter as altogether real. Moreover, and equally instructive for our thesis, the inspiration for the matter-disparaging outlooks usually comes from the East, often from India herself. For India, matter is a barbarian, spoiling everything it touches. By contrast, the West respects matter and takes it seriously, meshing nature and spirit wherever possible. Time and again she seems on the verge of slipping into the view that spirit is good and matter bad, but always she recovers. The Judeo-Christian Bible opens with the assertion that "God created the heavens *and the earth*," and before the chapter concludes it has God surveying all that He created, earth included, "and behold, it was very good." Good, moreover, not only for beholding, but as a field for endeavour; for in the center of that crucial opening chapter of Genesis humanity is commissioned to "have dominion... over all the earth," a commission later assumed to have been accepted and fulfilled: "Thou madest him to have dominion over the works of thy hands; thou has put all things under his feet" (Psalm 8:6). The Incarnation pays matter its highest conceivable compliment—it can become divine. The Kingdom of Heaven, from Jewish and early Christian apocalypticism right down to the social gospel, is to come *on earth*. Even in death the West will not desert the body. If there is to be life after death it, too, must be in some sense physical: hence, "I believe... in the resurrection of the body." Throughout the entire sequence runs the effort to maintain a sense of kinship between humanity and nature which totemism had earlier pointed up. Paul sees the entire cosmos as locked with people in their fallen condition, groaning and travailing as it awaits its redemption with and through theirs.[5] An earthquake forms the backdrop for the crucifixion. "Nature also mourns for a lost good."

It is unlikely that such a high regard for matter would have emerged in regions where nature confronted humanity as a holy terror. But in the parts of the Near East that cradled the Western religions, nature's guise was beneficent. Ancient historians have christened the arc that begins with the Nile, moves up the

Palestinian corridor, across Syria, and down the Tigris and Euphrates valleys "the Fertile Crescent," and it may even be no accident that the Garden of Eden story comes from this region, for nature here was in a most favorable mood—rich and joyous and treating humanity as a friend. To the Jews, Canaan seemed veritably to flow with milk and honey. There were problems to be met, challenges to equal; but their proportions were such as to coax rather than to discourage inquiry and advances. Matter appeared as a plausible matrix within which to continue the quest for human fulfillment.

India early ceased to think so, but China didn't. China resembles the West in seeking life's solution within a material context of some sort. But this isn't enough to define naturalism. A thoroughgoing naturalism requires not only that matter but that time as well be taken seriously, and Chinese religion implicates itself in time no more than does Indian.

(b) *Time.* To take time seriously is to be conscious of (1) the directional character of history, (2) the radical novelty it can introduce, (3) the uniqueness of every event, and (4) the potential decisiveness of some. Indian and Chinese religions stress none of these points. The Indian view of time is cyclical, reducing all that occurs to the anonymous insignificance of an ephemeral passage through illusion, while the Chinese tend not to generalize about time any more than about other things. For the East, time is a placid, silent pool in which ripples come and go. For the West, time is an arrow or river: it has origin, direction, destination, and is irreversible.[6] It is not difficult to see why. Judaism, the foundational religion of the West, was instigated by a concrete historical happening—the Exodus—as those of India and China were not. In addition, the basic concepts of Judaism were forged while the Jews, being either displaced persons or oppressed, were a people in waiting—first to cross over into the promised land, then to return to Jerusalem, then for the coming of the Messiah who was to deliver them.

This built into Judaism a future-oriented character[7] which was unique[8] until duplicated by Christianity which too is grounded in unique historical occurrences—the Incarnation and the Resurrection—and looks toward the future, in its case to the return of Christ and the coming of his kingdom on earth. The idea of progress, which arose in the West, and independently in the West only, is the secular offshoot of this Messianism, while the equally Western-originated Marxist vision of a classless society is its giant heretical facsimile.

(c) *Space.* The third property of nature is space, which has religious overtones because of its relation to individuality.

What distinguishes two persons most irrevocably is the fact that they are spatially discrete by virtue of occupying different bodies. It may be no accident, therefore, that the tradition which values individuality most and sees humanity's destiny to consist not in transcending the ego but in continuing and developing it, is the tradition in which space occasioned fewest problems because it was most plentiful. A recent report from India reads:

> "Too many people everywhere! Three servants for my simple hotel room. Seven or eight men, one of whom is working, in every tiny shop. The roadway invaded by a crowd moving in all directions, so that the passage of wheeled traffic is always obstructed. The pavements thick with sleepers at night. And I saw five people on one bicycle![9]

In such an everlasting swarm, there simply may not have been room for individuality to rise to its possibilities. The ideal breeding ground for individualism, as was earlier noted, is the frontier, and among the world's faiths it is Christianity that has been preeminently the frontier religion, moving first into the desolate swamps and forests of Northern Europe, and then across the waters into the Americas. The West's high estimate of the individual may be partly child of this fact. In the East everything participates in everything and nothing ever gets really detached from anything, neither a son from his father nor what is dead from what is alive; what is most prized in persons is the essence of their humanity which is shared in common with others. The West, by contrast, considers differences and distinctions to be virtues; the infinite worth which attaches to each individual derives in part precisely from the fact that everyone is unique and irreplaceable. This is part of the meaning of Kierkegaard's description of Christians as "joyful heirs to the finite"; they not only accept the finite, they rejoice in it. In death no less than in life, the West resists the East's temptation to merge the soul with the Absolute, insisting instead that it retains its identity through all eternity. The theological correlative of this concept of an individual soul is the concept of a personal God which again contrasts with Eastern, more impersonal, alternatives.

Western religion has involved itself more deeply, confidently, and expectantly in space, time, and matter, all three, than have those of India and China. Using "natural theology" in this special sense, we can identify it as the West's distinctive theological contribution.

III

East Asia, on the other hand, concentrated on social ethics; so much so, indeed, that it is often asked whether her basic philosophy—Confucianism—is rightly considered a religion at all.

At least two facts suggest that East Asia may have turned in this direction because nature looked less promising. The first of these is the Mongoloid physiognomy which bears marks of having originated under conditions of severe cold, probably in Siberia and eastern Central Asia where high winds were matched by temperatures which fell below minus 80° F. Such conditions were a far cry from the mild and sunny climes of the Mediterranean. They were so fierce that to this day the Mongoloid carries their impact on their faces. "There is no question," writes Walter Fairservis, "that the Mongoloid face is better equipped for cold weather than any other."[10] It has more protective fat, and its most exposed surface area, the nose, is reduced by the forward extrusion of the cheekbones and a retreat of the nose itself. Its eyes are protected by an extension vertically of the eye orbits and the whole area padded with fat, while the epicanthic fold which extends from the nose area over the upper eye narrows the slit of the eye and, with the fatty padding, acts as a kind of snow goggle against glare as well as an eye shield against the cold. Breathing through the nasal passages is facilitated by the retraction of the nose area into the face, while the banking up of nasal passages with fat provides maximum heat for the air on its way to the lungs. Face hair, which is a handicap in extreme cold because the beard stores breath moisture as ice which freezes the face, is reduced more than in any other human type.[11]

The other conspicuous fact is China's rivers. Chinese culture, like that of the West, is riverine in origin. But whereas the Nile, and the Tigris and Euphrates after their first cataclysmic floods, were well-mannered and orderly, China's rivers were unmanageable. The soil in the great treeless mountain ranges where the Yellow River and Yangtze rise washes badly, feeding into the rivers enormous quantities of yellow silt. The Yangtze dumps 400 million tons of this silt into the China Sea every year, while in the Yellow River it reaches 46% by weight and gives the river its name. Building up the riverbeds, this silt causes the rivers to flood inordinately. A single breach in the dikes, which in places have been built to heights of fifty feet to contain the elevated waters, can inundate hundreds of square miles and cut millions of farmers off from their sustenance. As resultant sedimentation can be as much as six feet deep, years may elapse before flood-ravaged lands can be cultivated again. I was myself living as a boy but twelve miles from the Yangtze during the catastrophic floods of 1932 which inundated an area equal to Missouri, Kansas, and Iowa combined and cost a million lives. The record of the Yellow River is even worse. Not without reason has it been called "China's Sorrow" "More than... any other great river, the Yellow River presents human-kind with a seemingly insoluble problem. Rulers of China have always faced but never conquered it."[12] Very early in China the rivers came to be symbolized by the dragon, which was also for centuries China's national emblem.

One stands in awe of dragons; one doesn't expect to tame them. We should be prepared to find, then, in China, a certain deference toward nature. There is a kind of naturalism in Chinese thought, but it is the naturalism of the artist, the nature lover, or the romanticist, rather than that of the scientist—the naturalism of a Wordsworth or a Thoreau rather than of a Galileo or a Bacon. Nature in China is something to be appreciated, intuited, communed with, or reverenced; there is no sustained notion that it might be mastered. A passage from the *Tao Tê Ching* puts the point in a nutshell:

> Those who would take over the earth
> And shape it to their will
> Never, I notice, succeed.
> The earth is like a vessel so sacred
> That at the mere approach of the profane
> It is marred
> And when they reach out their fingers it is gone.[13]

Chinese science, as a consequence, doesn't develop.[14] For a field of constructive endeavour the Chinese turned instead to society. They may have been lured in this direction by the fact that their population was racially homogeneous and so presented no surface discouragements to the natural wish for a harmonious society. But there were also factors which *forced* them to attend to the social problem. One was the crowded conditions under which they lived.[15] Another may have been the joint family system under which several generations and relatives as distant as third cousins might be grouped in a single household—three of Confucius' five famous relationships are concerned with the family. China's rivers may also have figured here, for from the beginnings of Chinese civilization they required vast, cooperative dike-building projects to keep them in their channels.[16] Finally, China's basic outlook was forged in the social furnace of her "Time of Troubles," those five convulsive centuries between 700 and 200 B.C. during which the Chou Dynasty was

in decay, centuries which culminated in the endemic violence of the
"Warring Kingdoms" in which anarchy was the order of the day. In
this context the burning question facing every responsible thinker
was the one which, on a smaller scale but under vaguely similar circumstances, faced Plato as well: How to save Athens?

The solution as it finally emerged gathered together many strands
but bore the distinctive stamp of Confucius' genius. It amounted to
nothing less than the attempt to 'Emily Post' an entire way of life in
which human relationships were always the focus of attention. Subtle
differences in relationship were delineated and prescribed to a
degree paralleled in tribes, but in no other civilization—witness the
complex vocabulary for distinguishing paternal from maternal
uncles, aunts, cousins, and in-laws, and for expressing fine distinctions in seniority. The prescriptions were enforced externally by sen-
sitizing individuals to the way they were regarded by others—'face'
in the peculiarly oriental sense of that word—and internally by delib-
erate self-examination.[17] Interests of family and community were
given precedent over those of the individual, and tested ways of the
past honored—by ancestor worship and filial piety—above innova-
tion and experiment.

The content of the life-pattern thus secured centered in the ideal
of the *chün-tzŭ*, or gentleman in the best sense of the term; the person who is completely poised, competent, confident, and adequate to
every social occasion; the one of perfect address, who is always at
ease within and therefore can put others at their ease. This attitude
toward others is that of *jen*, usually translated as benevolence, or
simply goodness. But the matter isn't left thus generalized. What *jen*
requires in specific instances is carefully prescribed by the delineation of "graded love"—that is, love for others according to one's
relationship to them, the five most important relationships being
those between father and son, elder brother and younger brother,
husband and wife, friend and friend, ruler and subject. The sum of
the conduct befitting these relationships is *li,* meaning propriety, but
significantly ritual as well, since it amounts to the ritualization of the
entire social process, from the way the emperor opens the doors of
the Temple of Heaven on great ceremonial occasions right down to
the way one entertains the humblest guest and serves tea. With
scholars placed at the top of the social scale and soldiers excluded
from it altogether, learning was revered[18] and violence despised. A
system of local and Imperial examinations, which made learning the
prime qualification for public office, opened the door to social mobili-
ty—the poorest peasant's son might aspire to high public office—

and produced the closest approximation to Plato's vision of the philosopher-king as this planet has seen. Age was respected, courtesy raised to the level of an art, and beauty admired to the point where the facility of an alphabet was rejected in favor of calligraphy, the most handsome, as well as most difficult form of written expression ever evolved.

If cross-cultural comparisons are difficult, cross-cultural evaluations are even more so. It is easy to say that China attended to social relationships more carefully than to science or psychology, and more carefully than did India or the West. But did China thereby achieve more in this regard? No judgment on this question can at this point pretend to be objective; too much depends on whether one favors dynamism, passion, tumult, creativity, and the individual (the West), or quiet, conservative good order. Avoiding comparisons, let me simply say that I find China's social achievement impressive. Chinese culture has a flavor all its own. It is a compound of subtlety, brilliance, and reticence that produces an effect that can be described only as good taste. Traditionally the Chinese have exalted the life of reasonable enjoyment and despised the destructive. As a consequence they have been able to unite an immense area of fertility and to create—if we multiply duration by size of population included— the most extensive civilization ever achieved, one which at its height included one-third of the human race. The political structure of this civilization alone, the Chinese Empire, lasted under various dynasties for 2133 years (from 221 B.C. to A.D. 1912)—a period that makes the empires of Alexander the Great and Caesar look insignificant. Its power of assimilation was equally impressive. Having the most open frontier of all great civilizations, China was subject to wave after wave of invasions by cavalried barbarians who were always ready to fall on the earth-bound agriculturalists. Always at their gates were the very Tartars whose one long-range raid inflicted a mortal wound on the Roman Empire. But what the Chinese could not exclude they absorbed. Each wave of invasion tends quickly to lose its identity. As the great sinologist Arthur Waley has remarked, there is scarcely a barbarian conqueror who came in purely for profit who within twenty years was not attempting to write a copy of Chinese verse which his master, who is also his conquered slave, might say was not wholly unworthy of a gentleman. And already the conqueror is hoping to be mistaken for Chinese. Here is a cultural furnace with enough heat to effect a real melting pot. There is no evidence that these barbarians were ever as impressed with what they found in Europe.

IV

Turning to the third great tradition, the Indian, we find neither the natural nor the social environment inviting India's primary attention. Geographically India today is a land of fierce extremes, running from the icy peaks of the Himalayas to the steaming jungles of Cape Cormorin. In summer, wrote Rudyard Kipling, "there is neither sky, sun, nor horizon. Nothing but a brown-purple haze of heat. It is as though the earth were dying of apoplexy." During this furnace season, millions of Indian villagers lie gasping in their mud huts. Wells dry up and fields blow away. When the monsoon rains come in the fall, the torrential downpours drown the arid land in surging floods. Only in the winter months does India appear comfortably livable and naturel kind.[19] We cannot, however, assume that nature was always this harsh. It is possible that with fruit that dripped from the trees and climate that demanded virtually no clothing, there was a time during which nature in India was so easy going that nature didn't challenge humanity in its direction at all.[20]

What is clear is that for one reason or another India bracketed nature. China in doing so turned its attention to society. But here India found itself facing the most devilish of all social problems, ethnic diversity. India is one of the greatest ethnographic museums in the world. An English anthropologist has likened India to "a deep net into which various races and peoples of Asia have drifted and been caught." The three main color divisions—yellow, black, and white— are represented, and these in turn have been further divided into seven distinct racial types.[21] No Indian ingenuity was equal to this problem. Caste was in part an attempt to deal with it, but instead of caste's solving the problem, in the end the problem took over caste, turning it into a device for perpetuating social distance. Relatively early, India abandoned hope of solving life's problem on the social plane.[22] Instead India turned inward, centering her attention on the psychological problem.[23] Nature? No; even at its best it drags us toward senility and death and leaves us with regrets. Society? No; as long as people are people there will be inequities and blockages on this front. But the individual—to the Indian the individual looked promising. If only we could discover who we truly are, might we not win through to an inner freedom beyond the opposites which block both nature and society?[24] The following lines from the *Katha Upansihad* will be recognized at once as typical of the Indian theme:

"...The senses turn outward. Accordingly, man looks toward what is without, and sees not what is within. [The wise man] shuts his eyes to what is without, and beholds the self."[25]

For the Indian, the senses are false witnesses.

"The world is not what it appears to be. Behind this surface life, where we experience the play of life and death, there is a deeper life which knows no death; behind our apparent consciousness, which gives us the knowledge of objects and things... there is... pure... consciousness... Truth... is experienced only by those who turn their gaze inward."[26]

As this conviction spreads, "such intellectual energy as had formerly been devoted to the study and development of a machinery for the mastery of the... forces of the cosmos... was... diverted inward.... The cosmic energy was being taken at its fountain head.... all secondary, merely derivative streams of energy... being left behind. In Indian thought... the whole outer world was dwindling in importance."[27]

India became, as a consequence, the world's religious psychologist. One evidence of India's preoccupation in this area is found in the elaborateness of its psychological vocabulary. Coomaraswamy, while curator of the Oriental Museum in Boston, used to say that for every psychological term in English there are four in Greek and forty in Sanskrit.[28] Mrs. Rhys Davids lists twenty Pali words whose subtle distinctions of meaning are obscured by single, indiscriminate English rendition as "desire" or "desires."

What India actually discovered of importance in psychology is, of course, a moot question. Elsewhere I have suggested eight specific insights which are remarkably contemporary to have been discovered in India over two thousand years ago.[29] Here I shall confine myself to a single point and several supporting testimonials. The point concerns the subconscious which breaks upon the West in the nineteenth century but in India before Christ,[30] with (in my judgment) two continuing advantages in India's favor: first, India's delineation of several layers of subconsciousness, not just one; and second, her greater awareness of the creative potentialities of the subconscious along with pathological ones. As for tributes, I shall content myself with three. It was the *Upanishads*' analysis of the self which caused Schopenhauer to stamp them "the product of the highest human wisdom," and Count Keyserling to say that Hinduism at its best has spoken the only relevant truth about the way to self-realization in the full sense of the word. The third tribute is the more impressive because it comes from the leader of the Barthian-grounded school which insists that religious truth is contained fully and exclusively in the Christian revelation. Despite this conviction, Hendrick Kraemer grants that "the wisdom of the East possesses a greater psychological virtuosity in analyzing man, in order to teach him to manage and master himself by spiritual and other kinds of training. As is well known, Eastern wisdom and spiritual experience meet here with the great discoveries in psychology and psychotherapy since Freud."[31]

Neither China nor the West have given a fraction of India's attention to the mind. Historically, India rightly deserves the title of the world's religious psychologist.[32]

V

We have suggested that each of the three great religious traditions has shown a unique specialization—the West in "religious naturalism." China in social ethics, and India in religious psychology. It remains to point out the inevitable price of specialization: ineptness in the subjects neglected. "Nothing fails like success." In the end all three traditions are brought to disaster or its brink because each succeeded so well on one front that it felt safe in neglecting the other two.

China and India have both neglected nature, the injunction to "have dominion." Consequently science has not developed, and the standard of living remains intolerably low. In China the problem periodically proved too much even for social genius. Between dynasties there was regularly a long period of civil strife which can always be correlated with population pressure on cultivated land which failed to increase productivity because improvement of agricultural technique was negligible. As for India, its only scientific contributions to the world at large have been in pure mathematics,[33] where India was dealing not with the outer world but with the resources of the mind.[34] In addition to ineptness toward nature, India adds social clumsiness, vividly illustrated by the present state of the caste system,[35] and China adds psychological naïveté.

Occasionally we catch glimpses in China of an interest in the mind and what it can do, as in the quietistic movement in the Chou Dynasty, the *Tao Tê Ching's* esoteric rendering of the idea of *te,* Mencius' passage on "the dawn breath," and Chu Hsi's discussion of "silent sitting." But the interest is never systematically pursued, and it usually takes a social turn: the mind is being inspected not for itself but for what it can contribute to social stability. One gets the impression that when China does get around to psychology, it is only social psychology that really interests it. East Asia's deficiencies in this field are seen most clearly in its failure to recognize the danger of repression. The Chinese scheme had no place for emotional carthasis, spontaneity, and unrepression. Consequently, negative emotions got damned up until eventually the dam gave way and the emotions came forth in terrifying form; Mao's Cultural Revolution of 1966–76 is the twentieth century's glaring instance of this. The pattern carried over to Japan where, as Robert Guillain has pointed out, a youth "received a Spartan training which developed his aggressive instincts and, at the same time, screwed down over his violent nature a sort of lid of blind obedience and perfect politeness. This made him an explosive creature, ready to burst like a bomb."[36]

The deficiencies of the West have been in psychology and sociology. Psychologically the West has been until recently merely inconspicuous, but in sociology one wonders if the West has not been delinquent. At least four facts must be faced as evidences of the West's ineptitude in social relations and lack of perceptiveness as to the forces that make for social cohesion and group harmony.

1. The first comes to light in simply comparing Europe's political map with those of China and India. Whereas Chinese civilization had the power to expand, uniting more and more people in a common heritage, and whereas Indian civilization could at least hold its own, the record of the West has been one of continuous secession. After the union of the Northern and Southern Kingdoms in Egypt, there is no further fusion in the Fertile Crescent. Instead, fission sets in. The Hebrews divide into Israel and Judah. "The fatal danger of Greece," writes Gilbert Murray, "was disunion as many see it in Europe now."[37] The Christian Church splits into East and West, the Western Church into Roman Catholic and Protestant, and Protestantism splinters. The Medieval Empire shatters into nations, and the process continues. Norway, Denmark, and Sweden, originally a Scandinavian unit, divide. Belgium and Holland, once united in the Netherlands, are apart. The British Isles have been plagued with separatist movements. The United States has had its Civil War and continuing North-South animosity. What has enfeebled and discredited us in our own day, writes Arnold Toynbee, "is the atrocious fratricidal warfare, within the bosom of our Western Society, since 1914.... We Westerners have fought among ourselves another bout of wars that have been as savage, destructive and discreditable as our earlier wars of religion."[38] Western history since the Middle Ages is one

long story of inability to inspire embracing loyalties strong enough to outweigh provincial attachments.

2. Western religion appears to have shared in this social ineptitude. The only large-scale persecuting religions have been those of the West—Judaism, Christianity, and Islam. Since the Middle Ages, Christianity has been divisive by itself. To continue with Toynbee: "For 400 years and more, from the outbreak of the struggle between the Papacy and Frederick II in the thirteenth century down to the end of the Catholic-Protestant Western wars of religion in the seventeenth century, the Christian Church in the Western World was a force that made not for gentleness and peace and concord, but for violence and dissension.... Before the end of the seventeenth century, the hatred, strife and atrocities inflicted on the Western World by Christian *odium theologicum* had become a scandal and menace to the Western Civilization."[39]

3. The West has invented the two things which, combined, most endanger the world's future: total war and religious nationalism.[40]

4. Eventually (one almost says inevitably) there emerges in Europe a social theory—or more accurately a religion, albeit a heretical one—which pushes the Western emphasis to its logical extreme. Paralleling the West's temptation to reduce psychology to physiology, Marx reduces sociology to economics. In the end, were one to believe him, there *is* no social problem. Once the material problem is solved, the social problem will automatically take care of itself and the state will wither away.

VI

We have suggested that each of the world's three great religious traditions has exercised a noteworthy influence on one of the basic human problems, but seems to have tended insufficiently to the other two. It would appear that an adequate civilization must strike all three notes as a chord. In developing this chord of a fully adequate world culture, each of the three great traditions appear to have something of importance to contribute. Perhaps each has something to learn as well.

Epilogue

Not often in discussions as general as this does one stumble upon evidence so clear-cut as to stand as independent verification for an entire thesis. But since completing the above, a point has occurred to me which seems to come close to this.

What is truth? The question didn't arise in our discussion. But if one does raise it, one finds the three civilizations answering along the lines we would expect. For the West, truth is essentially correspondence with a state of affairs that exists independently in nature or history (past nature). A Chinese, on the other hand, will feel that the primary objects to which assertions refer, and are responsible, are the feelings of persons involved. Hence the normality of white lies and keeping one's mouth shut when appropriate. India has a third criterion: to India truth is essentially spiritual pragmatism. One can generate little interest in India over whether Hindu myths are "true" in our Western sense—whether Krishna really lived, for example. The accounts are true to the needs of the human spirit. What could be more important?

NOTES

1. A number of thoughts here expanded and revised first appeared in "Accents of the World's Philosophies," *Philosophy East and West,* April–July 1957. For the quote from Dr. Charles Strong see "A Memoir" by Annie Worsley and Helen Strong, *Church Worship* (Melbourne: Melville, Mullen & Slade, 1892), pp. 5–6.
2. Zoroastrianism also belongs in this group, but is too small to bring into this general discussion.
3. William Temple, *Nature, Man and God* (London: Macmillan and Co., 1953), p. 478.
4. Denis de Rougement, *Man's Western Quest* (New York: Harper Brothers, 1957), p. 122.
5. Romans 8: 19–23.
6. Though the West's time-consciousness has been recognized, it has not always been admired. Schopenhauer, for example, considered Christianity's grounding in a unique historical event a weakness, contending that Buddhism shows a deeper wisdom by remaining aloof from such an unphilosophical encumbrance.
7. The great historian of Judaism, Salo Baron, goes so far as to *define* Judaism as the struggle between the 'ought' and the 'is,' "the struggle… between the ideal and the actual."
8. Hinduism looks forward to its *avatars* and Buddhism to its *Maitreyas,* but these are archetypical rather than decisive, recurring "every time that…".
9. Quoted in Denis de Rougemont, *op. cit.,* p. 13.

10. *The Origins of Oriental Civilization* (New York: The New American Library, 1959), p. 75.
11. Adapted from C. S. Coon, S. M. Garn, J. B. Birdsell, *Races* (Springfield: Charles C. Thomas, Publisher, 1950).
12. Edwin O. Reischauer and John K. Fairbank, *East Asia: The Great Tradition* (Boston: Houghton Mifflin Company, 1960), p. 20.
13. Witter Bynner, Trans., *The Way of Life According to Laotzu* (New York: John Day Co., 1944), p. 43.
14. I think this statement can stand despite Joseph Needham's monumental study of *Science and Civilization in China* (Cambridge: Cambridge University Press, 1956—[subsequently completed in six volumes]. For the general conclusion of this study appears to be that though China was far more ingenious than we had supposed in solving specific practical problems, she was disinclined to abstract from her concrete successes the general principles that might be developed into organized sciences concerned with broad domains of nature. Thus with respect to technical and mechanical skill, China and the West remained on a par until the Ming Dynasty opened in 1368. But before that dynasty ended in 1644, Europe was in possession of modern science and China was still in her Middle Ages.
15. "The crowding of people upon the land and in tight walled villages is not new in China's history. The Han Empire, which was contemporary with the Roman Empire, had a population of sixty million people, most of it concentrated in North China. Throughout their history the Chinese have habitually lived close-packed in their social and family relationships." Edwin O. Reischauer and John K. Fairbank, *op. cit.,* pp. 27–28.
16. "From earliest times Chinese administrators... have had to construct dikes to keep the Yellow River in its channel" *(ibid.,* p. 20).
17. "Tseng-Tzu [one of Confucius' chief disciples] said: Every day I ask myself three questions: Have I been unfaithful in carrying out my obligations toward others? Have I been insincere in my relations toward my friends? Have I failed to put what has been taught me into practice?" *Analects,* I. 4.
18. To this day there are Chinese who will not step on a piece of paper if there is writing on it.
19. *Cf.* S. Levi, *L'Inde et le Monde* (Paris: Champion, 1926), p. 90: "The civilization of India, alone, has grown up between the tropic and the equator in reaction against a nature which exceeds normal limits."
20. Arthur Basham sides with this view. "In 3000 B.C. (India's) climate was very different. The whole Indus region was well forested...and Baluchistan, now almost a waterless desert, was rich in rivers.... If the climate had any effect on the Indian character, it was... to devel-

op a love of ease and comfort, an addiction to the simple pleasures and luxuries so freely given by Nature" *(The Wonder that Was India* [New York: Grove Press, 1959], pp. 13, 4).

21. T. W. Wallbank, *A Short History of India and Pakistan* (New York: New American Library, 1958), p. 11.
22. Heinrich Zimmer speaks of "the blank pessimism of the Indian philosophy of politics, untouched as it is by any hope or ideal of progress and improvement" *(The Philosophies of India* [New York: Pantheon Books, 1951], p. 127). T. W. Wallbank says that a "Fundamental feature of the Indian traditional culture pattern has been its neglect of what we might call the science of society, and more specifically the art of government" *(ibid.,* p. 47).
23. *Cf.* S. Radhakrishana, *Indian Philosophy* (London: George Allen & Unwin, 1923), Vol. I, p. 28: "In India... interest... is in the self of man."
24. "What is the Oriental (read Indian) dream? We want to master *physis,* they *psyche* (Denis de Rougemeont, *op. cit.,* p. 193).
25. II.i.1. Swami Prabhavananda and Frederick Manchester, trans., *The Upanishads* (Hollywood: Vedanta Press, 1947), pp. 30–31.
26. Swami Prabhavananda, "Religion and Otherworldliness," in Christopher Isherwood, ed., *Vedanta for Modern Man* (New York: Harper and Brothers, 1951), p. 200. One is reminded of Gandhi's repeated admonition to "turn the spotlight inward."
27. Heinrich Zimmer, *op. cit.,* p. 357.
28. With regard to nature the ratio is reversed. Arthur Lovejoy has pointed out that there are 400 variations of the word "natural" in romantic poetry alone.
29. "Accents of the World's Philosophies," *Philosophy East and West,* April–July, 1957.
30. Eastern religious philosophies "have by their own power reached conclusions centuries ago (especially in the field of psychology and mystical intuition) to which the modern Western quest for knowledge and for explanation of the enigma of Mind and Matter often seems to lead with compelling logic" (Hendrick Kraemer, *World Cultures and World Religions* (London: Lutterworth, 1960). *Cf.* also Denis de Rougemont, *op. cit.,* p. 192: "The psychology of the unconscious, as inaugurated by Freud and developed by Jung, links up with the Yogis."
31. *Op cit.,* p. 374.
32. India's "great contribution to the world is a clarified and discerning understanding of the spiritual psychology of man." (Edwin A. Burtt, *Man Seeks the Divine* (New York: Harper and Brothers, 1956), p. 125.

33. Unless one includes methods of body-control as imbedded in *hatha yoga*. But note that these were originally developed as preliminaries which led on to controlling the mind. Characteristically the body was being investigated for its psychological consequences.

34. The Indians discovered the zero, the decimal place system, and the numerals which we call Arabic because we got them from the Arabs but which the Arabs got from the Hindus.

35. Nehru has asserted that when the caste system became rigid and inflexible, this led to a "decline all along the line—intellectual, philosophical, political, in techniques and methods of war, in knowledge of and contacts with the outside world." Quoted in Wallbank, *op. cit.*, p. 46.

36. Quoted in Werner Bishoff, *Japan* (New York: Simon & Schuster, 1955). p. 7. Cf. also Frank Gibney, *Five Gentlemen of Japan* (Tokyo: Charles E. Tuttle 1954), p. 33: "It has so often been Japan's tragedy that cruelty and atrocities have formed the one escape valve for the freer human feelings which a ruthlessly tight society did its unconscious best to inhibit or suppress."

37. *The Five Stages of Greek Religion* (London: Watts & Co., 1935), p. 81.

38. "Man Owes his Freedom to God," *Colliers*, 137, No. 7. (March 30, 1956), p.78.

39. *Ibid.*

40. Though his book is on the whole strongly pro-Western, Denis de Rougemont admits this. On p. 178 of *Man's Western Quest, op. cit.*, we read: "Europe...certainly invented total war;" and on pages 75–78 he says some very important things about nationalism becoming a religion *à la* the French Revolution, Hegel, and thereafter, first in the West, then to the East. Japan comes close to sharing the invention of religious nationalism, but until Japan caught the West's variety, hers is better designated as religious patriotism.

Truth in Comparative Perspective

My essay consists of four parts. Beginning with the comparative side of my theme, I divide this into a temporal, historical comparison (Part I) and a geographical, spatial comparison (Part II). In Part III, I turn expressly to our Western handling of the truth issue, reserving Part IV for pulling these various strands together.

I. Truth in Time

There was a time, lasting roughly up to the European Renaissance, when humanity was at one in its view of truth, though, of course, we did not know that fact. Not only did we not know that we were one, which is to say, alike; we were barely aware that we were multiple—Indian, Chinese, Western, and so on—while sharing, in our notion of truth, a view that was essentially the same. What this original, shared view of truth was, I shall say in a moment, but let me make sure that the strategy for this first section of my essay is clear. I am saying that the basic comparison, in this matter of truth, is not geographical or spatial, but temporal: we need to contrast an original, primordial time when our views of truth were virtually alike, with a later (let us call it modern) time in which they diverge. The essential point about our original, shared view of truth is that it gathered three things into its single corral: things, assertions, and persons; the last bridging the other two inasmuch as persons are those

This essay originally appeared in Philosophy East and West *30, 4 (1980): 425–437 under the title "Western and Comparative Perspectives on Truth." It had earlier been presented at a Washington cross-cultural symposium on truth.*

unique kinds of things that are capable of making assertions. In every civilization at its start, truth had this triple reference: to things, to statements, and to persons.

If this sounds surprising, I claim that fact as itself a support for my thesis. The surprise stems, I assume, from our assumption that only propositions are really *true* or false, so that in suggesting (as I just did) that these properties might also apply to persons and things, I must have been using the word loosely if not metaphorically, the way I would be using "crooked" if I applied it to a politician. I was not. I was not speaking metaphorically or even loosely; I was speaking universally. To lift from the pool of truth's total, undifferentiated meaning a single referent—propositions—and develop its meaning in that direction is our Western contribution to the subject.[1] Part III will be devoted to that contribution. Here our task is to see that it was a selective move. It involved, however unconsciously, a choice.

Let me back into my claim about truth's original, threefold referent. Though as Western philosophers we tend now to restrict truth to propositions,[2] if we widen our gaze to note the way the word functions in our language at large, we find clear signs that its earlier referent was much broader. In the category of truth as a property of things, we still speak of "true north" and "a true tone." Were a carpenter to validate that a "tabletop is true," we would understand that he meant that it is level. We speak of "true friendships," or a "true university." Statesmen and stateswomen tell us that "NATO must try to effect a true unity," and for some time we have been apprized that "beauty is truth, truth beauty." As for truth as a property of persons, we have Christ's claim that he was the truth ("I am the way, the truth, and the life," John 14:6) and that truth can be enacted ("He that doeth truth cometh to the light," John 3:21). We refer to so-and-so as being "a true gentleman (statesman, friend, whatever);" there is "true bravery" and "false modesty;" and since the rise of existentialism, authenticity has become a way of talking about being "true to oneself."

These may be residues in our language. If so, they hark back to a time when truth had a wider referent than it has in Western philosophy today. Nietzsche noted that when "members of the Greek aristocracy [spoke]... of themselves as 'the truthful'... the word they used was *esthlos,* meaning one who is, who has true reality, who is true; [only] by a subjective turn [did] the true later become the *truthful.*"[3] The Latin *verus* means true; it also means real, genuine, and authentic—properties that obviously are not restricted to statements. The same holds for the key terms in other civilizations. In Sanskrit *satya* doubles for both truth and reality, as the famous *sat-*

cit-ānanda (being-awareness-bliss) discloses immediately. "Etymologically, the Chinese character *chen*ᵃ in its original seal form denotes a loaded scale standing on a stool which implies full, real, solid, and therefore the meaning of true, as opposed to empty and unreal, i.e. *chia*ᵇ."⁴ Arabic has three basic terms that deal with truth: *ḥaqqa,* which leans toward the truth of things: *ṣadaqa,* which points toward the truth of persons: and *saḥḥa* which stresses the truth of statements. To elaborate only the first of these, *ḥaqq* denotes what is true in and of itself by dint of its metaphysical or cosmic status. This makes it supremely applicable to God: when Manṣūr al-Ḥallāj proclaimed in a moment of ecstasy *"anā'l-Ḥaqq,"* "I am the Truth," he was crucified, it being taken for granted by those who heard him that in so saying he had claimed that he was Allāh. As Wilfred Smith points out:

> *Al-Ḥaqq* is a name of God not merely as an attribute but as a denotation. Huwa *al-Ḥaqq*: He is reality as such. Yet every other thing that is genuine is also *ḥaqq*—and, some of the mystics went on to say, is therefore divine. Yet the word means reality first, and then God, for those who equate him with reality.⁵

To sum up this first section, originally truth was triple. Yet even then there were geographical differences.

II. Truth in Space

As far back as our historical eyes can see we find different emphases in peoples' notions of truth. At first these differences were small, but as the civilizations worked out their distinctive identities— or discovered their respective destinies, however you wish to put the matter—the differences became more pronounced. If we confine ourselves to the three civilizations that are being considered in this symposium—East Asia (China, Korea, and Japan), South Asia (India), and the West—we can risk the generalization that more than did either of the other two, India tied truth to things, East Asia to persons, and the West to statements.

INDIA

"To the knower of Truth, all things have verily become the Self," the *Īśa Upaniṣad* tells us. "What delusion, what sorrow can there be for him who realizes that oneness" (verse 7)? It is that oneness carried to its absolute, logical limit that gives India no alternative but to lodge truth primarily in things, for if "That One Thing"[6] is truly the only thing that exists, everything else, persons and propositions included, must be *māyā*. These latter are real in the empirical order *(vyāvahārika sattva),* but in absolute existence *(pāramārthika sattva)* they do not figure at all. Professor K. L. Seshagiri Rao makes this point explicitly in the "Dialogue on Truth" that appeared between him and Father Peter Riga in *Philosophy East and West:*

> The Hindu view is... that truth is not an abstract, intellectual formulation or proposition.... Truth... is not that which is... understood by the intellect. It is prior to all knowledge.... Being [and] truth... are interchangeable.... Reasoning is posterior and secondary to the fundamental experience of being (20, no. 4 [October, 1970]: 377, 379).

Buddhism's substitution of a process vocabulary (verbs) for Hinduism's nouns does not affect the point at issue: it, too, makes a state-of-affairs truth's basic home, as Nāgārjuna's twofold theory of truth (practical, conventional, world-ensconced *saṁvṛtti-satya* versus ultimate, highest *paramārtha-satya*) makes plain. "As long as 'truth' is regarded as an idea," it is at best inferior truth that we are dealing with; at worst such truth "can destroy a person 'like a snake wrongly grasped or magical knowledge incorrectly applied' *(Kārikās* 24.11)....'Emptiness' should not be regarded as another 'viewpoint'."[7] This basic Indian association of truth with being continues to the present. When Mahatma Gandhi turned *satyāgraha* into an international word which, among other things, was to play an important part in the Black Liberation movement in America, it was truth-*force* he was talking about. Truth as veridical concept and utterance were secondary.

EAST ASIA

My suggestion that East Asia lodges truth basically in persons should come as no surprise, given the social emphasis of its orientation as a whole. I assume that this social emphasis is generally recognized, but I shall cite several witnesses to it, to bring it to our direct attention. The following characterizations all focus on China, but they could easily be extended to cover Japan as well:

Wei-ming Tu: "Étienne Balazs, the brilliant sinologist, once characterized all Chinese philosophy as preeminently social philosophy."[8]

Arthur Waley: "All Chinese philosophy is essentially the study of how men can best be helped to live together in harmony and good order."[9]

Fung Yu-lan: "Chinese philosophy.... is directly or indirectly concerned with government and ethics.... All [its branches] are connected with political thought in one way or another."[10]

Wing-tsit Chan: "Chinese philosophers... have been interested primarily in ethical, social, and political problems."[11]

How this social preoccupation affected the East Asian notion of truth can be briefly summarized as follows: To begin with a negative point, the Chinese language does not appear to have been devised with an eye for dealing with abstract, intangible entities; absence of definite grammatical rules in ancient China and the ambiguity of individual ideograms and pictograms make it awkward for it to do so.[12] To cite but a single example, the closest Chinese comes to the Sanskrit *sat* and the English "being" or "existence" is *yu,* which basically means "to have" or "to possess." Possession implies a possessor and as persons are the kinds of possessors we tend to think of first, the word *yu* gives a personal flavor to even metaphysics' final generality and abstraction—I am thinking of Aristotle's definition of metaphysics as the study of being *qua* being.

As we turn from the notion of being to the notion of truth itself, that flavor increases.[13] I shall soon be arguing that our Western tendency has been to regard truth as the correspondence of an idea or utterance with an objective state of affairs which ideally could be captured on videotape. Using this criterion, Westerners have given Orientals bad marks for veracity. The following nineteenth-century missionary reports amount to outright condemnation:

> More unerradicable than the sins of the flesh is the falsity of the Chinese;... their disregard of truth has perhaps done more to lower their character than any other fault.[14]
> The ordinary speech of the Chinese is so full of insincerity... that it is very difficult to learn the truth in almost every case. In China it is literally true that a fact is the hardest thing in the world to get at.[15]

We would not expect Jacob Bronowski to be as biased as those missionaries were, but even he does not conceal his frustration:

Anyone who has worked in the East knows how hard it is there to get an answer to a question of fact. When I had to study the casualties from the atomic bombs in Japan at the end of the war, I was dogged and perplexed by this difficulty.... Whatever man one asks, [he] does not really understand what one wants to know.... At bottom he does not know the facts because they are not his language. These cultures of the East... lack the language and the very habit of fact.[16]

Pearl Buck knew East Asia well enough to see that it is different views of truth working against each other that give rise to criticisms like these. She writes,

We are often puzzled by the lack of what we consider truth-telling on the part of Asians. It seems at times impossible to get facts from Asian persons. The difference here is that [we have come] to consider truth as factual... whereas for the Asian truth is contained in an ethic. When we inquire of an Asian as to what may have happened in a specific incident, we grow impatient because we cannot get from him a clear and simple statement of fact. But for him... human feelings and intentions are more important than mere material fact.[17]

William Haas, whose neglected *Destiny of the Mind in East and West* I consider a minor classic in comparative philosophy, echoes Pearl Buck's point, which is also my point here:

Facts are sacred to the Westerner; they are less so to the Oriental, who has always been more interested in the psychological and human aspects of phenomena. What to him is important, what, as a matter of fact, is real, is not the object in its supposed "objectivity," but its significance for man. So in dealing with the Oriental there arise continually situations for which the Westerner finds himself wholly unprepared and for which he may propose all-too-simple interpretations.... The readiness with which the Oriental gives erroneous information instead of confessing his ignorance is motivated by reluctance to disappoint; this motive often makes him give an answer which he considers agreeable to the questioner. In such cases and many others the desire to please and to feel obliging has a tendency to make one ignore plain facts.[18]

There is not the slightest reason to suppose that virtue is unequally distributed around our globe. If All Asians have seemed unreliable to Westerners, that is because we have judged them by our Western standards. *We* think their utterances should conform to objective facts; *they* think it more important that they be tuned to the sentiments of the persons their words will affect. In both civilizations there are referents to which utterances should be responsible; in both, there can be strong temptations not to honor those referents and to become, thereby, untruthful. The difference lies in the nature of the referents themselves.

In saying that East Asia adopted a basically personal view of truth we should not, of course, read "personal" in our Western, individualistic sense. "To thine own self be true" is strictly Western advice; its East Asian counterpart might read, "To the selves of others—all whom your words and actions will affect—be true." This social rendering of "personal" gives the key Oriental virtue, "sincerity," a twist that comes close to being the opposite of that which the word carries in the West. In the West sincerity bespeaks fidelity to one's own, individually-arrived-at conscience and principles. In East Asia it involves bracketing these private preferences in favor of the outward-oriented social standards I have noted; to repeat, it involves optimizing the feelings of all interested parties, in accord with guidelines (we could go on to add) that have been impounded in ritualized customs *(li)*. Bertrand Russell failed to see the difference between East Asian and Western meanings of truth, when he wrote in his essay on "The Chinese Character": "Chinese life... is far more polite than anything to which we are accustomed. This, of course, interferes... with sincerity and truth in personal relations."[19]

Even a sinologist as on top of the issues as Donald Munro bows to the Western definition of truth when he writes in the Preface to his *Concept of Man in Early China*: "What were important to the Chinese philosophers, *where questions of truth* and falsity *were not*, were the behavioral implications of the statement of belief in question."[20] Later in his book, he raises by implication the possibility of an alternative, Chinese definition of the word when he writes that "in China, truth and falsity *in the Greek sense* have rarely been important considerations" (p. 55, italics mine), but he does not go on to develop that alternative. What we need to see is that, as someone has put the matter, for Confucius the important thing was not to call a spade a spade (that is, make statements conform to impersonal realities), but rather to *cheng ming*; for example, make (primarily personal) realities conform to their (normative) names—to have a father speak as a "father" should speak, his words governed by the sensitivities a father should possess or be working to acquire.

To summarize: truth for China is personal in a dual or twofold sense. Outwardly it takes into consideration the feelings of the persons an act or utterance will affect (one thinks of the normality of white lies and keeping one's mouth shut when appropriate). Meanwhile, inwardly it aligns the speaker to the self one ought to be; invoking a word dear to the correspondence theorists we can say that truth "adequates" its possessor to one's normative self.[21] The external and internal referents of the notion are tightly fused, of course, for it is primarily by identifying with the feelings of others (developing *jen*) that one becomes a *chun tzu* (the self one should be). If we are getting the feeling that the Chinese sense of truth opens onto its entire ethical system, this is as it should be, but I cannot exploit that virtue further here. There is space only to round off this section with a short, *staccato* coda. With truth as personally oriented as it was in East Asia, we should not be surprised to find *ad hominem* arguments counting for more there than they have in the West where they tend to be waived as logically irrelevant. As Henry Rosemont once put this point to me, if someone were to argue that the ideal form of marriage is monogamy while himself having three wives, the Chinese would consider this the best reason in the world not to take him seriously.

Against the background of these South Asian and East Asian notions of truth I proceed now to our Western vision.

III. Our Western Odyssey

I am not a Heideggerian, but I agree with Heidegger that the West's view of truth has been, distinctively, correspondence. Of the three theories of truth the Western-oriented *Encyclopedia of Philosophy* lists in addition to correspondence—coherence, pragmatic, and performative—the last is too recent and episodic to warrant space in an overview such as this. It burst on the scene in Strawson's essay on "Truth" less than forty years ago, and since he himself softened its original claim—that to say that a statement is true is not to make a statement about a statement but to perform the act of agreeing with, accepting, or endorsing a statement—it seems to be receiving decreasing notice. I do not think it will last as more than a footnote. The pragmatic theory has more substance, but it is shaking down into an epistemological *emphasis*. It continues, in Quine, for example, as a broad reminder that theorizing over experience is fundamentally motivated and justified by conditions of efficacy and utility in servicing our aims and needs, but as a theory that claims to say what truth as such *is*, I would say of it, as the *Encyclopedia of Philosophy* says of the pragmatic movement in general, that it "cannot be said to be alive today" (VI, 435). For one thing, it never did succeed in doing justice to aesthetic and disinterested truth, as William James himself recognized by introducing his "mechanical wife"— would the fact that she serviced me flawlessly show that she loved me? Edwin Bevyn argues the deficiencies of the pragmatic theory conclusively, and as his objection is aimed at the coherence theory as well, I quote it at some length.

> It may be that everything which has been said to show that the unsatisfactoriness of the correspondence theory of truth... holds good in regard to inanimate nature. But the moment one comes to the world of conscious Spirit, every theory of truth except the correspondence theory becomes absurd. If one thinks of the anxiety of the lover to know whether the person he aspires to win really loves him, it is precisely the question whether an idea in his mind, the image of the other person's state of mind, really corresponds with facts existing independently of his mind which torments him. What would the lover say if we told him not to be so concerned about reality apart from his mind; it would be enough for him to act as if the person in question loved him?... Does she really—really, apart from anything I may think—care for me? What really are her thoughts in themselves, her way of regarding me in herself?— that is his insistent cry. My belief about another human spirit, about what that spirit now thinks or feels or has experienced in the past is essentially belief about a reality existing apart from my own mind.... The desire to know the truth in this sense is raised to its greatest intensity in love.[22]

As I said, Bevyn's point is aimed as much against the coherence theory of truth as against the pragmatic, and it is this coherence theory which, in the West, has been the correspondence theory's major rival. But rival only to the extent of constituting its loyal opposition, which obviates my needing to deal with it further here. Chronologically the coherence theory emerges only in *modern* philosophy, and even here it has been confined to such metaphysicians as Leibniz, Spinoza, Hegel, and Bradley (all rationalists and idealists in the West's predominantly empiricist, realist tradition) and a few logical positivists (notably Neurath and Hempel) who have been attracted by its resemblance to theoretical physics and pure mathematics.

So I come out agreeing with Heidegger that the West has settled primarily into a correspondence theory of truth. In fixing on the way things are, this theory retains traces of the ontological emphasis India pushed to the hilt, while at the same time its concern for the way things appear to *human beings* aligns it to some extent with China's humanistic interests. But now the differences.

Against India, correspondence exempts truth from concern with the ontological status of things in themselves—the question of their genuineness. It brings the question down to whether we see a bed, say, as it actually *is*; the ontological status of the bed—if that phrase has meaning; I shall return to this question—is a separate issue. As for East Asia, though the correspondence theory sides with it (as I just said) in lodging truth in human beings, it does so with two restrictions—constrictions, I am tempted to say.

First, correspondence denies that truth pertains to persons in their entirety; it is imprecise, it holds, to speak of "true persons." (In holding that it *is* appropriate to do so, the Chinese perspective overlaps India's at this one point, in principle subscribing to a graded ontology of selfhood.) Rather than a predicate of selves, truth as defined by correspondence theorists is a predicate of *parts* of selves, their conceptual parts.

Second, these mental parts—I am using the phrase to cover images, ideas, propositions, statements, sentences, the entire corpus—are related (by the correspondence theory) to their referents *passively.* This elicited in the West the pragmatic theory of truth and notion of performative speech-acts as correctives, but these have neither unhorsed the correspondence theory nor (per impossible) been incorporated within it. The correspondence view does not say that thoughts must mirror things (the discredited 'camera theory' of naive realism), but however we conceive of "represent," it should represent them accurately. This puts the referent in the driver's seat; the job of true thought, we might say, is to settle down quietly in the seat beside it; that is, conform itself as fully as possible to the referent's nature. The East Asian view is more dynamic; pragmatic elements are built right into it, for it holds an act or utterance to be true to the extent that it 'gestalts' (composes, resolves) the ingredients of a situation in a way that furthers a desired outcome—in China's case, social harmony. Truth thus conceived is a kind of performative: it is speech or deed aimed at effecting an intended consequence.

Having devoted the first half of this section to agreeing with

Heidegger that our Western view of truth is primarily that of correspondence, I shall devote its second half to disagreeing with him on
when we settled into this position. I think we gravitated toward it
more gradually than Heidegger would have us think. Heidegger sees
the die as having been cast by Plato,[23] whereas it seems to me unlikely that we would continue to sign our letters, "Yours truly," speak of
lovers as being "true to each other," or refer to jurors as "twelve
good men and true" if we had turned our backs on truth's personal
and ontological referents twenty-five hundred years ago. Right down
through the Middle Ages, "goodness, truth and being are convert-
ible."[24] As for Plato, I side with Paul Friedlander in his criticism of
Heidegger's handling of that fount of Western philosophy. Plato did
not, as Heidegger claims, subordinate truth's ontological to its epistemological referent. "Truth in Plato's system," Friedlander writes,

> is always both: reality of being and correctness of apprehen-
> sion and assertion.... Plato's allegory of the cave [which
> Heidegger rightly focuses on] is characterized by the dual
> meaning of the hierarchical ascent: the ascent of being and the
> ascent of knowledge, both exactly related to each other.[25]

Nor was truth's third, or personal, referent lacking in Plato:

> As witness for these thoughts he chose Socrates, facing
> death for the sake of truth and reality. Thus, the dual meaning
> of the hierarchical ascent becomes three-fold if it is kept in
> mind that the allegory of unhidden and revealing truth is told
> by the truthful man.[26]

In sum, "in Plato... the ontological, the epistemological, and the
existential... facets of the Greek *alétheia*... are intimately united".[27] If
Plato had narrowed truth to its epistemological referent, as
Heidegger claims, we would have to assume that the move escaped
his pupil Aristotle, for to him too *alétheia* means, as in Plato, both the
nature of the real and the nature of a true statement.[28] Freidlander
thinks that in passing to Aristotle, *alétheia* suffered some constriction—"the existential aspect... represented in Plato through the figure of Socrates, has disappeared"[29]—but I do not see that even this is
the case. For, as Thomas Kasulis point out in his essay "The Zen
View of Truth," though correspondence theorists regularly take as
their point of departure Aristotle's assertion that "to say of what is
that it is not, or what is not that it is, is false, while to say of what is
that it is, and of what is not that is not, is true",[30] Aristotle himself

"goes on to speak in two further ways about truth. In the lexiconical section of the *Metaphysics* (1024b), he analyzes three senses of 'false': false as thing, false as an account and false as a man." The last of these seems to correspond to what Friedlander calls the existential meaning of *alḗtheia* In Aristotle's description,

> a false *man* is one who is ready at and fond of (false) accounts, not for any other reason but for their own sake, and one who is good at impressing such accounts on other people, just as we say *things* are false, which produce a false appearance.[31]

And again, in the *Nicomachean Ethics*: "The man who observes the mean [between 'boastfulness' and 'false modesty'] is true both in word and in life because his character is such" (1127a).

Professor Kasulis notes that Thomas says this also,[32] but this is not the place to go further into history. I hope that I have been clear. I do not deny that the seeds of our Western move—the extraction of truth from its original, threefold reference to lodge it in intellectual judgments that correspond with things outside themselves—can, with wisdom of hindsight, be found in Greek philosophy.[33] But I want to insist that these seeds matured slowly. It seems to me that there is a huge and precise block of evidence for this point that is so clear as to amount, virtually, to proof; it is not often in philosophy that one comes upon evidence that is so palpable as to feel crisp, but in the present case the feeling (for me, at least) pertains. Right "down to the late eighteenth century," Arthur Lovejoy tells us,

> most educated men were to accept without question the conception of the universe as a "Great Chain of Being," composed of an immense, or...infinite., number of links ranging in hierarchical order from the meagerest kind of existents... through "every possible" grade up to the *ens perfectissimum.*[34]

And what was the gradient for these grades to which Lovejoy refers? Can it be doubted that in last resort it was ontological; does not the very name, "Great Chain of *Being*" make this claim clear? Given truth's original involvement with ontology. I do not see how the word *could* have withdrawn its ontological claims as long as the Chain of Being being held firm. Or to transpose the wording, I do not see how that chain could have remained what it was, had it not been possible—natural, even—to regard its higher links as more genuine and real; in a word, more true.

IV. Return to the Center

It was not Plato, it was modern science that caused the West to contract its notion of truth until in philosophy it is now thought to refer strictly and properly only to judgments (or statements, or propositions). For in science the notion of degrees of reality (and its correlate, degrees of ontological truth) are meaningless: a state-of-affairs is a state-of-affairs, and that is the end of the matter. And with the demise of ontological truth—was it Eddington who proposed that "Reality" capitalized means nothing more than "reality followed by loud cheers"?—personal truth collapses as well. (In a last minute move, Kierkegaard tries to save it by proposing his notion of "subjective truth," but we know how little this influenced subsequent philosophy.) For persons, too, are ontological in the sense that they are beings; they are built of substance. I do not see how one can do anything but trivialize the notion of a "true *mensch*" if one undercuts the possibility that there is more *to* him, as we say, than there is to most men—that he is more substantial.

I think that we have been onto important things in this symposium.

> Little is more important about a culture, a century, a person, than its (or his) notion of truth. Pilate's unanswered question, What is Truth? whether expressed or latent, haunts every civilization, and finally... every man.

That statement comes from Wilfred Cantwell Smith, whose essays on "Orientalism and Truth"[35] and "A Human View of Truth"[36] have influenced this article in major ways. As the title of the second essay suggests, Professor Smith is primarily concerned with the depersonalization of truth in the contemporary West:

> Natural scientists deliberately and with success strive to construct impersonal statements, sentences whose meaning and whose truth are both independent of who makes them; and they see the truth of a statement as in large measure precisely a function of its impersonality. In the natural sciences this seems to do not only much good, but concomitantly little harm; elsewhere this is not clear.... There are some extremely important statements.... whose meaning and whose truth depend, and properly depend, on the moral integrity of who makes them, and who hears them (statements such as "I refuse to fight in Vietnam").

For a university or a civilization to set up impersonal propositions as the model of all propositions, and then to make these
the primary locus of truth and falsity, it is to exercise, wittingly
or otherwise, a remarkably decisive option in one's orientation
to the world ("Orientalism and Truth,"p.11).

It is indeed! And it is no less decisive to strip truth of its ontological reference, I would add, reducing thereby the Great Chain of
Being to its single, ground-floor level. How far the West has gone
down this road is shown by the fact that there are now Platonic
scholars—presidents of the American Philosophical Association, no
less—who can no longer comprehend how Plato could have been
serious in arguing that there are things more real (and hence more
true) than physical objects: Plato must have been linguistically confused.[37]

If, in broad outline at least, my paper is correct, its moral, I should
think, is plain:

No theory of truth works as well in the natural sciences as
does our Western, correspondence theory.

Only a profoundly personal theory of truth, such as was
developed in East Asia, can do justice to man.

Only a theory, like the Indian, that lodges truth in being, can
be metaphysically adequate.

I feel that our Society for Asian and Comparative Philosophy has a
message here for the philosophical community at large. All three
perspectives on truth are important. They need to be sounded as a
common chord.

NOTES

1. Confer the opening page of Eliot Deutsch's *On Truth: An
   Ontological Theory* (Honolulu, Hawaii: The University Press of
   Hawaii, 1979): "In recent decades, especially under the impact of
   positivism, which led philosophers to make a sharp division
   between cognitive meaning... and emotive meaning..., 'truth' has
   come more and more to be narrowly restricted to... propositions,
   with all other forms and usages of 'truth' taken to be metaphorical."

   Deutsch's book appeared after my article was written and is constructive rather than historical in intent, but as its subtitle indicates,
   it shares the concern I register at the close of my article to return

truth to its original ontological base. The statement I just quoted is followed by Deutsch's contention that "this restriction of the application, and narrowing of the meaning, of 'truth' (to the truth-value of propositions) is wrong and unfortunate: for it robs the concept of some of its richest possible meaning" (ibid.).

2. This seems self-evident to me, but to nail it down I shall add to Deutsch's confirming opinion (cited in note 1) another one which can be taken as typical. Nicholas Rescher's *The Coherence Theory of Truth* (Oxford: Clarendon Press, 1973) opens by saying that "Philosophical theories in general deal exclusively with the truth of statements or propositions—or, derivatively, such complexes thereof as accounts, narrations, and stories. Other uses of 'true' in ordinary language... are beside the point" (p. 1. Also Deutsch, *On Truth*, p. 121).

3. *The Genealogy of Morals,* trans. Francis Golffing (Garden City, N.Y.: Doubleday Anchor Book, 1956), p. 163.

4. From Professor Siu-chi Huang's paper, "Truth in the Chinese Tradition," which formed a part of the Washington Symposium but which, for reasons of space, unfortunately could not be included among the papers herein. a. 眞 b. 假

5. "A Human View of Truth," *Studies in Religion/Sciences religieuses* 1, no. 1 (1971): 7.

6. From what has come to be called the *Hymn of Creation in the Ṛgveda,* (X, 129) which goes on to say explicitly that "apart from it was nothing whatsoever." R. T. H. Griffith (trans.) *The Hymns of the Ṛgveda.* 2 vols. (Benares: E. L. Lazarus, 1920).

7. Frederick Streng, "Buddhist Doctrine of Two Truths as Religious Philosophy," *Journal of Indian Philosophy* 1, no. 3 (November, 1971): 263.

8. *Philosophy East and West* 21, no. 1 (January, 1971): 79.

9. *The Way and Its Power* (New York: Grove Press, 1958). p. 64.

10. *A Short History of Chinese Philosophy* (New York: Collier-Macmillan, The Free Press, 1966), pp. 7, 9.

11. Charles Moore, ed., *Essays in East-West Philosophy* (Honolulu, Hawaii: University of Hawaii Press, 1951), p. 163.

12. I do not think that this statement and the example that follows take issue with Henry Rosemont's point that too much has been made of the constraints archaic written Chinese is alleged to have imposed on Chinese thinking; see his "On Representing Abstractions in Archaic Chinese," *Philosophy East and West* 24, no. 1 (January, 1974): 71–88. In the end, people develop languages that enable them to do what they want to do, rather than being forced to do what their languages require.

13. One thinks of Confucius' statement, "It is not truth which makes man great, but man that makes truth great."
14. S. Wells Williams, *The Middle Kingdom* (New York: Scribner's, 1882; revised edition, 1907), 1:834.
15. Both cited in Derke Bodde, *China's Cultural Tradition* (New York: Holt, Rinehart & Winston, 1963), p. 8.
16. *Science and Human Values* (New York: Harper & Row, 1959), p. 43.
17. *Friend to Friend* (New York: John Day, 1958), pp. 121–122.
18. (New York: Columbia University Press, 1946), pp. 127–128.
19. *Selected Papers of Bertrand Russell* (New York: Modern Library, 1927), p. 232. Japanese politicians find it difficult to persuade voters to be sincere in the Western sense of voting by principle instead of by *giri,* which means, roughly, obligation as arising from *ninjo* or human feelings. On the eve of a national election in the 1960s, a prominent law professor pleaded the virtues of principle in a newspaper article which was strategically titled, "Private Giri and Public Giri" (J. O. Gauntlett, "Undercurrents in Japanese Social Behaviour," *Journal, College of Literature* 6, (1962): 15–16, Tokyo: Aoyama Gakuin University.
20. (Stanford, California: Stanford University Press, 1969), p. ix, emphasis added.
21. I am adapting to China the standard medieval formulation of the correspondence theory, *veritas est adequatio rei et intellectus* (truth is the adequation of a thing and intellect).
22. *Symbolism and Belief* (New York: Macmillan Co., 1938), p. 300.
23. "Plato's Doctrine of Truth," trans. John Barlow, in ed. Henry Aiken and William Barrett, *Philosophy in the Twentieth Century,* vol. 3 (New York: Random House, 1962), pp. 251–270.
24. Frederick Copleston, *A History of Philosophy,* vol. 2, part 2, p. 63. Copleston is describing St. Thomas's position.
   It is worth noting, though, that in the Platonic tradition ontological truth itself has a correspondence aspect where the created world is concerned. "Creatures have ontological truth in so far as they embody or exemplify [correspond to] the model in the divine mind" (ibid, 2, 1, p. 88, *a propos* St. Augustine.)
25. *Plato: An Introduction* (Princeton, New Jersey: Princeton University Press, 1958), pp. 225, 227.
26. Ibid., p. 225.
27. Ibid., p. 229.
28. Ibid.
29. Ibid.
30. See Thomas P. Kasulis, "Truth and Zen," *Philosophy East and West,* 30:4 (October 1980), Aristotle's words are from *Metaphysics,* 1011b.

31. *Metaphysics,* 1025a.
32. *Summa Theologica,* Pt. 2-2 Z 109, Art, 3 Reply Obj. 3.
33. *Why* the West moved in this direction, lies beyond this article, as do the questions of why India and East Asia moved in their distinctive directions regarding truth. I have toyed with answers in my "Accents of the World's Philosophies," *Philosophy East and West* 7, nos. 1 and 2 (1957); "Accents of the World's Religions," in John Bowman, ed., *Comparative Religion* (Leiden: E. J. Brill, 1972); "Valid Materialism: A Western Offering to Hocking's Civilization in the Singular'," in Leroy Rouner, ed., *Philosophy, Religion, and the Coming World Civilization* (The Hague: Martinus Nijhoff, 1966); "Tao Now: An Ecological Testament," in Ian Barbour, ed., *Earth Might Be Fair* (Englewood Cliffs, New Jersey: Prentice-Hall, 1972); and "Man's Western Way: An Essay on Reason and the Given," *Philosophy East and West* 22, no. 4 (October, 1972). I remain far from satisfied with my inroads on the problem, however.
34. *The Great Chain of Being* (Cambridge: Harvard University Press, 1936), p. 59.
35. (Princeton University: Program in Near Eastern Studies, 1969), privately distributed.
36. Op. cit.
37. I am referring, may he forgive me, to a friend, Gregory Vlastos, and his 1965 Presidential Address to the Eastern Division of the American Philosophical Association. An elaboration of his earlier "Degrees of Reality in Plato," appears in his *Platonic Studies* (Princeton, New Jersey: University Press, 1973). Take, he writes, "the 'real' bed in the *Republic,* which turns out to be not the one we sleep on.... How could a man who had so little patience with loose talk want to say in all seriousness an abstract Form is 'more real' than wood and glue?" (vii).

PART II

THE SPLENDID PRISM

East Asia

Transcendence in Traditional China[1]

China's regard for nature, as expressed (for example) in Sung landscape painting, is clear and well recognised. What the Chinese believed to exceed the natural world, the realm of 'the ten-thousand things', is less clear. The present essay tries to explore this question systematically.

We must first distinguish between the views of the peasants and those of the intelligentsia. Peasants believed the unseen world to be peopled by innumerable spirits, both benign *(shen)* and malevolent *(kuei)*, who could dwell in idols and natural objects and be used or warded off by magic and sacrifice. After Buddhism reached China the geography of the spirit world was mapped in 33 Buddhist heavens, 81 Taoist heavens, and 18 Buddhist hells. Divination, astrology, almanacs, dream interpretations, geomancy, and witchcraft all figured as ways of establishing relations with invisible powers.

We shall not linger over this popular view of the supernatural. In essence it is the Chinese version of folk religion which, where not dispelled by enlightenment modes of thought, has been universal throughout human history. What interests us here is the way the transcendent appeared to the Chinese intelligentsia—scholars, administrators, and landed gentry.

A common answer, from Voltaire to James Legge and Hu Shih, is that transcendence scarcely figured in the outlook of the literati at all. A representative statement asserts that 'Confucius confined his attention to reality, and his views are incompatible with religious matters'.[2] Chinese intellectuals, by this view, were humanists, ratio-

---

This essay originally appeared in Religious Studies *II (1967): 185–196 and was reprinted in James Liu and Wei-ming Tu (eds.),* Traditional China *(Englewood Cliffs, N.J.: Prentice-Hall, 1970).*

nalists, and moralists. When they referred to heaven or took part in sacrifices it was from force of mechanical habit, or to provide sops for the sentiments of the masses.

Four things work to encourage this interpretation of the Chinese outlook. (1) The social accent of China's outlook produced an unusual number of philosophers and schools that were purely utilitarian: the Realists, of course; but beyond them and within the Confucian stream itself such philosophers as Yen Yuan and Tai Chen in the Ch'ing Dynasty (1644–1912) and such schools as the Yung-k'ang and Yung-chia in the Sung Dynasty (690–1279).[3] (2) Chinese positions that are *not* exclusively utilitarian tend to appear more utilitarian than they are, because the general social bent of the Chinese mind inclines it to be more explicit about social matters even when it does not really wish to limit itself to them. (3) The utilitarian interpretation of Chinese thought fits nicely with the prejudice of modern academia which, inclining toward rational humanism, is pleased (as were Voltaire and the Enlightenment Sinophiles) to find this prejudice anticipated by the sophisticated Chinese. Concomitantly the interpretation suits the propensity of modern Chinese intellectuals who are eager to justify Chinese civilization in the face of the stronger and rationalistically oriented Western world which considers mysticism and faith in supernatural powers to be symbols of waywardness and inferiority. (4) Finally, Chinese thought patterns are apt to appear utilitarian when considered 'functionally' by social scientists. Social scientists study society. As a consequence their professional biases cause them to pay particular attention to, and therefore to see most distinctly, the social aspects of what they look at. When, therefore, they look at the metaphysical and religious dimensions of cultures, it is the social roots and consequences of these dimensions that leap to view. Durkheim's concept of religion, which for fifty years has dominated sociological and anthropological studies of the subject, is the classic formulation of this bias. 'The idea of society', he writes, 'is the soul of religion'.[4] The gods of religion are collective representations. This means most obviously that they are ideas imposed on individual minds by the group, and more significantly that 'they not only come from the collective, but the things that they express are of a social nature. The reality, which mythologies have represented under so many different forms, but which is the universal and eternal objective cause of these sensations *sui generis* out of which religious experience is made, is society'.[5]

Durkheim's mistake consists in passing from the truth that religion has social consequences and reflects social patterns in its imagery to the erroneous conclusion that it must therefore have arisen and developed for social purposes. This is like reasoning that because marriages usually produce children, children must be their object. In fact, couples often marry ahead of their schedule for children, with intent to have no children at all, or (as in old age) knowing they could not reproduce if they would. It is eminently the case that in China 'the religious factor plays an important role in justifying political powers, in establishing administrative authority, in maintaining peace and order, in upholding civic values, and in inspiring faith in the government and raising public morale during public crises'[6] But it is also the case that China's 'sacrificial and ritualistic activities were carried out for a sense of awe, wonder and gratitude toward an unfathomable power which can never be explained simply in socioeconomic and psychological terms alone'[7] Reviewing the role the Mandate of Heaven has played in Chinese history, a Chinese *sociologist* sees it as a device whereby 'the awe and respect for the supernatural... put... the coat of morality and honour on a dynastic founder, who was basically a master manipulator of force and violence'[8] The retort of a Chinese *humanist* is that 'what the [sociologist] has failed to see is that the person leading the rebellion is a man of his own age and beliefs and not of ours. He would not, therefore, even dare to start a rebellion had he not been assured that the Mandate of Heaven was with him. In other words, the Mandate of Heaven was not a device to achieve political ends, but something seriously believed by both the ruler and the ruled. It was religious in a... profound sense'[9] Actually the humanist overstates the case here. There doubtless were agnostics in every age who cynically played on prevailing faith to secure their worldly ambitions. But unless such cynics had been in the minority, there would have been no prevailing faith for them to play upon.

That the numinous was real for Taoism and Buddhism, no one doubts; it is in regard to Confucianism that the question arises. We read in the *Analects:*

> The Master did not talk about extraordinary things, feats of strength, disorder, and spiritual beings. (vii, 20.)
> While you are not able to serve men, how can you serve their spirits?... While you do not know life, how can you know about death? (xi, II.)
> To give one's self earnestly to the duties due to men, and, while respecting spiritual beings, to keep aloof [at a distance] from them, may be called wisdom. (vi, 20.)

But as H. G. Creel pointed out in a revealing study of this question a quarter of a century ago, of the pre-Sung commentators on these and similar passages in the *Analects,* not one saw in them signs of agnosticism, while among later commentators only four suggested that they contained such signs.[10] The Romans may have assumed that human being is the highest being there is; the Chinese, Confucians included, would have sided with the Greeks who considered such a notion *atopos,* 'absurd' (Aristotle). 'In spite of its preoccupation with this-worldly matters, Confucianism cannot be considered a completely rationalistic system of thought'[11] Confucius carefully kept the numinous alive, in his admonition to 'respect the spiritual beings', in his close attention to sacrificial ceremonies, in his watchfulness toward Heaven and its decrees. The formalised Confucianism about which we sometimes read, the Confucianism, that is all exterior with no sensitivity to inwardness and the hidden mystery into which all of life's roots ultimately invisibly descend— this is fossilised Confucianism where it is Confucianism at all. The *li* which stood at the heart of Confucianism-alive was a tap-root fixed in the mystery of the Tao which, where not cut by selfishness, kept both individuals and society in living touch with Heaven's majestic will.

We labour this point because it constitutes the chief barrier to accurate assessment of the traditional Chinese outlook. No more than the masses did the Chinese intelligentsia see the world as a disenchanted causal mechanism floating on a foundation of nothingness. The principal terms by which they referred to the transcendental 'more' that envelops and permeates the phenomenal world were *T'ien* (Heaven)' and *Tao* (Way)'. The former tends to be associated with Confucianism, the latter with Taoism. The differences between these complementary strains in the Chinese persuasion are more than terminological. The Taoists were in love with nature, the Confucians with history. This meant that the Taoists tended to stress the importance of keeping human nature, 'the uncarved block', undefiled, while the Confucians searched the past to discover which social patterns reflected *T'ien* most faithfully. 'The essential difference is the difference between Lao-tzu's direct way to the *Tao* and Confucius' detour by way of the human order... Lao-tzu immerses himself in (the *Tao),* while Confucius lets himself be guided by his awe of [it] as he moves among the things of the world'.[12] But the differences are in approach and emphasis only. No more than Lao-tzu did Confucius take the commmunty as an absolute. Both believed humanity and nature to be undergirded by an eternal numinous reality from which life proceeds and which inclines it toward harmony.

We can summarise the metaphysics of the Chinese literati in five points:

1. Both human beings and Heaven, both the phenomenal realm and the noumenal realm, are real. Underlying the visible is something of immense importance that is invisible.

2. The essential relation between the two is unity or non-duality. Life's dependability, mingling with nature's, betokens a hidden oneness in the bosom of the multiple, a total interdependence at the heart of the spheres. In this respect Chinese metaphysical thought simply instances the correlative character of Chinese thought generally. Many Chinese terms, such as *'li* (principle)', *'ming* (ordinance)', *'tao'*, *'teh* (power)', and *'yang-yin'*, apply to Heaven and humanity equally. *Tien ming,* for instance, the Heavenly Ordinance, 'exists neither externally in Heaven only, nor internally in humanity only; it exists, rather, in the mutuality of Heaven and humanity; i.e., in their mutual influence and response, their mutual giving and receiving'.[13] Other terms, like 'God *(ti)'*, 'pneuma *(ch'i)'*, 'grand polarity *(t'ai-chi)'*, 'non-polarity *(wu-chi)'*, 'the Origin *(yuan)'*, and 'non-being *(wu)'*, refer primarily to Heaven but are manifest and function in humanity also. Still others, such as 'mind', 'emotion', 'desire', and 'ambition', denote human qualities while connoting that these qualities have their sources in Heaven. A rhythm falls upon the visible, breaking it into day and night, summer and winter, male and female, but these divisions are caught up and ordered in a superior integration, the *Tao,* which resolves the tensions and reconciles the apparently irreconcilable. As the *Great Commentary* puts it: 'Now *yin,* now *yang:* that is the *Tao'.* Heaven and earth agree. They are united in a hymn for a double choir, an antiphony on a cosmic scale. A paradigm of correlative thinking appears in those strikingly un-Semitic instances—e.g., the Chou rites for King Wen as well as for his ancestor Hou-chi—in which the Chinese joined humanity with Heaven and sacrificed to both in the same act.[14]

3. In keeping with another general theme in Chinese thought, that the mutual reciprocity that pervades all things is in most instances between unequals, the relations that link humanity and nature are not symmetrical. Heaven is clearly the senior partner. As Confucius says: 'Only Heaven is great... The superior man... stands in awe of its ordinances' *(Analects,* xvi, 8).

4. Heaven's grandeur does not, however, force it into the foreground of human thought. The Chinese perspective remains humanistic in the double sense that (a) humanity is more often than Heaven the explicit object of attention, and (b) when the Chinese mind does think explicitly about Heaven it usually gets at it through human

beings by considering Heaven's relation to and import for humanity.[15] Again Confucius is paradigmatic. 'He who lives by *jen* has but one anxiety in his heart: not to know man' *(Analects* i, 16). In short, the Chinese were interested in humanity as human beings appear against a noumenal backdrop. Humanity is smaller than the backdrop, but humanity stands out more clearly in our attention. Or if we prefer a musical analogy, the note the Chinese sounded was human, but it carried numinous overtones. The overtones were more majestic, but the note actually sounded was more distinct. 'The wise man vibrates the heart of man and the universe harmonises. The one who can understand these resonances is able to understand what moves the celestial, the terrestrial, and all of creation in its multiplicity' *(I Ching,* Commentary on hexagram 31).

5. The weighting of explicit attention towards humanity as noted in the preceding point causes the numinous to receive in Chinese thought less sharp, objective symbolisation than it does in either India or the West. In ancient Chinese thought the numinous was personified: the character for Heaven was originally a rough sketch of a human being, and in the *Odes,* the *Book of History,* and the *Tso Chuan,* Heaven loves the people and metes out rewards to the virtuous. The coming of philosophy dissolved not only this kind of anthropomorphism but all attempts to describe the numinous explicitly. Confucius never made last things his direct theme. At the approach of the ultimate he grew diffident. Seldom did he speak directly about Heaven, death, or the *Tao.* When asked about such matters he gave answers which left the questions open. We have noted the rationalist's tendency to conclude from such evasions that Confucius was a politically-minded positivist: he did not believe in the numinous but had sense enough to realise that it would be unpolitic to say so outright. For our part, having found reasons to reject this agnostic interpretation, we look to other explanations for his reticence. The principal one we have already named: his refusal to let his direct gaze be distracted from humanity. But beyond this, Confucius' answers to questions about the numinous left the questions open because the subject imposed such answers. Like the Buddha whose teachings were to move in and take their place beside his own, Confucius was aware at some level of the extent to which human beings are led to ultimate questions by inauthentic motives: idle curiosity or the wish to circumvent responsibilities at hand and thus detour the road into life. Confucius had no wish to pander to such motives. More important, he sensed intuitively what philosophers today, be they phenomenologists or analysts, are coming to see explicitly: the impossibility of discussing objectively what can never

be the object of such discussion. In our time Heidegger, Jaspers, Buber and Wittgenstein have all stressed the violation that is wrought when one tries to discourse objectively about what can never, properly speaking, become an object. Ulitmately it is the same perception that prompts both the *Tao Te Ching*'s opening warning that 'the *Tao* that can be expressed in words is not the eternal *Tao*' and Confucius' refusal to speak directly to metaphysical themes. No more than 'Lao-tzu' was Confucius indifferent to the unknowable. He became chary at its mention because he was unwilling to deform intimation into pseudo-knowledge and lose it in words. 'For him the Encompassing is a background, not a theme to work with; it is the limit and foundation to be considered with awe, not the immediate task.' His certainty was rooted in the Encompassing, but it enjoined him to turn to humankind in the actual world. So we discern the presence of last things in his outlook only indirectly, 'in his pious observance of customs and in maxims which, without explicitly saying much, suggest a way in critical situations'. His direct concern was for beauty, harmony, integrity, and happiness in the world, but all these were grounded 'in something that is not made meaningless by failure and death.'

What Karl Jaspers says of Confucius in these last three quotations[16] can be said of the Chinese intellectual position generally. The spiritual 'upholds all, is imminent to all, and nothing can be separated from it' *(Doctrine of the Mean,* xiv). But it is a zone which 'one contemplates without seeing, listens to without hearing' *(ibid.).* Like the cosmos itself which both manifests the Tao and conceals it, sages can allude to the numinous but are quickly brought to silence. 'When one has examined the universe closely—the perfect alternation of day and night, of heat and cold, their constriction as they go, their unbending as they come [again]—one reaches a point beyond which one cannot go' (paraphrased from the *I Ching,* Great Appendix, chapter v, by Confucius or his school). To understand the depths of *Tao* or the decrees of Heaven is impossible for human beings. 'The *Tao!* How deep and unfathomable!' *(Tao Teh Ching,* Giles translation). 'Heaven is what it is' *(Doctrine of the Mean,* xxvii).

So the literati alluded to Heaven more than they defined it, and they sensed it more than they alluded to it. At the same time they were shrewd enough to realise that they could not eschew symbolisation entirely or deference would turn to forgetfulness. So they sacrificed. When the Emperor offered the annual sacrifices to Heaven and magistrates gathered villagers around mounds to sacrifice to earth, peasants may have visualised gods being fed and buttered up generally to ensure their continuing benefactions. Most scholars would have had no such anthropomorphic imaginings, but they would not for this reason have deemed the sacrifices less important nor valued them solely for their effects on the masses. For gentry no less than peasants, 'sacrificial and ritualistic activities were carried out for a sense of awe, wonder, and gratitude toward an unfathomable power which [could] never be explained simply in socio-economic and psychological terms'[17] Sacrifices represented the community's collective recognition that it was not autonomous, that it was enveloped by a 'more' that nurtured it as long as its divine imperatives were honoured. They constituted the Chinese way of expressing the feeling 'this nation, under God'.

To summarise: For the literati the noumenal was (1) real, (2) organically related to the phenomenal, (3) more majestic than the phenomenal while being (4) less in focus or rewarding for direct attention and (5) better intimated than explicitly described, better sensed than thought. What the sense provided above all else was the awareness of being related. According to a contemporary psychiatrist, this awareness is humanity's fundamental want. 'A longing for knowing that one has roots, that one's existence reflects the order and trustworthiness and utter 'sanity' of the universe itself... a longing for some absolute awareness of relatedness [is] man's deepest need[18] China's concentric vision, the vision of society set like a stone in nature and nature set similarly in the deep repose of eternity, filled this need. If everything is tied together in an organic system of interdependent parts, human life shades into eternity. The concept inspired a medley of profound religious intuitions. One sensed the blessings of Heaven and Earth as they flowed into the society which sustained one's life. Or if taste tended toward monism, one sensed the soul of humanity as identical with the soul of Heaven and Earth and all things. Security was assured, for society was no holding operation, pieced together against chaos by some precarious social contract. It was humanity's natural condition, the condition to which cosmic sources naturally inclined humanity if human beings did not wilfully and selfishly divert them. But security was not the vision's only yield. Relatedness gave life meaning as well. An important reason for existential despondency in the contemporary West is the existentialists' conclusions that humanity's values are free-floating, that they have no grounding or sanction beyond one's own private regard. The Chinese saw things otherwise. The values that rightly order society imbue everything. They are rooted in being itself. "The Heavenly *ming* (Ordinance)... and... 'what one's heart feels peace in'... are two aspects of one thing.[19] When Confucius extolled the legendary founders of Chinese civilisation it was no idiosyncratic inventiveness that he praised. He revered them because, having perceived the eternal archetypes of heaven, they ordered their lives by them to the point where they became transparent through them. 'Only heaven is great; only Yao was equal to it'. These psychological benefits which the Chinese derived from the transcendent were important, but equally important was the way it reenforced the dutiful, social conduct they prized so dearly.

First, it provided grounds for their conviction that the social norms *(li)* which individuals should strive to exemplify in their conduct toward one another were not arbitrary. Had the Chinese suspected that these norms were not more than conventions or, worse, had been perpetrated by a segment of society to shore up its privileged position, they could have regarded them more lightly. As it was, they saw them as sanctioned by the cosmos: they were natural law. 'The "rules"… have their origin in Heaven and Earth, ie., in "the central harmony between Heaven and Earth".[20] When society is ordered as it should be, when persons behave human-heartedly toward one another, when rulers govern wisely and sacrifices are observed in spirit as well as form, then society, nature and cosmos combine to function like a beautifully synchronised machine. But deviate from the heaven-appointed pattern and everything will go wrong. Wars and pillage will abound. Even nature will be thrown off its track and erupt in plague and rampage.

It is in this connection that we have our best chance of understanding Confucius' 'reversed time orientation', for it was in the human record that Confucius thought human beings have the best chance of perceiving what the Heavenly sanctioned values are. If Confucius has been mistaken for a rationalist, he has been mistaken oftener for a conservative. The mistake is understandable for he did characterise himself as 'a transmitter and not a maker, believing in and loving the ancients'.[21] But we must be careful in reading this sentence, making sure in particular that we balance it with his seemingly opposite assertion that 'a man born in our days who returns to the ways of antiquity is a fool and brings misfortune upon himself.[22] As no uncomplicated conservative could have said that, we do better to read Confucius' attitude as historical rather than conservative in any mechanical sense.[23] He loved the past, but not for itself so much as for the fact that it is there that we see the woof of humanity's doings laid out on the warp of eternity. This makes it the place where normative values become most clearly evident, ideally through exemplification, but if not, then through their conspicuous absence. To embody these values in the present calls not for blindly reduplicating the past but for translating what was good within it into contemporary idiom. Repetition of the eternally valid, this rather than imitation of empirical history was his object. Only on this interpretation could Karl Jaspers say of him: 'Here for the first time in history a great philosopher shows how the new, merging with the tradition flowing from the source of eternal truth, becomes the substance of our existence.[24]

If the Confucians loved history, the Taoists loved nature. Here we come upon a second way in which the Chinese sense of the transcendent supported appropriate social conduct; namely, by imbuing her people with the sense that human nature inclines toward appropriate conduct in a kind of natural tropism. Instead of scanning the past to see which attitudes and acts go well and which do not, the Taoists advocated centering down to 'the uncarved block', humanity's original unspoiled, Tao-endowed nature, believing that if we could unburden ourselves of society's warping effects we would all behave very well. Though the Taoists were unique in staking everything on this 'return to the source', the notion that humanity is naturally inclined toward virtue is widespread in Chinese thought. Very early the *Odes* tell us that 'Heaven gives birth to the people. If there is a thing there is a rule for it; therefore the nature of the people will naturally incline to virtue'. Confucius continued the refrain—'True goodness springs from humanity's own heart... Is virtue so far away?'—while Mencius went 'much further than Confucius in his insistence upon the goodness of human nature... teaching... that since human nature is endowed by heaven, it must be good'[25] 'Humanity's natural tendency toward goodness is like the water's tendency to find the lower level', he wrote. The ancient sage kings were simply men who fully developed their innate goodness.

With the passing of the centuries the debate over whether the human is innately good was to deteriorate into pedantic bickering and trivial scholasticism. But in the formative stages of Chinese thought the question was vital. For our image of ourselves affects our conduct: we do not always behave like the kind of person we think we are, but we tend to do so. To believe that one's fundamental nature participates in the transcendent source of all goodness, call it Tao or T'ien, is to be disposed to some extent to act accordingly.

Though humanity is naturally inclined toward virtue, this inclination is at birth, as Mencius says, only a tender shoot which must be nurtured and developed. This brings us to a third way in which the transcendent reenforced appropriate social conduct: it rewarded virtue's cultivation. In ancient times this reward meant worldly prosperity. Thus we read in the *Book of Odes* that Heaven cherished the illustrious virtue of King Wen, and so the Heavenly Ordinance *(ming),* which would ensure a successful reign, came upon him. With the coming of sophistication, Heaven's reward came to be conceived more inwardly, moving toward a Chinese version of virtue as its own reward. It continued to be assumed that the Heavenly Ordinance would descend on the one who cultivated virtue, though it might be clearer at this stage to say that the virtuous person's life would become aligned with the *ming;* but the *ming* for the individual (the *ming* for the ruler was a different matter) no longer implied worldly success. 'It does not necessarily follow that upon the one who "receives the Heavenly *ming*" God will definitely bestow wealth and high rank, and make him the actual king... [Being] unlimited... the... Tao may be realised equally in the outward success and the outward failure of men'.[26] This drift of thought led directly to Chuang Tzu's concept of the person of virtue as one who is in complete harmony with whatever transpires. Through unswerving loyalty and filial piety human beings become indifferent to both pleasure and grief. The person who preserves inner harmony and spiritual glory will be so attuned to the operation of *ming* amidst variable circumstances that he or she will be in accord with whatever happens. From this premise Chuang Tzu proceeds to his ideas of 'enjoying one's heart in accordance with things as they are' and nondifferentiation of things leading to a state of untroubled ease'. The one whose heart has come to rest in *ming* is indifferent to circumstances in pursuing duty, even to death. 'Death and life are great considerations, but they could work no change in him. Though Heaven and Earth were to be overturned and fall, they would occasion him no loss.'[27] I and Heaven and Earth are born together, and I and all things in the universe are in a state of unity.'[28] Amidst these changing concepts of the character of reward, the constant element was the notion that things in their widest and most ultimate context are set up in such a way that, whether visibly or invisibly, grossly or subtly, outwardly or inwardly, virtue brings satisfaction.

Fourth, the transcendent supported social conduct by encouraging its development beyond any given stage that it actually reached. This comes out in the idea that 'the Heavenly *ming* is not unchangeable' *(Book of Odes* and *Book of History).* Were it unchangeable, one who had developed a modicum of virtue could rest on one's oars, content with the Heavenly blessing that came with the virtue he had acquired. In point of fact, however, '"acceptance of the Heavenly *ming*", in its true meaning, is... the starting point of something to be done, rather than a terminal point of something already accomplished.... Once one has received *ming* one must further cultivate his virtue."[29] The reason human beings must do so can be stated both positively—'the more fully men cultivate their virtue, the more fully will heaven confer its mandate on them'[30]—and negatively: those who fail to keep cultivating their virtue will find Heaven's blessing withdrawn.

Such statements obviously point to a relationship in which 'there is mutual influence and response between Heaven and human beings.[31] In his discussion of 'correlative thinking' and 'resonance' in the second volume of *Science and Civilization in China,* Joseph Needham describes this relationship with great penetration.[32] Here, with limited space, we try to reach its essential point through cybernetics:

> Cybernetics is not just a technological revolution; it is a revolution in our way of thinking....
>
> Western man has traditionally thought... in terms of cause and effect going in one direction. That is, if A causes B, B cannot cause A. The reason for this assumption is that event order has been confused with logical order; Western man has assumed that because 'circular argument' is prohibited in logic, there cannot be circular causal relationships in natural or social events.
>
> But not everyone has thought this way... Peoples in pre-communist China... have seen the universe as a mutual process of... influences in harmony and occasionally disturbed harmony—in complementary balance rather than in vertical oppositon...
>
> In a sense they have been living cybernetically... Cybernetics [in one of its aspects] is concerned with the growth, development, and the rise of complex structures resulting from *mutual* interactions between components which do not fall into a causal hierarchy.[33]

The relation between the Heavenly *ming* and human effort constituted an important instance of such mutual interaction. The more human beings exerted themselves in the cultivation of virtue the more the Heavenly mandate blessed their efforts and strengthened their continuance. The more their efforts slackened, the further the mandate receded and the more difficult it became for them to renew their moral exertion.

Finally, in all of the four ways we have enumerated, the transcendent encouraged political as well as private morality. The Emperor's position was not simply that of the person who had risen to the top of violence's heap. The Emperor ruled with the Mandate of Heaven for the benefit of the world under Heaven. As this Mandate is unceasing—'Heaven constantly loves the people and therefore looks on all parts of the world to find a dwelling place for its mandate, which it confers unceasingly.'[34] If one Emperor's regime ceased to furnish the Mandate a fitting abode, Heaven would be forced to spot and back to victory a new Emperor whose regime would renew the hospitality.

NOTES

1. I am indebted to my colleague, Professor Nathan Sivin, for a number of helpful suggestions bearing on this study.
2. Liang Ch'i-ch'ao as quoted by C. K. Yang in John K. Fairbank (ed.), *Chinese Thought and Institutions* (Chicago: University of Chicago Press, 1957), p. 270.
3. See T'ang Chun-i, 'The Development of Ideas of Spiritual Value in Chinese Philosophy' in Charles Moore (ed.), *Philosophy and Culture: East and West* (Honolulu: University of Hawaii Press, 1962), p. 228.
4. Emile Durkheim, *The Elementary Forms of the Religious Life* (London: Allen and Unwin), p. 419.
5. Ibid. p. 418.
6. C. K. Yang, *Religion in Chinese Society* (Berkeley: University of California Press, 1961), p. 175.
7. George Ling, 'Functional Interpretation of Chinese Religon', *Quarterly Notes on Christianity and Chinese Religion*, XII, 2 (July 1963), p. 8.
8. C. K. Yang, *op. cit.* p. 132. George Ling, *op. cit.* pp. 8–9.
9. George Ling, *op. cit.* pp. 8–9.
10. 'Was Confucius Agnostic?', *T'oung pao*, xxix (1932), pp. 55-99.
11. C. K. Yang, 'The Functional Relationship between Confucian Thought and Chinese Religion' in John K. Fairbank (ed.), *Chinese Thought and Institutions, op. cit.* p. 272.
12. Karl Jaspers, *The Great Philosophers* (New York: Harcourt, Brace and World, 1957), p. 70.
13. T'ang Chun-i, 'The T'ien Ming (Heavenly Ordinance) in Pre-Ch'in China', *Philosophy East and West*, xi, 4 (January 1962), p. 195.
14. Tang Chun-i, *op. cit.* p. 201.
15. Cf. William S. Haas, *The Destiny of the Mind: East and West* (New York: Macmillan, 1956), p. 149: 'The Eastern [read East Asian] mind is not interested in... an independent object.... From the very begin-

ning the main problem was to secure an unassailable position for man in the face of all that exists within and around him.'

16. *The Great Philosophers* (New York: Harcourt, Brace and World, 1957), p. 70.
17. George Ling, *op. cit.* p. 8.
18. Robert Murphy, *Psychotherapy Based on Human Longing* (Pendle Hill. Pamphlet III. September, 1960), p. 12.
19. T'ang Chun-i, *op. cit.* p. 213.
20. *Ibid.,* p. 208.
21. *Analects* vii, I.
22. Quoted in Karl Jaspers, op. cit. p. 54.
23. The attitude of Confucianism, as distinguished from that of Confucius, is another story well reviewed in A. T. Roy, 'Confucianism and Social Change', *The Chung Chi Journal,* iii, I (November 1963), pp. 88–104. His conclusion: 'Confucianism... cannot be labelled as hopelessly conservative. Yet... its role in Chinese history has been largely that of conserver'.
24. *Op. cit.* p. 54.
25. Lee Shiu Keung, 'The Doctrine of Man: Confucian and Christian, *Quarterly Notes on Christianity and Chinese Religion,* V, 2 (June 1961), p. 1.
26. T'ang Chun-i, *op. cit.* Part I, p. 201; Part II, p. 32.
27. *Chuang Tzu* ch.v.
28. *Ibid.* ch. ii.
29. T'ang Chun-i, *op. cit.* pp. 201, 203.
30. *Ibid.* p. 202.
31. T'ang Chun-i, p. 203.
32. Cambridge University Press, 1956; especially pp. 279-91.
33. Magoroh Maruyama, 'Cybernetics', *NEA Journal* (December 1964), pp. 51–2. By the same author, 'The Second Cybernetics', *American Scientist,* li, 2 and 3 (1963).
34. T'ang Chun-i, *op. cit.* p. 203.

Tao[1] Now:
An Ecological
Testament

The rise of ecological concern in the West—swift, emphatic—is one of the striking developments of our times.[2] My wife and I return from a year abroad to find a sign over our kitchen disposal instructing us to "Save all garbage for compost recycling—thanks a heap!" We open our mail and find political candidates promising: "Not ecology rhetoric but ecology action.... Stiffer sanctions against industrial pollutors.... The right of private citizens to bring suit against violators." On my way to my office I note that a storefront in Central Square has been converted into Ecology Action; it is bustling. On reaching my office I find the top item on the mountain of accumulated mail to be a house organ report of the 1970 Clean Air Car Race. My own institution's showing in the race appears to have been spotty. Of the forty-three entered vehicles, M.I.T.'s steamer didn't quite make it to the starting line, and its electric hybrid, plagued by hard luck all the way, was barely maneuvering Oklahoma City as competitors crossed the Cal Tech finishing line. Its turbine, on the other hand, did well—a sure winner, being the only entry in its class.

What should we do? Our first impulse is to put on the brakes through legislation. This is obviously needed: private citizens won't come to heel without it any more than will the large pollutors. Legislation not only gets results by virtue of the teeth in it; it also educes willingness. I resent paying 3¢ more for Amoco gas when the result is imperceptible, but I would do so with a will if my act, joined by that of my fellow citizens, were party to decreasing the lead content of my atmosphere appreciably. It's the difference between throwing my pennies away and buying clean air for that little.

This essay originally appeared in Ian Barbour (ed.), Earth Might Be Fair *(Englewood Cliffs, N.J.: Prentice-Hall, 1962.*

Still, legislation is limited. Pressure groups keep it from being fully equitable, loopholes can be found, and there will always be a time lag between the discovery of new ways to violate the environment and laws to curb these ways. So while applying the brakes we need concomitantly to press the accelerator. This means research: substantial allocation of public and private monies to see how technology's usurpations and fallout can leave our environment intact if not actually improved. The guiding principle here is the closed system. Instead of pouring industrial wastes and sewage into our waterways and puffing smoke into the atmosphere, convert the pollutants mechanically and chemically into useful substances and loop them back into the nutrient cycle. "Pollutants are resources out of place" is one of the heartening discoveries of our time, but the discovery didn't fall into our laps. It required work—work that has only just begun. So prohibiting legislation (injunctions) must be joined by enabling legislation for research, including research on how to keep our economy prosperous without built-in obsolescence. Luddite negativism is no answer.

I. The Need for a New Consciousness

Prudential measures of this sort are important, but they need to be undergirded by an altered stance toward nature itself. At least three ingredients of our present posture could stand improvement. The first of these is our presumption that nature has no claims, only uses. In antiquity each tree, spring, grove, and hillock had its own *genius loci,* its guardian spirit. Before one cut a tree, mined a mountain, or dammed a brook, it was important to placate the spirit animating the domain in question. *Moira* (fate), the Greek's earliest and ultimate posit, was at root a spatial concept, referring originally to the division of the world into distinct spheres or provinces, each with its attendant rights and taboos. Nemesis grew out of this notion. Originally she was a woodland goddess. As such she personified the woodland's sacred presence, a dangerous power not to be entered, not to be set foot on by persons who were not themselves sacred, sanctified, or ceremonially brought into a state in which contact with the mysterious power was no longer dangerous. When the profane did trespass, she became Avenging Anger and, as an extension of this, the goddess of retributive justice. Such views are far removed from technological human beings who, in Heidegger's phrase, have come to regard the world as a huge filling station.

Second, as nature is devoid of purpose, it is without compass or rudder. If left to its own devices, it cannot be trusted. This, too, represents a departure from earlier suppositions. At the start of Western philosophy, Thales announced that *physis,* the ultimate 'nature' of all things, is water and concomitantly is alive, 'has soul in it' in the same sense that there is a soul in the animal body. As organisms are remarkably resilient, homeostatic, and solicitous of their members, the thought that the world is alive inspires trust.

All in all, our emptying the cosmos of rights and life has positioned us toward it in a stance that is uncomfortable. For evidence I shall content myself with the balance of this single sentence: Heidegger's report that the world is that in the face of which one experiences anxiety, Beckett's key line in *Endgame* ("You're on earth, and there's no cure for that"), and Camus' reference in *The Myth of Sisyphus* to "this world to which I am opposed by my whole consciousness." Out of this discomfort grows the third aspect of our stance toward nature, which, in distinction to the foregoing two that are philosophical, is psychological and largely unconsicous. Nature is that which we devour in our efforts to assuage our "dis-ease": its fruits to fill our emptiness, its distances to still our restlessness. Towards our planet's fare our civilization has come to exhibit the pathology of neurotic eating.

If our ecological difficulties stem in part from our outlook on nature, from whence might a different outlook derive? One possibility is that we could simply invent it, or conjure it up; but this possibility is more logical than feasible. To be more than fiction such a creation would have to derive from a myth maker the stature of which the world has seldom seen. More promising than an empty canvas as a starting point is our human past. In looking thereto we shall step back, as it were, in order to move forward, as when we retreat a little to take a running jump. No past perspective can fit present needs exactly, but there is the possibility that one might be updated. Moreover, the past has the advantage that in dealing with it we can be certain that we are dealing with more than fiction. Its contents grabbed humanity; at some stage of its development it connected with the wellsprings of humanity's being. As we are members of the same species, we have a chance of finding in the outlooks of our ancestors elements that at some level of abstraction might speak to us also.

In scanning the past for suggestions it might seem sensible to begin with our own tradition, it being presumably more accessible. I do not discount this approach; other contributors to this volume ply it with results that are useful. It is not only to avoid duplication, however, that I propose myself to try a different tack. As our Western present has evolved evolved from our Western past, that particular past may not be the best resource for advancing us beyond it. As it happens, my next section *will* be devoted to the West, but not in search of the clues we need. Rather the opposite: I want to show why, Western civilization having produced features in our worldview that are giving us trouble, to counter these it may be helpful to look outside that civilization altogether.

II. The West's Distancing From Nature

The earliest respect in which the West showed signs of differentiating itself from the common stream of human development was in distancing itself from the given. Until the West took this fateful step—stepping back, as it were, to place at arm's length and survey for the first time circumspectly and critically the milieu in which life was set—humankind everywhere had lived under the spell of the cosmological myth. According to this myth, the given was God-given. Humanity's primal matrix was the living womb that sustained all. It existed to nurture humanity, not to be challenged, defied, or refashioned.

The Jews effected this distancing through Yahweh, a god who, unlike Baal and Astarte, did not evolve out of the natural processes of life and the soil but sprang into being through an extraordinary *un*natural occurrence: the improbable escape of a feeble, half-formed Hebrew tribe from the Egyptian juggernaut. Elsewhere in the Fertile Crescent, gods and nature fused. Not so in Yahweh; Yahweh was lord *of* events, deeds, history, and eventually of creation. Yahweh was forever commanding his people to do exceptional things, things that differed from the natural in the sense of the normal and conventional—what was already standard practice. "Get thee up. Go to the west to spy out the land. Go to the west, the fields are waiting."

What distanced the Greeks from the given is less clear, for by the time we first catch sight of them they seem already discernibly estranged. Hesiod's posit of a Golden Age was dropped in favor of Homer's less rosy view. The mythic ancestry of the Greeks is rife with crimes and perversities. Flagrant injustice abounds. Even the gods are party to it, impelling humanity to evil without purpose. And over it all broods Moira (fate), inexorable master of human beings and gods, making puppets of both. When the Greeks looked outward onto their neighbors, the given that greeted them was no prettier than that in their own past, for their tiny landmass caused them to be ringed by foreigners who, partly in fact and even more in fearfilled fancy, were (in the word they coined) barbarians.

A small band set in a sea of 'given' that didn't comfort or appeal; what was the alternative? For the Jews it was Yahweh, his commanding and saving will. For the Greeks whose gods were accomplices in the given, this recourse wasn't open. If there was to be an alternative, it would have to come from human beings.

Reason was the logical candidate. Among human faculties, mind has the largest purview: it can see backward through memory, forward through foresight, and to either side by entertaining its neighbors' interests even where it cannot feel these interests as its own. What better instrument for bringing order out of chaos?

It was all, as we say, so reasonable. But now we come to a key sector in our review. We must look at the notion of reason itself.

Intelligence is a generic human capacity, spread over the globe (as far as we can tell) in equal proportion; if Confucius or Kobo Daishi or Ramakrishna were not intelligent, then no one is intelligent and the word has no meaning. But intelligence can take many forms. We shall never understand our Western civilization in the sense of discerning the ways in which, and extent to which, it is a human option until we understand the peculiar *genre* of intelligence that has informed it. To denote this Western genre of intelligence I shall use the word 'reason'. How it developed out of the generic pool of human intelligence, delineating step by step its distinctive contours, is a story too involved for the telling here, even the parts we know. I shall content myself with indicating how the West's notion of reason derives fom the Hebraic/Hellenic distancing from nature and doubles back to enlarge that distancing itself.

I back up for a running start. Mind advancing into increased self-consciousness is part of the meaning of civilization. By virtue of this advance, people confront the given as if it were laid before them. As assessment is inevitable, some stance toward it is required. On reaching this choice-point, civilizations jumped differently. Asia retained a deep, unquestioning confidence in nature, appreciative of it, receptive to it. Had the Chinese and Indians not risen above the natural plane at all, they would not have spawned civilizations. The way in which they did transcend it, however, was by confirming it. They dignified it by affirming it consciously. By contrast the West opposed herself to nature in a stance that was reserved and critical. Its civilization receded progressively from the natural and instinctive and set itself up against them.

Consider the following contrast. On the eve of battle, Krishna is

trying to help Arjuna, who is assailed by waves of pacifism, to discern his duty. It is axiomatic that his duty must be in accord with his
nature. Plato assumes the same: intellectuals should rule, the courageous should guard and defend, and those of appetitive nature
should produce. But how is one's nature to be ascertained? In India
the answer is embedded in the given, specifically in the caste into
which the individual is born. The possibility that an individual might
be miscaste doesn't arise. Arjuna is a Kshatriya; Krishna's directive
follows from that fact: "Therefore fight, O Bharata!" With Plato
things are not this simple. Children will as a rule inherit their parents' natures and hence social positions, but this can't be counted on.
In the *Gita,* "ought" follows from "is"; Given (what one should do)
and given (one's social position) converge. In the *Republic,* not necessarily.

The difference is indicative. Asia's social philosophy has been
more conservative throughout, and eminently natural in the sense of
being grounded in strong instinctive drives. In the political sphere
Asia never seriously questioned the natural extension of the tribal
chief: autocratic monarchy. Power being a fact of social life, it is best
to have it focused. A monarch effects this focus while monarchy as
an institution extends it through time, across the generations. Closer
to home, in the intimate sphere, China grounded social life in the
family; India (with more ethnic and racial differences), in clusters of
families or caste. All three forms keep within natural bonds; nowhere
did Asia consider it humanity's function to interfere with existing
social forms. Reform to Asia meant change in personnel—turning
the rascal out—not institutional change. So ideology was left for the
West where it flourished. Starting with Solon in Greece and the abolition of kingship in Rome, social and political movements were
planned and carried out with increasing intensity in the name of theories, principles, and basic rights. How little Western people felt
bound by natural ties, how much at liberty to replace them, is evident from the start. Plato doesn't hesitate to disrupt the family; reason can devise institutions that are better.

III. An Estranged and Estranging Epistemology

The West's compulsion to disengage from nature, to break from
its womb and launch on an independent career, is not without effect,
I am arguing, on its notion of reason—which notion, once formed,
will influence everything that follows, the whole of Western culture.
The effect was, in a word, to make division reason's basic operation.

Intelligence deploying itself in the context of the West's distancing penchant was commissioned more for distinctions than for commonalities; it was by disposition better primed for analysis (the drawing of distinctions) than for intuition and synthesis (pulling together gestaltwise, at a glance and partly unconsciously, the multiple factors that converge in situations and require response). If Asia chose not to deploy intelligence primarily down reason's whole-splitting path, this was not entirely out of oblivion to the possibility. Partly it was because Asia sensed at some level the dangers that lurked.

From this foundational operation of reason, the drawing of distinctions, five other features emerge.

1. Clarity. Where distinctions are prized, clarity will be prized also. We are accustomed to the phrase "clear distinctions," but its words are really redundant. Insofar as it is genuine, every distinction is clear; to the degree that it is indistinct, the distinction itself is questionable—borderline cases are an embarrassment. When the father of modern philosophy, Descartes, built his methodology on clear and distinct ideas, the basic conjoint characteristic of Western reason surfaced to full consciousness.

2. Generalization. The distinctions of reason do not move toward indicating the individuality and uniqueness that each event possesses but rather in the opposite direction, toward isolating properties that members of the same class share in common. Ontologically reason strives for universals in objects, epistemologically for universals in thought, being interested (for example) in what treeness means for people generally and relatively uninterested in what a single tree might mean for me personally by virtue of the fact that I happen to love it. "From Socrates downwards," William James observed, "philosophers have vied with each other in scorn of the knowledge of the particular, and of adoration of that of the general." Far from being inevitable, he adds, this directionality is an "idol of the cave" and "hard to understand."

3. Conceptualization. Articulation and communicability go with this, for language and conceptual thought proceed together. When Socrates argues that every effective shoemaker will know his intended product and the use to which it is to be put, he speaks for human experience universally; but when he includes as integral to this knowledge the ability to describe these features of the product clearly, he speaks as architect of the specific version of knowledge that reason produces and the West promotes. This version is not the only kind of knowledge. There comes a point at which every craftsperson reaches the limits of language and must say in effect, "I can't tell you what you are doing wrong, but let me have the chisel and watch how I shape that line," or "Let me have the keyboard and listen to how I take that passage." China with her "Tao that can be spoken is not the true Tao" and India's Upanishadic truth that can be comprehended only through living in the presence of a life through which it actively shines *(sad* = sit, *upani* = near to, under) hold closer to these tacit dimensions of knowing.

4. Implication. Western reason is interested in entailment, the if then propensity, the impulse to see if from truth in one area anything follows about truths in areas that are adjacent and contiguous. This too derives from reason's proclivity to separate and divide, for unwinnowed experience is too complex to serve as the basis for inference. There are no laws of history, we say, giving evidence thereby of our realization that entailments hold only hypothetically or in restricted areas of actual experience. In demarcating these areas, separating reason establishes conditions wherein entailments become more readily evident.

5. Control. This too derives from reason's penchant for division; "divide and conquer" applies to the theoretical sphere no less than to the political. Life can be responded to as a whole, but it can be controlled only piecemeal: try to get it all out in front of you to order it about and you will be left with nowhere on which to stand. At least two distinctions are built into the very notion of control: the distinction between the way things are and the way they should be reordered, and the distinction between what is to be controlled and what will remain stable to provide footing for the operation.

In ways like these control requires distinctions, but distinctions need not in themselves awaken desires to control. They do so in reason because there they get implicated with the West's experience of the given as basically antipathetical and hence in need of monitoring. Several sentences rearranged from Chapter 5 of Herbert Marcuse's *Eros and Civilization* bring out the controlling coloration that reason early acquires, as succinctly as any I could compose to that precise end.

When philosophy conceives the essence of being as Logos, it is already the Logos of domination—commanding, mastering, directing reason, to which man and nature are to be subjected.

Nature (its own as well as that of the external world) were 'given' to the ego as something that had to be fought, conquered, and even violated. The struggle begins with the perpetual internal conquest of the 'lower' faculties of the individual: his sensuous and appetitive faculties. Their subjugation is, at least since Plato, regarded as a constitutive element of human reason. The struggle culminates in conquest of external nature which must be perpetually attacked, curbed, and exploited in order to yield to human needs. The ego experiences being as 'provocation' (Gaston Bachelard), as 'project' (J. P. Sartre); it experiences each existential condition as a restraint that has to be overcome, transformed into another one. Whatever the implications of the original Greek conception of Logos as the essence of being, since the canonization of the Aristotelian logic, the term merges with the idea of ordering, classifying, mastering reason. And this idea of reason becomes increasingly antagonistic to those faculties and attitudes which are receptive rather than productive. The Logos shows forth as the logic of domination.

Civilizations are obviously too complex to evolve in any simple, linear fashion. They show few straight lines; usually it is a mélange of hens and eggs, circles, vicious and benign, and constant feedback. Thus the West's distancing of the given shapes its reason, while reason in turn pushes the given back still further, turning it into object. By "pushing back" I am thinking here primarily of psychological distance, but physical distance provides an accurate and influential analogy, for things must be held more or less at arm's length before they can be recognized as objects in their own right. The emergence of self-consciousness necessarily creates some gap between humanity and the world, but in the West the gap is greater.

The attitude that derives from taking the nonsubject to be fundamentally an object is, of course, objectivity. It involves, to begin with, a directionality, a mind that faces primarily outward. In alien territory or even in "no man's land" one needs to be wary; protracted introspection could divert attention from an environment that needs monitoring. So in contrast to Asia which focuses on the subject, the West concentrates on the outer side of the divide. It does so not only out of watchfulness and prudence but because the object, once on stage, actively invites attention. An immediate consequence is that disinterested thought becomes both natural and pertinent. Western epistemology develops along primarily realistic lines; buttressed by the Judeo-Christian doctrine of creation, this encourages pure knowledge, not only applied. It also encourages philosophy to develop along lines distinct from theology and psychology, both of which, being soteriological, are subject-preoccupied. In Asia the three never divide.

Modern science and a penchant for the physical are only the most evident examples of the West's urge to posit objects everywhere, to confer on everything she encounters the form and existence of external entities. So when the West turns from the outer world to inner experience—the object-oriented West always gets around to humanity after nature, whether the seminal period in question be Greek, Renaissance, or modern—the mind carries its objectivizing propensity with it. Thoughts come to be regarded as mental objects, universals as 'eternal objects', feelings as data. This doesn't require that these objects be physical in character; it's just that wherever the mind moves, it casts what it encounters into the mold of objectifiable phenomena. So literature and science vie with increasing vigor to unveil the variety and intricacies of the human soul—psychology and psychiatry, biography and autobiography, history, drama, and the novel, all get into the act. Asia shows little interest in this kind of phenomenology, contenting itself with a limited number of archetypical examples, for the most part ones that bear on edification. In the West the disclosures are valued for themselves, for they help fill in the map of existence, which, if the West had its way, would lie unrolled at its feet, complete. A mirror would make an even better image, for it would reflect everything precisely as it is, distorted ideally only in proportions to render the small visible and the large comprehensible. This is the logical goal of the objectifying intellect, the final desideratum of its unceasing urge to confront reality as a totality of concrete, preferably picturable, objects.

What happens to truth when intelligence takes the form of reason with its separating bent and the world takes on the guise of object? At the onset of all civilizations, truth is interchangeable with reality: Whether we look at *satyam* in Sanskrit, *haaq* in Arabic, or *verus* in Latin, the matter is the same: all of these words denote what is real, genuine, and authentic on the one hand, and what is valid and accurate on the other. In Asia this generous denotation persists, but in the West it has shriveled; truth (and its opposite, falsity) are now taken by the West to be strictly predicable of statements only. Two simple steps led to this conclusion. In the first step, the West's objectifying penchant depersonalized truth. Traces of the earlier referent linger in phrases like "to thine own self be true," "true courage," "true to one's wife," and the New Testament reference to "doing the truth", but philosophy comes to dismiss these as metaphorical and not really legitimate—only propositions are *really* true or false. The remaining step was to withdraw truth from impersonal reality. As long as the Great Chain of Being was in place, reality admitted of degrees; so it made sense to speak of God as more real than human and of human beings as more real than artifacts. Truth's accountability to such ontological gradations continues, too, as in our allusion to "true tones," or "true north." But since the West's objectivizing tendency pushed reality beyond the pale of value entirely, these statements too are taken to be bred of confusion if intended literally. Notions of degree have no place in reality. A state-of-affairs is a state-of-affairs; it either exists or it doesn't. How then can it be either true or false?

For a civilization to relegate truth to the realm of impersonal propositions is to position itself toward the world in a special and far-reaching way. In the natural sciences this positioning does much good and no harm; elsewhere this is less clear. Gandhi could mobilize an entire people around *satyāgraha*, "truth-force," and in doing so liberate a nation. Our canons have no room for such a notion; to us it appears a pastiche, a conflation of intentions and dispositions that a clear mind will distinguish and lay out in patterned array. Thereby again our ties to the given are loosened and neurotic eating continues.

Objective knowledge, taken as a paradigm, points in the same direction. As with the notion that truth is impersonal, the notion that knowledge ideally is objective is unexceptionable in technology and the sciences; but when it is extended to knowledge of meanings and values, it produces unanticipated consequences, ones so important that they have provoked an entire movement to counter them. The concern of existentialism with such topics as dread, death, choice, and the self has not been out of interest in these subjects as self-contained; at bottom it has been because these topics, being intensely personal, provide natural entrées for challenging the claim of objectivity to be the only reliable route to knowledge. For objectivity pulls counter to selfhood. Selves are individual; as no two have the same genetic composition or are shaped by the same ontogenetic influences, so none ever beholds the world with eyes identical to another's. Objectivity seeks to remedy this perspectival "defect" by seeking knowledge that is valid for everyone. To maintain that such knowledge can do justice to selves in every important respect entails the view that their differences are not important; it is like holding that a single GI-clothing issue can suit all bodies. As individuality is too much a part of our constitution to be thus discounted, objective knowledge cannot be wholly satisfying. It holds, moreover, a specific danger: If extended unduly it leads, as Nietzsche saw, to nihilism. For if, per the objectivist ideal, we were to succeed in getting all our values out in front of us, completely visible to our conscious understanding, one decisive move would remain—to espouse them or to shrug and walk away.

IV. The Turn to the East

Nothing is gained by turning intelligence off, but sometimes it needs to be deconditioned. With this profoundly subversive intent I propose now to cut out of Western civilization completely, to prune back its impersonal truth, objective knowledge, and its view of reason as dividing and controlling, so that I can touch base with the common water table of humankind, the primeval outlook from which all civilizations evolved. This archaic outlook I have called the cosmological myth; it depicted nature, society, and self as fused in a more or less compact unity. Moreover, having worked our way back to this primordial base. I propose to veer sharply to the East. For although even archaic humanity has had thoughts that could help us, there is an obstacle. We are civilized. China, I suggest, may help us across the gulf this poses. For China developed the cosmological myth, neither staying with it as did the tribes that remained oral, nor veering from it as did we in the West. My hope is that in our time of ecological need it may prove suggestive to see how the primordial philosophy out of which all civilizations evolved looks when it is updated, modulated by cultivated expression within the bosom of a full-fledged civilization.

China developed the cosmological myth by viewing the universe as an organic system of interdependent parts. This view disclosed the individual as being in the first place the recipient or heir to an endless flow of blessings issuing most noticeably from one's parents but behind them from one's ruler and from heaven and earth in their entirety. By virtue of these benefactions, the individual owes a debt of service to those from whom they issue. In particular one owes debts of filial piety to one's parents and loyalty to one's ruler. Where life is in balance these debts will be repaid spontaneously, motivated by the gratitude that the benefactions instinctively awaken in the recipient. Expressed metaphysically, the view led to the notion of the fundamental unity of all things in their essential aspects. The individual who seeks for their own true soul will discover it to be the same as the soul of heaven and earth and all things. The quest partakes of mysticism, but in East Asia, not a world-rejecting mysticism. Once the individual discovers one's supreme identity, one is able to live in harmony with one's social and natural environment.

To designate this complete divine ecology, the Chinese used the word Tao. What can we say of it?[3]

The first thing we must say is that it is impossible to describe it objectively, that is to say, in a way that will be publicly convincing. This is obvious when we think of the world's worth; if I were to claim I could persuade someone recently disillusioned in love or someone saddled with a deplorable self-image that life is a magnificent adventure, you would think me mad. Any objective description of the world would have to be value-free. But the world is not value-free; to assume that it is, is the ontological dead end into which we Westerners have been driven by our peculiar canons of knowing. Another way to indicate that the Tao eludes objective demonstration is to say that knower and known are correlative. We see what we are capable of seeing, know what we can know. But the Tao, according to one thoughtful soul, Dwight Goddard, "is the name given to perhaps the grandest conception the human mind has ever conceived." It would be puzzling, therefore, if it *were* in focus to casual, surface inspection.

The Tao cannot be objectively described, then, in the sense of being depicted in a way that is logically consistent and intuitively plausible to all. To assume the contrary would be (to repeat) to perpetuate in the Western objectivist mistake. The only approaches to it are the way of letters and the way of life. The way of letters is the poet's way: by verbal wizzardry to trigger an astral projection of our moods and imaginings to another plane. The way of life is different. It requires long years of cultivation, for it requires altering not one's imagination but one's self; transforming one's sentiments, attitudes, and outlook until, a new perceptual instrument having been forged, a new world swings into view.

This world of the accomplished Taoist, of the one whose psychic integration has progressed to the point where not only are one's inner forces harmonized but the sum of these are attuned to one's enveloping surround—what is this world of the perfected Taoist like?

It is the Realm of the Great Infinite. Here too let us acknowledge that even the accomplished Taoist can have only the slightest sense of what this realm is really like. We approach it as human beings, with minds and senses that suffice for our needs but fall as far short in their capacity to discern reality's ultimate nature as an amoeba's intelligence founders before Einstein; if physicists like David Bohm and Phillip Morrison can suspect that the levels of size in the universe—transstellar, mega, macro, micro, subquantum—are infinite, a sage may be pardoned the hunch that its value-reaches are comparably beyond our ken. To be in any way manageable our question must be modified to read: What is the profoundest view of the Realm of the Great Infinite available to human beings?

1. It is a realm of relativity. Perhaps, as Kierkegaard put the matter, existence *is* a system—for God; for people, who are within it, system it can never be. Within it, all is perspectival. The flower, in front of the candle to me, is behind it to my wife. One stone is light compared to a second, heavy compared to a third. The pitch of a locomotive's whistle is constant for the engineer; to a bystander it falls. Nothing can be absolutely positioned, for we lack the absolute framework such positioning would require. If this is true of perception and thought, it must also hold of course for language. It being impossible to say everything at once, every statement is perforce partial; it is one-sided. But the world itself, being in us and and around us, is not one-sided. All this holds, of course, for the present statement. Naturally I shall try to make my account of the Tao as cogent as possible, for if I begin to fail glaringly, I shall lose interest as quickly as will you. Still, somewhere in my words there will be a flaw—that's a priori; somewhere in my depiction is a value counterpart of the surd Goedel spotted in mathematics: a point that contradicts something I say elsewhere or collides with a piece of your own considered experience. We should not bemoan this buckle in our logic, for it keeps us moving, keeps us from settling down, insists on an extension in our horizons if it is to be smoothed out. If it doesn't show itself today, it will tomorrow.

2. It is a realm of interpenetration and interdependence. It is not one in a simple sense that excludes distinctions and could be visualized as the clear light of the void, a sky unflecked with clouds, or the sea without a wave. Distinctions abound, but the domains they establish cohere. "Heaven and Earth and I live together, and therein all things and I are one" (Chuang Tzu).

> Thirty spokes joined at the hub.
> From their non-being [i.e., the point at which their
>   distinctnesses disappear in the hub itself]
> Comes the function of the wheel (Lao Tzu).

Multiplicity is itself a unity. As nothing exists by itself, all things being in fact interdependent, no phenomenon can be understood by divorcing it from its surround. Indeed, it is the underlying unity that provides the possibility *for* distinctions. Thus even parts that appear discordant unite at some level to form a whole: "Tweedledum and Tweedledee/*Agreed* to have a battle." Or like elderly chess players who, having done their utmost to vanquish each other, at the game's end push back the board, light up cigarettes, and review the moves as friends. Being is organic. Peculiarities dissolve, parts fuse into other parts. Each individual melds into other individuals and through this melding makes its contribution, leaves its mark.

This complementary interpenetration is symbolized in many ways in China. One of the best-known ways is the *yin-yang,* a circle divided into black and white halves, not by a straight line but by one that meanders, leading white into the black domain and allowing black to lap back into the white. Moreover, a white dot stakes its claim in the deepest recesses of black, while a black dot does likewise in the central citadel of the white. All things do indeed carry within themselves the seeds of their own antitheses. And the opposites are bonded; banded together by the encompassing circle that locks both black and white in inseparable embrace.

On a two-dimensional surface, no symbol can rival the yin-yang in depicting the Great Infinite's complementing interpenetration, but because it is two-dimensional, it needs supplementing. Our two cats when they overlap each other in sleep form a three-dimensional yin-yang, and indeed when they fight they form a four-dimensional one. But people need to feel the play of these forces within them, kinesthetically, not just observe them in others. So the Chinese created *Tai Chi,* the Great Polarity, a discipline that cuts right across our disparate categories of calisthenics, dance, martial arts, and meditation. In lieu of a film strip I insert here some notes I once jotted down at a Tai Chi class:

> Everything a little curved; nothing extended or pushed to the limit. Expansive gestures (out and up) are yang, ingathering gestures (down and in) are yin. No side of the body exclusively one or the other. Yang dissolves at once into yin, yin gathers strength to become yang. Down becomes up, up down. All is lightness and freedom. As soon as it's done, stop; no sooner heavy than grows light. Strong, then immediately release. Energy reserved, highly volatile, capable of being deployed in any direction, at any point. So finely balanced that a fly cannot alight nor feather be added.

Apocryphal like all such stories, yet making its point, is the account of the great master, Yang Chien Ho. Birds were unable to take off from his palm because as their feet pushed down to spring, his hand dropped concomitantly. Drawing a cocoon thread is another image; if there is no pressure the thread isn't drawn, but the instant there is too much the thread snaps.

3. Viewed extrovertively, under the aspect of yang, the interrelatedness of existence shows forth as the Great Creativity. From a single primordial atom the entire universe derives: galaxies, nebulae, island universes, pushing forward faster and faster. Potentiality explodes into actuality, infinitely. Every possibility must be exploited, each nook and cranny filled. Thereby diversity is accomplished. When attention shifts from this multiplicity to its relatedness, the Great Sympathy comes into view. As sympathy, Tao synthesizes, as creativity it proliferates. The two movements complement; creativity flows from one to all, sympathy from all to one. Without sympathy multiplicity would be chaos, whereas without creativity sympathy would lack province. They proceed together, hand in hand, partners in the Tao's sublime ecology. Chuang Tzu's illustration, characteristically homey, is the centipede. At the points at which they touch the earth its legs are a hundred or so, but on a higher level such orchestration! It is through the many that the one enacts its versatility.

Perceived thus in the context of the Tao, nature to the Chinese was no disenchanted causal mechanism floating on the foundation of nothingness. It was undergirded by an eternal numinous reality from which life proceeds and which inclines it towards harmony. Underlying the visible—our phenomenal world, the "realm of the ten thousand things"—is something of immense importance that is invisible. The essential relation between the two is nonduality. Life's dependability, mingling with nature's, betokens a hidden oneness in the bosom of the multiple, a total interdependence at the heart of the spheres. A rhythm falls upon the visible, breaking it into day and night, summer and winter, male and female, but these divisions are caught up and ordered in a superior integration that resolves the tensions and reconciles the irreconcilable. Heaven and earth agree. They are united in a hymn for a double choir, an antiphony on a cosmic scale. It is a concentric vision, the vision of society set like a stone in nature, and nature set similarly in the deep repose of eternity.

V. The Ladder of Ascent

To experience reality as just described results in sensing a friendly continuity between one's own life and the Tao, and a willingness to

blend with its ways. There comes also a shift toward *yes* and away
from *no* where the claims of the nonego are concerned and a consequent freedom and elation as the boundaries of confining selfhood
melt down. A generalized sense of life's enlargement and well-being
commences. How to get into this state—the question of method—
lies outside the scope of this paper, but I will note five stages through
which the aspirant is said to pass.[4]

1. The aspirant begins with the world as it appears to human
beings generally, composed of discrete and apparently self-subsisting
entities that are related only in such ways as empirical observation
discloses.

2. The second stage involves a dramatic awakening in which the
world's undifferentiated aspect is realized. This is the world known
to mystics and a good many artists. Individual selfhood vanishes; one
becomes merged with the Great Self, Emptiness, or the Void.

3. But we live in the everyday world, the world of relativity and
separate things. So the next step is to realize that noumena and phenomena, the relative and absolute worlds of stages one and two
respectively, are but two aspects of one reality. With feet planted in
the absolute the aspirant is directed to look anew at the relative
world that one previously took to be the only world. The aspirant
must come to see that the phenomenal is in truth but the aspect
under which the noumenon is perceived. Absolute and relative completely interpenetrate without obstruction or hindrance. They are
one and the same thing. With this realization the aspirant discovers
that everything in the world around, every tree and rock, every hill
and star, every bit of dust and dirt, as well as every insect, plant, and
animal, self included, are manifestations of the Tao and their movements are functionings of the Tao. Everything, just as it is, is in
essence holy.

4. But more lies ahead. One must come to see that the things that
have already come to be recognized as manifestations of the Tao
together form one complete and total whole by means of harmonious
and unobstructed penetration, interconvertibility, and identification
with each other. Everything in the universe is realized to be constantly and continuously, freely and harmoniously interpenetrating,
interconverting itself with every other thing. A favorite symbol here
is India's net, each intersection of which lodges a jewel that reflects
all the other jewels in the net together with the reflections each of

them contains. The problem with this symbol is the same as that which we encountered in connection with the yin-yang: a net, too, is static, whereas the point is to grasp dynamically the Tao whose nature is always to move on. This requires that the grasper also be forever in the mood of moving, this being the character of life itself. Taoist terms are, for the most part, dynamic rather than static, terms like 'entering-into' and 'being-taken-in', or 'taking-in', 'embracing-and-pervading' and 'simultanous-unimpeded-diffusion'.

5. Finally, and characteristically Chinese, there is 'the return to the natural'. Having come to recognize every element in the world and every act as holy and indispensable to the total universe, as this realization deepens and grows increasingly profound, it is no longer necessary to think explicitly about such things. It is enough for things to be affirmed in their own right; each moment can be responded to naturally and spontaneously as sufficient in itself. It is in this culminating state that one realizes with Master Nansen that "the everyday mind is Tao." Trudging through the snow a master and disciple were surprised by a rabbit that sprang out of nowhere and bounded across their path. "What would you say of that?" the master asked. "It was like a god!" the disciple answered. As the master seemed unimpressed with the answer, the disciple returned the question: "Well, what would you say it was?" "It was a rabbit!"

VI. Quietism: The Test of the Theory

Every position has its problematic, a shoal that, navigated or foundered upon, determines whether the system stands or falls. For Taoism the danger is quietism, the reading of its pivotal *wu wei* (no action) doctrine as admonishing us to do as little as possible or in any case nothing contrary to natural impulse. If everything is an aspect of Tao and thereby holy exactly as it is, why change it? Or to put the question another way: Since, although the Tao's parts are always in flux, its balance of forces is constant, why try to shift its parts from one place to another?

The path that winds past this precipice is a narrow one, and time and again China fell off it. Indeed, one can read the entire history of philosophical Taoism, as well as Buddhism in its Taoist variant (Ch'an), as one long struggle to keep from reading Chuang Tzu's "Do nothing, and everything will be done" as counselling sloth and rationalizing privilege. What other reading is possible? If the answer is "none," the jig's up. If Taoism ends up admonishing us to lounge around while tsetse flies bite us, to sink back in our professional set-tees, handsomely upholstered by endowments amassed from exhor-bitant rents in ghetto slums; if Taoism suggests that we rest on our oars while our nation mashes peasant countrysides in Vietnam, the sooner it is forgotten the better.

The doctrine cannot be stated to preclude such misreading, but the misreading itself can, with care, be avoided. Helpful to doing so is the realization that Taoist assertions are made from the far side of the self/other divide, being in this respect the Orient's equivalent of "Love God and do what you will." *Wu wei* can be read unequivocally only after one has attained Tao-identification. At that point one will continue to act—the Tao, we recall, is never static; to be in it is to be always in the mood of moving. But the far shore attained, one need do nothing save what comes naturally, for what needs doing will claim one's will directly. Unobscured by attachment to ones own perquisites, the suffering of the dispossessed will draw one sponta-neously to their side. Until that point is reached there must be labors that are not wholly spontaneous as we try to act our way into right thinking while concomitantly thinking our way into right action.

The Tao is not unilateral yin. Sensing that even in China when the Tao hits one's mind it tends to enter a yang phase, Taoism sought to redress the balance, but the balance itself was its true concern. "Now yin, now yang: that is the Tao" *(The Great Commentary)*. The formulation is exact; countering the disposition to put yang first, Taoism throws its ounces on the side of yin, but to recover the origi-nal wholeness. That emphasis is what we Westerners need as well. "Heroic materialism" is the phrase Kenneth Clark used on the con-cluding program of his *Civilization* series to characterize our Western achievement; pointing to the Manhattan skyline he noted that it had been thrown up in a century, about a third of the time it took the Middle Ages to build a cathedral. With an impunity Asia would not have believed possible, we have indulged ourselves in a yang trip the likes of which was never before essayed. And we are still here; we haven't capsized. But if we have arrived at a point where taste as well as prudence counsels a redressing, the Tao stands waiting in the wings with "now yin" as its first suggestion. It doesn't ask us to dismantle our machines; civilization needn't be de-yanged. Its call is simply to open the sluice gates of our Great Sympathy to let it catch up with our Great Creativity. The virtues of mastery and control we have developed to near perfection, but life can't proceed on their terms alone.

To enter a friendship, to say nothing of marriage, with an eye to control is to sully the relationship from the start. Complementing the capacity to control is the capacity to surrender—to others in love and friendship, to duty in conscience, to life itself in some sustaining way. The same holds for possessions and complexity; we know well the rewards that they can bestow, while knowing less well the complementing rewards that derive from simplicity. When a Western musicologist was seeking help in deciphering the score of certain Tibetan chants, he was informed by the Karmapa that they "could only be understood by a perfect being, there being so much to hear in a single note." And fronting Eiheiji is Half-Dipper bridge, so-called because whenever Dogen dipped water from the river he used only half a dipperful, returning the rest to the river. Such sayings and behavior are difficult for us to understand; they tend to be beyond our comprehension. But if we were to feel the beauty of the river and a oneness with the water, might we not feel its claims on us and do as Dogen did? It is our own true nature, our natural 'uncarved block' as the Taoist would say, to do so.

Simplicity and surrender can appear as high-ranking values only in a world one trusts and to which one feels at deepest level attuned. If the Taoist approach to nature was not based on reasoned strategy and well-planned attack, it was because such stratagems appeared unneeded. Western civilization has tended to regard the world either as mystery to be entered through religious initiation or as antagonist to be opposed with technological adroitness or stoical courage. Greek tragedy and philosophy set the tone for this; modern science and technology have amplified it a hundredfold. Western peoples have been at heart Promethian; therein lie both their greatness and their absurdity. Taoism does not try to beat or cajole the universe or the gods; it tries to join them. The Western stoic tries this tack too, but from the premise of antagonistic wills to be reconciled by obedience or overcome by dogged refusal. To Asia the problem is a matter of ignorance and enlightenment. If seventeenth-to-nineteenth-century science saw the world as mechanism and twentieth-century science is seeing it (with its holism, reciprocity, and growth) as resembling more an organism, is it possible that the twenty-first century will see it as—what? Is the savingly indefinite word "spirit" appropriate? "If I could say impersonal person, it would be that" (Sokei-an).

> There is a being, wonderful, perfect;
> It existed before heaven and earth.
> How quiet it is!
> How spiritual it is!
> It stands alone and it does not change.

It moves around and around, but does not on this
    account suffer.
All life comes from it.
It wraps everything with its love as in a garment, and
    yet it claims no honor, it does not demand to be
    Lord.
I do not know its name, and so I call it Tao, the Way,
    and I rejoice in its power.[5]

NOTES

1. It is now common knowledge that the Chinese character anglicized
as "Tao" is pronounced "Dow." But for American students, especially radical ones, "Dow" has come to denote Dow Chemical and,
derivatively, napalm. Within this simple phoneme the opposites
have met.

2. In progress, this statement formed the substance of the 1971
Mendenhall Lectures at DePauw University, Gates Lectures at
Grinnel College, Merrick Lectures at Ohio Wesleyan University, and
Distinguished Lecture Series at the University of Oregon. I am
indebted to audiences at those institutions for criticisms that helped
to shape the present formulation.

3. What I say of it here is what *I* shall be saying. This is not an historical study; if it were, the entire space could be devoured by the question of which Tao to describe—that of the Six Classics, of
Confucianism, of Neo-Confucianism, of the Chinese Buddhism that
caused Dwight Goddard to include the *Tao Te Ching* in his *Buddhist
Bible*? If the response is "Not these, surely, but the Tao of the
Taoists themselves," there is still the question of which Taoist:
philosophical, mystical, or popular-religious? (See my chapter on the
subject in *The Great Religions*.) What follows is a composite that
draws mainly on the *Tao Te Ching* and Chuang Tzu, more on the
former than the latter, but it follows their seminal intuitions as these
saturate other strands in the Chinese fabric, notably Ch'an
Buddhism. In addition, the statement undoubtedly contains
emphases occasioned by the angle from which I am approaching
the subject. I am looking for a concept that might speak to us in our
ecological need. I find this concept in the Tao that emerges from my
Chinese meditations; but if a reader wishes to object that it is difficult to match my depiction to a single concept, individual, or school
in classical China, he may be right.

4. The first four steps are taken from the *Hua-yen school,* which, building on Buddhism and hence indirectly on India's willingness to attempt to conceptualize positions the Chinese would have left intuitive, articulated the doctrine of "perfect mutual unimpeded solution" more explicitly than did any other school in East Asia. The fifth step is added by the Ch'an school.

5. Adapted from K. L. Reichelt's translation of the Twenty-fifth Chapter of the *Tao Te Ching,* in his *Meditation and Piety in the Far East* (New York: Harper & Row, Publishers, 1954), p. 41.

A Note on Shinto

All life-forms look out upon the world from a center of individual identity, and this holds for collectivities as well as for individuals. For the Japanese people Shinto constitutes their identity while Buddhism opens them to the world—most directly to the peoples of China and Korea, but beyond those to India and all Asia. Thus while Buddhism is centrifugal, Shinto is centripetal; at heart it is reverence and love for things Japanese. Spatially this reverential love is directed towards the land, the Japanese islands. Temporally it focuses on a genealogy which, beginning at home and in neighborhoods with family and clan, moves through the myths of the imperial family to the Sun Goddess Amaterasu, symbol of the metaphysical reality from which all things proceed.

Actually, the land too is included in this lineage, for the *Nihonji* reports that the islands of Japan arose from drippings from a jeweled spear that Izanagi and Izanami plunged into the briny sea. By virtue of that miraculous origination, nature in these islands is sanctuary, a truth that finds expression in *tori-i* placed to frame sacred landscapes, and in the designation of notable natural objects—mountains, groves, springs—as *kami*. One of the most treasured objects in my own home, the gift of a Japanese professor who visited me while I was teaching at the Massachusetts Institute of Technology, is a *kakimono* whose handsome inscription reads 天地有情 (The universe is spiritual). I treasure it for its beauty, but even more for its message as a corrective to the lifeless, mechanistic cosmology that scientism has foisted on the West.

This note is excerpted from the Introduction to the projected Japanese edition of Smith's The World's Religions. *It was pre-published in the* Atheneum Society Review *(Spring 1985), pp. 79–80.*

Returning to the human side of the sacred genealogy, we notice that veneration mounts as we travel backwards in time: ancestors are more esteemed than the living, age is exalted over youth, and parents are more respected than children. As this "reverse time orientation" runs counter to the modern myth of progress, historians of religion have saddled it with the epithet "ancestor worship," the implication being that in East Asia human progenitors double for the divine, taking its place and serving as its substitute. Asians see the matter differently. Rather than standing in for the divine, ancestors constitute a bridge to it. There is something metaphysically sound in this institution that, as the world and its spinnings derive from divinity, those who stood closer to creation were closer to the Creator as well and more bathed in its light. Whether they were actually better than we are—whether "there were giants on the earth in those days" (to quote the Biblical version of this myth) that were morally as well as physically our superiors—we cannot know, but to think that there were, buttresses our sense of the sacred. For if the heroism of patriarchs derived from their proximity to the point of origin, two things are accomplished in a single stroke: the origin is honored by being credited for their heroism, while we for our part are accorded noble pedigree. We derive not from some primordial ooze, but from the gods themselves. The notion strengthens us for the nobility that is required of us, for if our nature is noble we feel both that we should act nobly, and that we can so act. The exemplary models our ancestors provide are relevant. To be true to them is, at the same time, to be true to ourselves and true to God.

From the two preceding points, the sacred origin of the Japanese islands and the Japanese people, a Shinto ethic derives. It is an ethic of purity, sincerity, and simplicity. That two of these three words duplicate Dr. Suzuki's characterization of Zen Buddhism should not surprise us, for the degree to which Shinto and Buddhism coalesce in the lived lives of the Japanese people has already been remarked. On NBC's 1958 "Wisdom" series, Dr. Suzuki characterized Zen as consisting of simplicity, sincerity, and freedom.

Purity ties in with the sacredness of nature, as the phrase "virgin nature" attests, but in a way simplicity is fundamental. When on one occasion I mentioned to Prof. Ono Sokyo, author of *The Kami Way,* that I could find no English exposition of Shinto theology, he said that the reason was clear: Shinto has no theology. And in ethics, he added, its precepts reduce to purity and sincerity. The parsimony in these answers is reflected in Shinto sanctuaries which are virtually empty, and in the Japanese esthetic sense generally which is world renowned. Everyone has heard of at least one Japanese principle of flower arrangement: compose the flowers as they should be, then remove half of them, then half of what remain. In the tea ceremony we find the same understatement and paring back to essentials. If we see in this austerity a naturalness that derives in ways from nature, its connection with ancestors is even more apparent, for whether they were better than we are, their lives seem clearly to have been simpler, and thereby exempt from the complications and attendant ambiguities and compromises that bedevil so much of modern life.

Spiritual Discipline
in Zen and Comparative
Perspective

To the honor that has been accorded me in the invitation to deliver the opening paper in this important symposium I shall add a liberty. Though the symposium is on Zen Buddhism, in exploring the subject of spiritual discipline I shall not restrict myself to Zen's mode of spiritual training. This is partly because I am a comparativist rather than a Buddhologist or specialist on Japan, but the decision is also prompted by the thought that before we center down on Zen proper it might be useful to consider our topic in the context of humanity's religious venturings as a whole.

To launch me on that project, let me invoke a wry comment the American novelist John Updike once made. "A lot of people are looking at maps," he said; "few seem to be going anywhere." This is a useful opening because it shows us at once why spiritual disciplines are important. An oasis is of no avail while it is distant, and the same holds for reality; for it to empower us we must be joined to it. But we are normally not well joined, as the myths of exile and fall, of sleep-walking and forgetting, persistently remind us. Something must be done to effect the needed union, and discipline is a name for that doing. It is the journeying that carries us from exile to our spiritual home.

This essay originally appeared in The Eastern Buddhist XVI, 2 *(1983): 9–25. It had earlier been presented at the International Symposium for Religious Philosophy (Kyoto Zen Symposium) held under the auspices of the Institute for Zen Studies, Hanazono College, Kyoto, Japan, in March 1983. A briefer version of this essay, entitled, "In Defense of Spiritual Discipline," appeared in James Duerlinger, (ed.),* Ultimate Reality and Spiritual Discipline *(New York: Paragon House, 1983).*

I. Discipline as Requisite

To say that this journeying is always in order is an understatement; it is needed, for never for long are we exactly where we should be. There are intervals when we *seem* to be where we should be; these are the "times of inherent excellence" Wallace Stevens speaks of,

> As when the cock crows on the left and all
> Is well, incalculable balances,
> At which a kind of Swiss perfection comes...[1]

Such times do indeed come, and when they do we do not know whether the happiness they bring is the rarest or the commonest thing on earth, for in all earthly things we find it, give it, and receive it. But we cannot hold onto that happiness. This hardly needs arguing, but two giants can be quoted to drive the point home. "Whoever thinks that in this mortal life a man may so disperse the mists of bodily and carnal imaginings as to possess the unclouded light of changeless truth, and to cleave to it with the *unswerving* constancy of a spirit wholly estranged from the common ways of life," St. Augustine wrote, "he understands neither what he seeks, nor who he is who seeks it" (italics added). St. Teresa's formulation of the same point is as follows: "If anyone told me that after reaching this state [of union] he had enjoyed *continual* rest and joy, I should say that he had not reached it at all" (again, italics added). There seems to be no permanent abode this side of Eden. Even Jesus prayed, and the Buddha continued to sit after his enlightenment.

This initial point is important enough to repeat, exchanging the metaphors of travel, oases, and home for the actual object of the spiritual quest, which is knowledge. No desire is more deeply embedded in us than the desire to know; to see things as clearly and completely as is possible. Buddhism recognizes this by asking us "to see things in their suchness," while a *hadith* of Muhammad runs, "O Lord, show me all things as they truly are."[2] In our present state, though, as St. Paul admits, "we see in a mirror dimly" (I Cor. 13:13). As a boy growing up in China, that was a vivid image for me, for quicksilver mirrors had only recently arrived and the reflections afforded by the traditional mirrors of burnished bronze were murky at best. To "see face to face" is not our present lot, but we can polish our mirrors, or (in Blake's alternative wording) cleanse the doors of our perceptions. If we take seriously our human opportunity (which the Indian tradition never tires of reminding us is "hard to come by") we may wonder whether anything unrelated to this cleansing is worthwhile.

Light cannot penetrate a stone, and is barely reflected from a black surface. For truth's light to enter us, our petrified selves must be turned into crystal; correlatively but in altered imagery, if our lives are to reflect truth's light, black bogs must be changed into fields of snow. Such alchemical changes require doing. In the language of our title, they require discipline.

II. Objections to Discipline

Those who have urged the importance of spiritual disciplines—be they the Buddha's Eightfold path, Patanjali's Raj or Astanga Yoga, Buddhaghosa's Visuddhimagga (Path of Purification), Saint Ignatius' spiritual exercises, or John Wesley's Method-ism, to name but a representative sample—have had to face a number of objections, three of which are recurrent.

1. The first of these is the charge that such regimens preempt for human beings the credit for change that belongs to God. Approaching salvation as if it were a condition to be achieved rather than a gift to be received, they shift the accent from grace, where it belongs, to self-effort.

A number of rejoinders are in order here, and I will proceed from the most obvious to ones that are less so.

To begin with, not all disciplines have subjective change as their aim. When the Qur'an enjoins the Muslim to "hymn the praise of thy Lord when thou uprisest, and in the night-time also hymn His praise, and at the setting of the stars" (LII: 48–49), it foreshadows what is probably the most widely practiced spiritual discipline on our planet today—the canonical prayers of Islam. These prayers unquestionably have an effect on those who offer them, but that effect is not their direct intent which is, rather, to honor Allah with the adoration that is Allah's due. A cynic could of course claim that though that is the right reason for prayer, the real (in the sense of operative) reason is the celebrant's wish to get to heaven. To this the answer is: Doubtless this is so for some, but motives for praying cover a wide spectrum, reaching to the prayer of the Sufi saint Rabi'a, which has become classic:

> O God! If I worship Thee in fear of Hell, burn me
>   in Hell;
> And if I worship Thee in hope of Paradise, exclude
>   me from Paradise;

But if I worship Thee for Thine own sake, withhold
not Thine everlasting beauty!

Proceeding to the more subtle point, even when discipline does
include self-transformation in its object, it does not follow that the
program excludes grace or even tips the scales away from it.

The model in this second instance is the athlete. No one supposes
that an Olympic contender can stay in the running unless he or she
works out regularly. Are we to suppose that spiritual attainment is
less demanding; that it does not require its "spiritual exercises," to
invoke Ignatius' phrase which fits perfectly here? Both cases call for
effort, but athletes are not normally concerned with the relation of
that effort to empowerment from other sources,[3] whereas "spiritual
athletes" have to give thought to that question because "relation to
reality" is their central concern. Where do they come down on the
question? What *is* the relation between grace and self-effort?

It is easiest to state the conclusion negatively. The relation is not a
disjunctive one, such that the more you have of one the less you
have of the other. It's closer to the opposite: not either/or, but
both/and.

Given a space that is finite, say, an empty hat box, the more black
marbles it contains the less room there will be for white ones, and
vice versa. But for the way human activity is related to God's, this
model won't work: a different logic is required. To begin with, there
is no human action which is not divinely empowered, which makes
every human act in some way God's act as well. This initial point is
simple, but it opens quickly onto paradoxes and then mysteries.
There is no hope of fathoming these here, if indeed the rational mind
can ever dissolve the mysteries that are involved. What it can do, to
repeat, is see clearly that either/or logic in this domain is "pre-
Riemannian." With Ramakrishna's "the winds of God's grace are
always blowing, but you must raise your sail" and St. Paul's "in His
service is perfect freedom" we approach paradox, but if we keep
going we are confronted with what, to the rational mind, must look
like absolute contradictions. Spinoza's equation of freedom with
determinism is one of these; Pauline theology another. I once heard
a New Testament scholar compress the latter into a sentence that
was vivid, though earthy: "You have to work like hell because it's all
been done for you."

In an important essay that originally appeared in 1968 but has
recently been republished,[4] Marco Pallis details the reciprocal relationship between grace and self-effort as they interact in Buddhism.

Early Theravada Buddhism provides a good test case on this issue, for a perspective that does not include the idea of a personal God seems at first glance to leave little room for the idea of grace as well. Can merciful action from above, defined as an unsolicited gift that is extended to human beings independent of their own effort, be reconciled with the workings of karma as the inexorable law of moral cause and effect? Pallis shows that it can be. For as the Buddha said: "There is, O monks, an unborn, an unbecome, an unmade, an uncompounded," without which there would be "no escape from the born, the become, the made." This "uncompounded" on which the Buddhist quest is founded and to which it leads, stands prior to all human doings as something that is simply given to us. Our discernment of this uncompounded sunyata initiates our spiritual quest, but again we must ask into the anatomy of this discernment. When we gaze on the Grand Canyon, how much of what we see is of our own doing? We make the journey to see it, we can say; but would we have done so had we not heard reports of it and been endowed with sensibilities to respond to those reports? Above all, would we have journeyed and responded had it not been *there*? In the case of enlightenment, were it totally beyond our reach we could no more respond to its summons than an ox can feel drawn to astronomy, which shows that the capacity for enlightenment has been given us as a gift. Meister Eckhart put this matter in perspective when he wrote that "in the course of nature it is really the higher which is ever more ready to pour out its power into the lower than the lower is ready to receive it"; for as he goes on to say, "there is no dearth of God with us; what dearth there is is wholly ours who make not ready to receive his grace." Eventually this point finds Buddhist statement in the assertion that the Buddha-nature is with us from the start.

All of the Buddha's emphasis on self-effort and exertion—"be ye lamps unto yourselves"; "work out your salvation with diligence"— should be seen in the context of a gracious matrix that inspires the religious quest and assures its fulfillment. There is not space here to go into Pallis's discussion of the ancillary "means of grace" in Buddhism; the *upayas* (skillful means) that range from the compelling example of the Buddha's own life, through the sutras and other scriptures, to art (notably the sublime iconography of the Buddha himself) which can put us ahead of ourselves by relaying to our dispositions the beauty that impacts our senses. Even if we do not include the Bodhisattvas who are grace personified, these gifts are strewn about almost carelessly in Buddhist civilizations, free for the taking. But though I must pass over these proximate supports, I do want to note before completing this Buddhist excursion that

Marco Pallis's analysis was in important ways foreshadowed by D. T. Suzuki's study of Shin Buddhism. As a development that stresses other-power *(tariki)*, Shin had from the first to argue that it is truly Buddhist, for original Buddhism (as we have seen) *seemed* to lean heavily towards self-power *(jiriki)*. Suzuki argues Shin's case historically by saying that in our preoccupation with the Buddha's teaching we should not overlook his example which leaned heavily towards helping others. From the moment of his enlightenment, he was occupied with his mission: What he could do for others and the benefits that could accrue to them from that doing. But beyond this historical point, Suzuki argues the logical point we have seen Pallis making: self-power and other-power, self-effort and grace, prove under inspection to be reciprocal; each entails the other in principle. Other-power must be *received*, while self-power rides on a supporting context that *is* received inasmuch as the self did not create it. Moreover, it is possible to advance to the point where each component is recognized as its opposite. The Shin believer pronounces the *nembutsu* (formula that saves), yet he or she doesn't; Amida, the saving Buddha, pronounces it using the believer's lips while being simultaneously the faith/compassion that rises in the believer's breast.[5] Meanwhile the Zen Buddhist, whose strenuous zazen places him or her at the opposite end of the grace/self-effort spectrum, is brought to the same point the Shinnist reaches. Zen urges self-effort, but what happens to self when it discovers that it is nothing less than the Buddha-nature in phenomenal guise?[6]

I have spent what may seem like disproportionate space on the interplay of discipline and grace because, respecting the topic at hand, this is the point at which theological confusion is most likely to arise. In four steps, let me summarize the argument I have used Suzuki and Pallis to set before us:

a. We begin with segments of experience suffused with feelings of effort or ease that can stand in sharp contrast. There are times when it seems that if anything is to come our way it will have to be through our own initiative, and there are times when we simply sit back and ride the Glory Train—Shinran's image is taking a boat ride; it is so easy and pleasant.

b. These episodes do not last, however. Effort eases, but then that ease too crumbles like something in a fairy tale when the clock strikes twelve. Nothing in life can be understood without introducing the element of time, and time brings rhythms and oscillations. We wake to work; later we lie down to sleep. We stretch our legs and then relax them.

c. But even apart from these pendulum swings which show both reception and exertion to be parts of life's story, we can see, if we look closely, that self- and other-power entail each other in principle. Even benefits that are transmitted to us through other-power *(tariki ekō)* must, we have seen, be received; and self-power presupposes a supportive context which the self did not create.

d. The culminating stage is reached when each of the two components is actually experienced as being also its opposite. Whereas the preceding point was that Amida's saving power requires the *nembutsu,* now the point is that in pronouncing that formula the Shinnist realizes that Amida is pronouncing it through the believer. Comparably with the Zennist. It is not just that zazen presupposes a supporting context. The line between one's sitting and what cushions that sitting, we might say, disappears.

2. Disciplines have been subject to a second criticism; namely, that they are prompted in the end by a subtle form of willfulness.

A natural tendency of the ego is its wish to have things differ from the way they are. The West is inclined to see this as a problem because we want things to differ in *our* way, not God's way, but there is a view that holds that the problem lies deeper. According to this second view, the ultimate cause of the human problem is our wish to have things differ in *any* way from the way they are. Buddhism argues this most explicitly with its claim that the source of *dukkha* (suffering) is *tanha* (desire or craving), but we can find the point in every tradition if we look carefully enough. Eckhart's teaching that we should not even wish that we had not sinned is readily misunderstood, but in the context of his complete theology its function is to take the final step in closing the ought/is divide. Beginning by acknowledging God's omnipotence—recognizing that in last analysis God is the author of everything—it goes on to affirm that that omnipotence is perfect. Islam, for its part, compresses the logic in question into its very name. Unique among the world's faiths in being named by a common noun, that noun designates (as we know) a spiritual attitude: submission. Uncapitalized, *islam* simply means submission; capitalized it designates the company of those who have dedicated their lives *to* submission.[7] Run-of-the-mill understandings of submission ride on master/servant imagery, but metaphysically submission calls for aligning the human heart with the way things are. The test of this alignment is total affirmation; not passive acceptance, but the active affirmation of everything, exactly as it is and will be.

The bearing of all this on discipline is not far to seek. To the extent that spiritual exercises aim at self-change, this second criticism argues, they exacerbate the ought/is divide rather than ameliorating it. That the posited "ought" is in this instance a noble one—self-improvement and eventually liberation—only camouflages the trap it overlays: the ego has a deep-rooted tendency to co-opt and appropriate even the process of liberation; it thrives on such appropriations and we have here a clear instance. In Buddhist terms, the desire to be desireless is itself a desire and therefore contradictory. The Sufi Hasan Esh-Shadhili makes the same point in theistic idiom when he writes: "The desire for union with God is one of the things which most surely separates from him."[8]

As in the first charge against disciplines, there is much in this second charge that is true—everything, in fact, save its presumed conclusion: that spiritual disciplines are misguided. "To desire to be desireless" may sound contradictory, but until we *have* transcended desires[9]—while we continue to dangle from their puppet strings—it is crucial to discriminate among them. Some desires—the Bodhisattva's vow to save all sentient beings, and yes, the desire to reach enlightenment oneself—are better than others; they are, as the Buddhists say, "wholesome states." To overlook this simple fact is to betray one's ignorance, the deadliest form of which is to think that one has completed the spiritual journey when one is still a traveller on its way.

As for the Sufi version of the warning-against-desire that was quoted above, is it true that desire for union with God actually separates us from God? The answer depends on the nature of the union anticipated. If it focuses on a finite ego which is destined to be flooded with rapture and who knows what other good things when the beatific vision dawns, desire for a union that places this grandiose ego stage center does indeed separate. Disguised egoism, it is simply another variant of Chogyam Trungpa's "spiritual materialism." But if eyes are kept steadfastly on God, allowing God's presence to expand until, filling the horizon, it leaves no room for the self that inherits the view, it is difficult to see how this second mode of desire, radical to the point of seeking the ego's extinction *(fana)*, could backfire.

Though it was cast in different terms, the dispute between the Northern and Southern Schools of Ch'an Buddhism in the T'ang dynasty was over issues that are very close to ones we are involved with in this second objection to method. When Hui-neng countered Shen-hsiu's admonition to keep the mirrors of our minds brightly polished, he seemed to be challenging the importance of method, which challenge was to prompt burlesques of zazen as tile-polishing and sitting like Sengai's frog. But these challenges were not categorical. The issue is as subtle as any that can be posed, and a look at the way it was handled in the "gradual versus sudden" controversy can help with the problem we are working on.

The Southern School is said to differ from the Northern School in advocating sudden rather than gradual enlightenment; as *The Platform Sutra* puts the point, "Why not from your own natures make the original nature of true reality suddenly appear?" We can translate this temporal (gradual versus sudden) distinction into spatial imagery and think of gradual enlightenment as the horizontal dimension of Zen, and sudden enlightenment as its vertical dimension. Roshis use a homely illustration to bring out the difference.

I break a bowl. On the one hand I can say that I should have been more careful and can resolve to be more careful in the future. On the horizontal, linear plane where past and future figure, this is all as it should be. Nevertheless—here the vertical dimension enters—at the moment the bowl was breaking, bowl-breaking was all there was. Self-nature (the Buddha-nature, *sunyata, pratitya-samutpada,* whatever terms we wish to use) was manifesting itself in just that way. Enlightenment is to see that. Such seeing can occur whenever and wherever. And when it does occur, it occurs in an instant, which is why the philosophy that stresses this point came to be known as the sudden school. The point for this paper on spiritual exercises, though, is that the defenders of sudden enlightenment do not repudiate gradualism. Hui-neng continued to sit and practice other austerities, and I should never give up trying to be careful not to break more bowls. But no amount of caution will ever guarantee that my fingers will never again slip. This is simply a concrete way of saying that I will never become perfect. In Buddhist terms, no amount of practice—gradualism—will make me a Buddha; no amount of zazen will carry me to enlightenment. If the Buddha is to arrive he must do so not at the end of my life, as the terminus of my horizontal, linear effort. Buddha must arrive vertically, where I am right now, in the midst of my imperfections. He (or it) must arrive in an instant, in a sudden flashing insight that cuts through the distinction between present and future and collapses the distinction between practice and what practice seeks.

3. A third charge against disciplines is that they foster spiritual pride. This is indeed a danger; spiritual pride is pride's subtlest form. But the religions have known this, while adding that this final adversary is best countered with a light touch. When William Law proposed some measures for deepening the contemplative life a clergyman responded with an angry sermon "On the Wickedness and Presumption of Attempting to be Righteous Overmuch." Law replied, "Perhaps, Sir, if you try to be a saint, you may succeed in being a gentleman."

To summarize this central section of my paper: If the reproaches that have been directed against disciplines are read as warnings they can be useful. It would be a mistake, though, to see them as proscriptions. The alternative to discipline and the effort it requires is "quietism," a technical term in the vocabulary of mysticism for a state that comes perilously close to doing nothing. Even Taoism, whose concept of *wu wei* skirts the brink of that state, recognizes that the state itself is disastrous.

III. The Common Thrust of
Spiritual Techniques

Having devoted most of my space to answering objections to spiritual disciplines, I can only touch on four other points, beginning with the sense in which such disciplines point in the same general direction.

To broach the prospect of unity in the world's religions is to raise the spectre of syncretism, but guidelines are available for avoiding its pitfalls.[10] Syncretism plays upon universal yearnings for brotherhood and understanding to reduce the "strong meat" of divine revelation to innocuous pablum; it levels the great traditions to their lowest common denominator, as if there were nothing more to God's (in ways terrible) word than the Golden Rule and vague belief in "a something or other" that is greater than ourselves. In important ways the historical religions are *not* alike, and to insist prematurely on their resemblances is to play down these "importances" in favor of resemblances that are secondary and derivative. The most vocal champions of ecumenism often turn out to be persons who, having lost faith in the revealed character of traditions per se, their own included, have retreated to commonsense values—brother/sisterhood and understanding—which are secure in that no one could possibly take exception to them. Thanks to its advocates of this stripe, ecumenism (for all its lofty ideals) often spreads relativism and strengthens secularism's already heavy hand.

Still, it seems most unlikely that there is not some important sense in which the great religions are one; in theistic terms, would God have permitted them to endure for millennia, nourishing the lives of untold millions, if they were not in some sense vehicles of God's all-including will? The way to acknowledge this authentic unity while avoiding the pitfalls of syncretism is to locate the unity in a transcendent realm, beyond the kataphatic, positive (as in *via positiva*), articulated theologies whose differences should be honored while being kept sharply edged.[11] Heinrich Ott has made a parallel move by suggesting that interfaith dialogue be anchored in the notion of mystery.[12] If, as Noam Chomsky and his fellow transformational grammarians are arguing, human languages with their surface variations derive through the application of unconscious rules or "transformations" from a deep linguistic structure that is common to the human species—programmed into its members, one might say—might there be a comparable universal religious "grammar" which the great religions illustrate as different languages?[13]

This is not the place to explore that question, and in any case I have already argued my (affirmative) answer in a book-length study, *Forgotten Truth: The Primordial Tradition* (Harper & Row, 1976). I shall note only that, as respecting the question of disciplines, a common direction in which they point seems clearly discernible; it comes to view when we attend to the virtues they all seek to cultivate. Asia, characteristically, describes these negatively by way of the vices that stand in their way; in Buddhist terms these are the Three Poisons: greed, hatred, and ignorance. The West is less reticent about invoking the virtues directly; they are humility, charity, and veracity, and it is easy to see that they are simply direct expressions of the virtues Buddhism approaches indirectly. Selfishness or greed is the opposite of humility which has nothing to do with low self-esteem but is rather the capacity to distance oneself from one's private, separate ego—to realize *anatta,* we mights say—to the point where one can see oneself objectively and therefore accurately, as counting for one, but not more than one. Obviously love *(metta* or *karuna)* is the opposite of hatred, and veracity or truth the opposite of ignorance.

IV. Variations on the Universal Theme

Several times I have acknowledged that not all disciplines aim at self-change. The belief that pious observances, regularly performed, are "the food of the gods" is widespread, and in disciplines thus outwardly directed the accent is on the objective, cosmic consequences of our acts, not their subjective deliveries.[14] But discipline tends to suggest self-discipline, and admittedly it is this side of praxis that this paper has primarily in mind. When the Surah of the Rock tells us to "worship God till certainty comes to thee," an important reflexive consequence of worship, balancing its objective, "food of the gods" intent, is brought squarely to view.

The preceding section called attention to the uniform direction in which spiritual disciplines point, but the invariance of that direction does not preclude significant differences in the multiple paths that honor it. These paths can be identified as the world's great religions; as they differ from one another in ways that are isomorphic with the differences in the civilizations they serve,[15] we are not surprised to find that each has its own distinctive *marga,* or path, as well. Thus orthodox Judaism centers in a discipline which, in its call for observance down to the Torah's minutest details, conforms the self to a holy mold which prayers *keep* holy. Christianity, by contrast, foregoes a good part of that Law to focus on an inward spirit which, through love and devoted service, it seeks to open to Christ's incursion. Buddhism takes yet another tack; the distinctiveness of its discipline emerges in its attention, not to what the mind believes, but to how it works. If we could understand this working, not just theoretically but experientially, we would see how we bring our unhappiness on ourselves and would be released from our self-imposed sentence. Islam's distinctive mode is anchored in its Five Pillars. The *shahadah's* twofold testimony fixes the Absolute in its place and, through its Messenger, anchors the relative world in that Absolute. Prayer marks the submission of the relative to the Absolute. Fasting is detachment with regard to desires and so with regard to the ego. Almsgiving is detachment with regard to things, and so with regard to the world. Finally, pilgrimage is return to the Center, to the Heart, to the Self.

A different typology emerges if we attend, not to differences between religions as integral wholes, but to different spiritual personality types that surface in varying ratios everywhere. With the theory of the Four Yogas, India has taken the lead in this way of "slicing the pie." *Jnana yoga* is for those who want most to know God, *bhakti yoga* for those who want to love God, *karma* for those who want to serve the Lord, and *raj* for those who want to experience God directly through psycho-physical exercises; in this classification, Zen is a version of *raj* yoga. My colleague Agehananda Bharati insists that this scheme goes back no further than to Swami Vivekananda, but the fundamental division, between *bhakti* and *jnana,* can be traced at least to the Upanishads.

Returning for a moment from diversity to oneness, the universality of invocation is too conspicuous to forego mention: the *mantram* in Hinduism, Islam's *dhikr,* and the "Jesus Prayer" of Christianity; in Buddhism, does the *mu* koan qualify alongside the *nembutsu* and *Om mani padme hum*? "There is a means of polishing everything, and of removing rust; what polishes the heart is invocation...." "The invocation of Allah," that *hadith* concludes, but each tradition could provide its own appropriate ending.

V. Stages on the Path

If an intentional or disciplined life, taken as one that places itself under a rule involving prescribed acts in some kind of time frame, is likened to a journey with a destination of some sort in view, a question suggests itself. Does the journey admit of stages? Does the scenery change in predictable ways? Are there landmarks that show how far one has come and how far one has yet to go?

Of the several facets of our topic that I have touched on in this paper, this is the one I am least clear about. One reads of demarcations, beginning with the traditional Hindu claim that the *varnas* (castes) themselves show how far one has progressed on life's total odyssey. If for present purposes we pass over that reincarnational claim and content ourselves with the present life, we can begin by noting the sequences in Patanjali's *raj yoga,* the final steps of which are roughly parallelled by Buddhism's higher *jhanas,* most clearly delineated perhaps by Buddhaghosa. Beginning with unwavering attention to a single object, one proceeds in this program to eliminate first the subjective awareness of oneself as the meditator who is experiencing the object being attended to, and then that object itself, whereupon the "intentionality" of Brentano and his phenomenological successors collapses and one is left with a state that Franklin Merrel-Wolff analyzes in his *The Philosophy of Consciousness Without an Object* (New York: Julian Press, 1973). In Christian spirituality we encounter the stages of vocal prayer, mental prayer, affective prayer (prayer of the will), and the prayer of simplicity wherein words are silenced and images foregone. Covering not prayer only but the aspirant's life as a whole are the stages of purgation, proficiency, and union. The Sufi counterpart of these is more complex, but its subdivisions fall into two categories: stages *(magamat)* and states *(ahwal)*. The former of these are the stages through which the wayfarers must pass in striving after perfection and in their efforts to dispose themselves for the flooding of mystical graces. Being moral and spiritual purifications and realignments that can and must be effected by the disciple's own efforts, they are said to be "acquired" rather than "infused," and are subject to slippage. In these respects they differ from the states which are mystical graces: sheer gifts of divine grace and generosity to a soul which has stripped itself of all self-seeking and self-regard. Henceforth it is not so much the earnest striving and pressing forward of the pilgrim that is in the foreground; it is the victorious and irresistible attraction of the divine beloved, sweeping the traveller off his/her feet and carrying him/her along in states that are not easy to describe. The clearest account of these stages and states that I have encountered is in *The Persian Sufis* by Cyprian Rice (London: George Allen & Unwin, 1964) where the stages are listed as seven[16] and the states as ten,[17] but there are many variations.

In Zen's depictions of the stages of the journey, we have the famous division between the times when mountains and rivers are, then are not, and finally again are mountains and rivers; the Oxherding Pictures further divide these three stages into (most popularly) ten. Hakuin staked out stages in Rinzai Zen practice that move through five kinds of koans:

1. *hosshin,* which introduce us to the undifferentiated realm of the Dharmakaya and help us familiarize ourselves with it as our original home;

2. *kikan,* which help us to understand the differentiated world and its complex interlockings;

3. *gonsen,* which are concerned with the meaning of words and thereby help us to understand the subtlest insights in the patriarchs' utterances;

4. *nantō,* which are the most difficult because they ask us to replicate not just the patriarchs' understandings, but their experiences; and

5. *goi,* which relate to the Five Ranks of the Apparent and the Real: the apparent within the real, the real within the apparent, the coming from within the real, the arrival at mutual integration, and unity attained.[18]

To try to coordinate the milestones on the spiritual paths that have been established by the leading traditions is an undertaking that is beyond my capabilities. I do not have a firm grip on this matter of progression. Being very much a novice on the path myself, reports of its further reaches lack traction; they sound stylized and abstract. And when they are not "archetypal" in this way, the idiosyncratic biography and imagery of the reporter so colors his or her account that I have difficulty pegging it on a universal scale. Finally, my own odyssey has been so filled with ups and downs and the unforeseen, including sharp reversals at times, that it seems presumptuous to try to delineate the stages of pilgrimage in any but a very general way.

NOTES

1. *Collected Poems* (New York: Alfred A. Knopf, 1955), p. 786.
2. Sayyid Haydar Amuli, *Jamehal-Asrar wa Manbuh al-Anwar* (pp. 17, 89); *Rasa'il-e Shah Nimatullah* (Vol. 1, p. 209; Vol. 4, p. 23). Shabistari's gloss on this *hadith* reads:

   > Leave behind both worlds and reside
   > on the highest peak of His threshold.
   > God will bestow upon you whatever you want
   > and show you all things as they truly are.

   Quoted in Javad Nurbakhsh, *Traditions of the Prophet* (New York: Khaniqahi-Nimatullahi Publications, 1981), pp. 32–33.
3. I say "not normally concerned," but actually such concern may be more common than we suppose. Michael Murphy has made a study of star athletes which shows that a large number of them were seriously occupied with forces beyond themselves which they felt worked in their behalf at crucial junctures.
4. "Is There Room for Grace in Buddhism?" in Marco Pallis, *A Buddhist Spectrum* (New York: Seabury Press, 1981).
5. The Islamic version of this is contained in the *hadith,* "I have known my Lord by my Lord," which is anticipated by the Qur'anic verse, "He turned to them that they might turn" (IX: 119). "For," as Abu Bakr al-Kalabdhi explains in commenting on that verse, "the cause of everything is God."
6. Suzuki's full analysis of the *jiriki/tariki* relationship is summarized on pages 142–47 of my "Four Theological Negotiables: Gleanings from Daisetz Suzuki's Posthumous Volumes on Shin Buddhism," *Eastern Buddhist* X, 2 (October 1977).
7. Arabic has no capitals. I have converted the case into English.
8. Quoted in Frithjof Schuon, *Spiritual Perspectives and Human Facts* (London: Perennial Books, 1969), p. 162. It will not have been lost on the reader that in introducing examples to illustrate the points of this paper I often match East with West, in keeping with the dictum: "And to God belongs the East and the West. Wheresoe'er ye turn, there is the Face of God" (Qur'an, II: 109).
9. The word "transcended" is important because it is also possible to sink to a condition that is *below* desire's reach. Both cases involve a levelling process, but in the second a dead level is reached, the psyche having lost its capacity to respond to anything. The difference is the absolute one between finding God everywhere and finding him nowhere.

10. See S. H. Nasr, *Knowledge and the Sacred* (New York: Crossroad, 1982), Chapter Nine.

11. To speak of transcendence is to suggest a hierarchical view of reality, and some will see this as relativizing the Schuon/Nasr solution (to which I also subscribe), inasmuch as it will be acceptable only to those who buy into its ontological premise. But speaking from inside that perspective, I see things differently because I do not see how it is possible to deal philosophically with spiritual matters without a hierarchical ontology. Whether it is possible to have a religion without a philosophy is a separate but equally important question. In the emphasis it places on Bodhidharma's "direct transmission outside the scriptures" and the Noble Silence of the Buddha himself, Zen may come closer than any other historical religion to claiming that religion without philosophy is possible, but I do not see even Zen pushing that claim to the limit. On the issue of hierarchy (which this footnote introduces), there are, in Buddhism, *ontologically,* the doctrine of the Three Kayas, and *psychologically,* the levels of consciousness—phenomenal, mano-vijnana, alaya-vijnana, and a fourth that goes beyond these three—which the Yogacara or Vijnaptimatrata (Consciousness-Only) Schools developed. The latter, in particular, was important for Zen. See Toshihiko Izutsu, *Toward a Philosophy of Zen Buddhism* (Tehran: Imperial Iranian Academy of Philosophy, 1977), Essay Two, Part II.

12. Heinrich Ott, "Does The Notion of 'Mystery'—As Another Name for God—Provide a Basis for a Dialogical Encounter Between the Religions?" in Frederick Sontag & M. Darrol Bryant (eds.), *God: The Contemporary Discussion* (Barrytown, NY: The Unification Theological Seminary, 1982).

13. Irene Lawrence has recently pressed this possibility in her *Linguistics and Theology* (Metuchen, NJ: Scarecrow Press and the American Theological Association, 1980).

14. Some lines by Aldous Huxley, quoted in the Summer 1982 issue of *Parabola,* will remind us, if reminder is needed, that this view is not naïve: "Intense faith and devotion, coupled with perseverance by many persons in the same forms of worship or spiritual exercise, have a tendency to objectify the idea or memory which is their content and so to create, in some sort, a numinous real presence, which worshippers actually find 'out there' no less, and in quite another way, than 'in here.' Insofar as this is the case, the ritualist is perfectly correct in attributing to his hallowed acts and words a power which, in another context, would be called magical. The *mantram* works, the sacrifice really does something, the sacrament confers grace *ex opere operato*: these are, or rather may be, matters of direct

experience, facts which anyone who chooses to fulfill the necessary conditions can verify empirically for himself."

15. The isomorphism is not surprising, given the fact that the religions spawned their respective civilizations.
16. Repentance or conversion, fear of the Lord, detachment, poverty, patience, trust or self-surrender, and contentment.
17. Watching one's consciousness, realization of the nearness of God, love, fear, hope, longing or yearning, loving familiarity with God, security and serene dependence, contemplation, and certainty.
18. Isshu Miura & Ruth Fuller Sasaki, *Zen Dust* (New York: Harcourt, Brace & World, 1966), Part Two.

"Celestial Mirages":
Reflections on Thought and Truth

D. T. Suzuki's two posthumous volumes on Shin Buddhism—his *Collected Writings on Shin Buddhism* and translation of *The Kyōgyōshinshō*[1]—have "opened yet one more treasury of Buddhism to the Western world," as Nishitani Keiji rightly observes.[2] Alfred Bloom has already reviewed the set for this journal,[3] and qua review his statement needs no supplement. My object is different: to look, not so much at these books as through them into humanity's religious consciousness generally, for the books have helped me see things about that consciousness I had not heretofore noticed—not, at least, as clearly. If the view I report proves helpful to others, Dr. Suzuki will have helped to open to the world another treasury, not just of Buddhism but of the human spirit.

In the West Daisetz Suzuki will probably always be remembered as the man who singlehandedly, it almost seemed, brought Zen Buddhism to America, this being the side of himself which, in the English writings that appeared in his lifetime, he turned in our direction. But his *Japanese Spirituality*[4] which he wrote for his own people joins the two volumes here in focus to show that his full concern was in fact polar. While he was interpreting Zen to the West he was quietly sounding, deeper and yet more deeply, the Pure Land schools of Hōnen and especially Shinran who "took Pure Land Buddhism to its highest point" (Nishitani, p. ix).[5] But more. It was not just that he was determined to neglect neither of these superlative expressions

This essay originally appeared in The Eastern Buddhist *X, 2 (1977): 140–154 as "Four Theological Negotiables: Gleanings for Daisetz Suzuki's Posthumous Volumes on Shin Buddhism." The image of "celestial mirages" that occurs in the present title is from Frithjof Schuon,* In the Tracks of Buddhism *(London: George Allen & Unwin, 1968), p. 128.*

of the Japanese spirit. He wanted to fathom their relation. Professor Bloom puts the point precisely when he writes: "Through all his work, Dr. Suzuki's purpose in expounding both Zen and Shin Buddhism was to show the essential *oneness* of Mahāyāna Buddhism" *(op. cit.,* p. 164).

There Dr. Suzuki's interest in convergence stopped; when he alluded to other traditions, chiefly Hīnayāna Buddhism and Christianity, it was usually to show how they differed from Mahāyāna. For my part I wish to suggest that the convergence Dr. Suzuki so perceptively spotted in Mahāyāna Buddhism can serve as paradigm for tempering four controversies that have dogged theology across our globe:

I. Is God personal or transpersonal?
II. Is God without (transcendent) or within (immanent)?
III. Is God substance or process?
IV. Is God realized by grace or self-effort?

That says abstractly what I want to do, but my project will be more graphic if I link it to a concrete image, and one is at hand. This essay, as it happens, is being written on an ocean voyage. Considering its subject it is appropriate that the passage is from Japan to America, but the immediate point is another one. When I boarded this ship in Kobe my thesis was at best hazy, but I came upon an item that brought it to sharp relief: a freak of navigation that was recounted in the "Welcome Aboard" folio that greeted my wife and me as we entered our cabin.

It seems that at the exact turn of the last century—Daisetz Suzuki would then have been a young man nearing thirty—an Australian passenger steamer, the *Warrimoo*, found itself in interesting waters. Recognizing that fact its captain managed with a bit of maneuvering to set his ship precisely astride the intersection of the Equator and the International Date Line. The consequences of this bizarre position were interesting. The date in the forepart of the ship was January 1, 1900; in the stern it was December 31, 1899. Passengers in the front were in the southern hemisphere in the middle of summer, while those behind were in the northern hemisphere in the middle of winter. Thus the passengers were not only in two different hemispheres, two different days, two different months, two different seasons, and two different years, but in two different centuries. Yet the differences were experienced simultaneously and on the same ship.

The moral for my thesis is obvious. However different the theological alternatives I listed above may seem—and in ways are—those who are divided by them are on the same ship; in the same boat, we might say. The differences are negotiables in the sense that it is possible for passengers at either end of the ark to understand and respect the alternative positions even if they are not their own. In pursuing this claim I shall, as I have said, be using Dr. Suzuki's posthumous volumes as my map, and their author as my guide.

I. Are We Saved by Self-Effort or Grace?

In introducing the four theological alternatives I listed this one last because unlike the others it focuses not on God but on humanity's appproach to God. In examining the "negotiables" through Dr. Suzuki's eyes, however, it should head the list, for it is the one he treats most explicitly.

Are human beings saved through grace or works? Every religion runs up against this question; all agree that both are necessary;[6] and all contain strands that veer toward one side or the other—the way of the monkey whose young must cling to their mother's neck, or the way of the cat whose kittens simply dangle from their mother's mouth. But Buddhism is especially interesting on this point because its strands are so clearly divided. The Buddha appears to have allowed no room for grace, while the largest surviving sects of his followers—Pure Land (J., Jōdo) Buddhism and especially Shin— seems to allow for nothing else. T. I. Stcherbatsky's account of the transformation has become classic:

> When we see an atheistic, soul-denying, philosophic teaching of a path to personal final deliverance, consisting in an absolute extinction of life and a simple worship of the memory of its human founder—when we see it superseded by a magnificent High Church with a supreme God, surrounded by a numerous pantheon and a host of saints, a religion highly devotional, highly ceremonious and clerical, with an ideal of universal salvation of all living creatures, a salvation not in annihilation but in eternal life—we are fully justified in maintaining that the history of religions has scarcely witnessed such a break between new and old within the pale of what nevertheless continues to claim common descent from the same religious founder.[7]

Dr. Suzuki acknowledges the change: "There is no doubt that… in the beginning there were no indications in the teaching of the master which betrayed the 'other-power' *(tariki)* elements of later

Buddhism" *(CW,* 15). His originality consists in arguing (more systematically than anyone else I know) that "the two systems apparently contradicting each other [are] really working in unison" *(CW,* 12).

The grounds for his arguments are both historical and logical.
Beginning with history, he grants that "we have no mention of... the
idea of pranidhāna[8]... in Pāli literature" *(CW,* 17); even so, he
argues,[9] the founders of the Pure Land school were quite right in
believing "that everything they had in the way of 'tariki' faith came
from the teaching of Śākyamuni himself" *(CW,* 10). The reason is
that the teachings of a founder cannot be limited to his words.
"There is no doubt that Buddha was a wonderful personality: there
must have been something in him which was superhuman, impress-
ing his immediate disciples with a supernaturally overwhelming and
entirely irresistible power" *(CW,* 38), and central to this power was
his example.[10] Resisting the temptation to proceed directly from his
enlightenment into parinirvāṇa, he chose instead to devote forty-five
arduous years to sharing with his followers the yield of his disciplined labor. However discontinuous this example may seem from
his counsel to "be... lamps unto yourselves" and "work out your own
salvation with diligence," both the words and the example emanate
from the same person and can be shown to be inseparable.
Practically, his words could not have had a fraction of their impact
had they not been backed by his example, while in principle his central teaching—*anatta* (no substantial soul) in its negative formulation; *pratītya samutpāda* (dependent co-origination) when expressed
positively—precluded the possibility of an enlightenment that is self-
contained. Enlightenment is not of the intellect only; it includes the
will. And

> according to Buddhist interpretation, the first thing the Will
> as embodied in an individual being wishes to achieve after...
> release is to do to others what it has done for itself. As enlight-
> enment has made it known to the Will that there is no real and
> impassable gap between oneself and others, the Will feels now
> no need of asserting itself blindly, that is, following the dictates
> of the principle of individuation. [On the contrary,] the efforts
> of an enlightened consciousness are to lead others to the reali-
> sation of a similar state of release *(CW,* 20).

If the Buddha did not spell all this out in so many words it must
have been because of circumstance, not principle. He repeatedly
stressed the need for *upāya*: knowledge must be shaped to the vessel that is to hold it. He also explicitly stated that the teachings he

imparted were but a handful of leaves compared with those of the forest. If we accept Hīnayāna as primitive Buddhism, Mahāyāna obviously follows it chronologically. But it also follows it in the sense of adhering to its trajectory. It discloses the full, though partially unrecognized, implications of what was present at Buddhism's start.

This is Dr. Suzuki's historical argument for his claim that Shin's stress on other-power is as genuinely Buddhist as Hīnayāna's stress on self-power. Turning to logic, he argues the dialectical interdependence of self-power and other-power themselves.

Obviously there are times when only one of the two is in view: times when it seems that if anything is to come our way it must be through our own doing and other times when we simply sit back and ride the Glory Train—Shinran's image is taking a boat ride; it is so easy and pleasant. But these are isolated episodes. No one can live durationally without alternation. Life is subject to rhythm: we wake and we sleep, we stretch our legs and relax. In the soul as in the world, things proceed in waves. And even without getting into time, if we look deeply into action and passion, giving and receiving, we find that each *in principle* involves its opposite. The whole thrust of Jōdo is from self-power to other-power, but to take effect this other-power must be received and this reception is itself a kind of doing.[11] As the reception requires faith, indeed absolute faith, it "is not... easy" *(CW, 117)*. It is not *dolce far niente*—pleasant relaxation in carefree idleness; literally, sweet doing nothing. "There has to be a strong effort to obtain it. So in the end it may be as difficult as the efforts of Self-power sect believers" *(ibid.)*. But quite apart from ratio, the point is that both components must figure to some degree. Even Shinran who carried other-power to its logical limit conceded that a supplicant had to pronounce the *nembutsu* at least once, and if we pick up the stick from its Zen end we find that it leads to the same middle. Zen stresses *jiriki* (self-power), but a clear giveaway shows this self-power to be planted in other-power soil.

> There is much bowing in Zen training [and] bowing the head is an age old gesture of laying down 'I'... in respect for something perceived as greater than 'I'.... In the training, so much depends on one's own effort that there is an ever present danger of 'I' getting a swollen head. Hence... bowing... is indispensable.[12]

There is one more step to be taken. Beginning at the most superficial level with (a) discrete experiences in which self- and other-power *feel* completely sealed from each other, we introduced time to show

(b) that sequentially they must alternate. But having used time as an entré, we stepped back and found it dispensable. Our initial atemporal reading was superficial and therefore onesided. Even without introducing time, (c) self- and other-power prove under inspection to entail each other in principle: other-power must be received, and self-power rides on a supportive context which the self did not create. The last step is taken when (d) each component is sensed to be its opposite.[13] The Shin believer pronounces the *nembutsu* and yet he or she doesn't: Amida pronounces it using the believer's lips while being simultaneously the faith/compasion that rises in the believer's breast. The Zennist mirrors this gestalt. He or she discovers that he or she *is* the universe that supports the finite ego.

This may be the last step but it is not the last word, for partisans of either side can still claim that the *feel* of the two approaches are different: in Shin the self is nothing and Amida everything, whereas in Zen the self is it-Self everything.[14] This is so; the difference is real, which is why there are two paths, not one. Dr. Suzuki never wished to obliterate differences, only to soften them—or better, to understand them as deriving from a common ground. He couched his basic point abstractly in what he called the logic of prajñā-intuition *(soku-hi)*: "A is not-A, therefore A is A."[15] In present context, tariki is not-tariki, therefore it is tariki. That is, only to the extent that we succeed in seeing tariki as not set off from what we normally assume is other-than-tariki, in this case, jiriki, do we understand tariki's true nature. We can see, I think, why Thomas Merton wrote in his Introduction to *The Shen Hui Records*: "The religious genius of the Far East, China and Japan, is the *only one* that has so far achieved... perfect resolution of any possible conflict between action and contemplation" (italics in original).

II. Is God Without or Within?

This question is closely related to the preceding one, for if God is outside us God's power will come to us as tariki, whereas if God is the deepest stratum of our selves we will sense that power as our own. There is a difference in angle, however. The jiriki/tariki question asked from whence we experience God's power as coming, whereas the present one asks what the God/humanity relation is. Both questions are posed in spatial terms, but space of course is not the issue. In the realm of the spirit space figures only symbolically.[16] The question is not whether God is literally located inside or outside the human frame, but whether in last analysis the two must be distinguished.

With rare exceptions—Dionysius the Areopagite and Meister Eckhart come at once to mind—Western theology insists that the distinction must hold to the end. The Christian treatise I happen to have read most recently is one I have already cited in a footnote. Titled *Prayer,* it is by a Jesuit theologian, Hans Urs von Balthasar, and I shall quote him as representative on the point at hand.

Father Balthasar recognizes, of course, that as the ground of our being, God is not set off from us in the excluding way in which an apple, say, is demarcated from an orange or from the bowl that contains them both.

> The Son... is no finite Thou marked off in contradistinction to us, but the origin and ground in which our whole being with all its roots is fixed, from which it draws its sustenance and derives all the best characteristic features...."I in them and thou in me" (John XVIII. 23). The person who contemplates has not to strive laboriously to enter a region wholly alien to him.... In a profound, supernatural sense, he enters into himself. [God's] eternal word of love... is more interior to me than I to myself (pp. 49–50).

This shows emphatically that the West's God/human distinction is no simple-minded one. God "is no mere Other; he is the eternal Thou, who spans the dreary barrier between me and the not-me" *(ibid.,* 54). Yet even in a formulation as discerning as this, a distinction remains. "The pure soul is, indeed, a mirror, a resplendent image and symbol of the eternal Spirit but only a mirror" *(ibid.,* 207).

In Shin, of course, the distinction likewise figures; if anything, it is more pronounced than in the Christian formulation I have just quoted, and for rank and file Shinnists it is doubtless final. For Dr. Suzuki, however, it is only provisional. The "ego is called by Shin philosophers *ki,*" he points out *(CW,* 159), as contrasted with *hō* which "is 'Dharma,' 'Reality,' 'Amida,' and 'the other-power'. This opposition appears to our intellect as contradiction" *(Kyōgyōshinshō,* 284; hereafter cited as *K),* but at the deepest level of spiritual awareness the contradiction is resolved. "[In] 'Namu-amida-butsu'... the oneness of *ki* and *hō* is embodied: 'Namu' is *ki* and 'amida-butsu' is *hō....* The *hō* is the absolute self while the *ki* is the relative, conceptual self. Shin teaches that the *hō* and *ki* are one" *(CW,* 160, 156). To those who might object that this conclusion is more Dr. Suzuki's than Shin's, we have already admitted that not all Shinnists would accept it. But this does not make it idiosyncratic, or even confined to Shin esoterism. Myōkōnin are a class of Shin devotees whose simplicity and near-illiteracy align them closely to the common people, and one of the best loved modern myōkōnin concluded exactly as Dr. Suzuki does. *"Ki* and *hō* are one" (from a song by Asahara Saichi, quoted in *CW,* 161).

As Zen begins where Shin thus ends—in Zen's words, with the not-twoness of small mind and Big Mind—"there is... a difference metaphysically between Zen and Shin in this respect. While Shin [normally] regards... the Other [as] standing in opposition to 'I', Zen merges the 'I' in the Other" *(CW,* 97). This difference gives us a provisional line-up of Zen and Suzuki's Shin on one side and Christianity and conventional Shin on the other. But if we have watched Shin span this divide, reflection shows that Zen does so as well. With all its efforts directed toward having us realize experientially that we *are* the Buddha-nature, Zen stands emphatically on the "God-within" side of the divide that is now before us. But the Self which it equates with the Buddha-nature is obviously not the self we normally experience—in Shin vocabulary, it is not the *ki.* So in both schools we find distinction and indistinction. In Zen and Suzuki's Shin the distinction is between the apparent self and the Self that is finally real; in conventional Shin the distinction is between karmic mortals and Amida—the element of indistinction in both camps we have already noted. Here as before we must add that these similarities do not conform Shin to Zen. Differences remain, but they are now traceable to differences in spiritual personality-types rather than views of reality.[17] They are negotiable.

III. Is God Personal or Transpersonal?

All of the dichotomies I am considering are sharper in the West than in Asia, which makes it not surprising that it is from an Asian source that I think I find clues for tempering them. In the West the personhood (personal nature) of God is axiomatic. The Christian Creeds proclaim God in three persons, and when pronouns are used to refer to the deity, personal ones are almost always employed. But whereas in the West, use of the pronoun "it" for God is likely to bring charges of pantheism, Dr. Suzuki alternates between "he" and "it" freely; causally, we might almost say. Most of the time he uses "he" to refer to Shin's Amida Buddha and "it" for Zen's Buddha-nature, Big Mind, and Dharmakāya, but this usage is not inflexible.

God is the most worthful of all realities—about this there can be no two opinions. As persons are the most worthful realities we tangibly encounter, it is logical that the most worthful object we can conceive should be an extension in their direction. Take all that makes

persons the noblest of God's creatures that we know concretely—
their sensitivity, their responsiveness, their capacity to love and create. Purge these human virtues of their attendant all-too-human
limitations, elevate the cleansed remainder as far as mind can reach,
and the object in which these exalted perfections converge is God.
The God that emerges from this approach is personal or he/she is
nothing.

The approach is so plausible that we have to work a bit to realize
that there are some who cavil. What these objectors fear most obviously is the slough of anthropomorphism into which personalism can
readily slide. The concept "person" originates with a human referent:
can it move beyond that referent without carrying finite human bag-
gage with it? We need not join the Greek satirists and imagine Being
Itself itching or The Nature of Things tippling in the wine bowl in off
moments—we have said that the concept of a personal God begins
by screening out human impurities. The problem is that even human
virtues fall so short of God's that it seems presumptuous to class the
latter under human labels. Knowing is an almost miraculous capacity, but compared with the divine omniscience human knowing is
almost nothing. A knowing that comprehends everything—the
entire past and future in a single incandescent sweep—is so removed
from the way persons know that we may well wonder if the term
"personal" should be applied to it.

This is the first consideration that can cause minds to balk at the
idea of a personal God. A second runs deeper. Persons are social
creatures. As social psychologists like Charles Cooley and George
Herbert Mead gave their lives to demonstrating, they are created by
a dynamic context of exchanges, an unending series of give-and-take
interactions. Feral children who are deprived of this interpersonal
exchange do not grow up to be persons; their minds and "personalities" are arrested at a sub-human level. All this adds up to the fact
that personal implies interpersonal. And the concept "interpersonal"
encounters difficulties when applied to God because it violates the
divine unity or simplicity, for in Father Balthasar's words, "in... the...
Infinite... there is no... quantitative multiplicity" (p. 210). If there is
nothing outside God; if (to take the case most immediately at hand) I
myself am not outside him, he being "more interior to me than I to
myself" *(ibid.,* 51), where, for God, is the other on which the notion
of interpersonal builds? What it would be like to be a person and
have nothing outside myself to work on and deal with, eludes me
completely.

In the face of these objections Western theologians continue to
insist on the personhood of God because, I should like to suggest,

the West's alternative to "person" has become "thing"—a brute, inanimate object such as a stone or magnetic field which, having no sentience whatever, is emphatically *sub*human. But this, as I say, is a Western opposition. Buber's dichotomy between I-Thou and I-it relations was born of a tradition which, on the trail of modern science, progressively "disqualified" nature until apart from humanity—or animals in general if you think Descartes went too far—nature came to be seen as housing primary qualities only.[18] A Japanese Martin Buber is scarcely conceivable, and despite Japan's admiration for German philosophers I have not heard that he has much of a following there. For to repeat, the "it"—the spectre of "dead matter" deriving from what Whitehead called "the fallacy of misplaced concretion"—has never haunted the Orient. A Japanese visitor once presented me with a *kakemono* (that is, a vertically hanging scroll) which has become one of my most treasured possessions. I have less than an amateur's knowledge of Chinese, but in this case I could make out that its first three characters 天地有 added up to "Heaven and earth have...," or "The entire universe is imbued with..." When I asked the meaning of the remaining character 地, my friend groped for an English equivalent and finally resorted to the German "gefühl" (feeling, sentiment, consciousness).

In Part Four of *The Kyōgōshinshō* Shinran writes: "Because the Dharma-nature is tranquillity *(nirvāṇa),* the Dharmakāya is formless. Because it is formless, it assumes every possible form. Therefore, the Dharmakāya provides itself with form." To which Dr. Suzuki adds: "Now the Dharmakāya is a person" *(K,* 190). Thus casually is the question of God's personhood handled in Shin. God is personal in that, like us, God is aware. Infinitely so; in the Hindu ternary *sat-chit-ānanda* awareness is *chit.* At the same time God is not personal insofar as that term implies human limitations (anthropomorphism) or relationality for as we have seen, in the final analysis there is nothing outside God for God to relate to. One is free to come down on either side of the ledger.

IV. Is God Substance or Process?

Like the preceding question this one has a Western ring, for it is in the West that Process Theology has emerged as a movement to challenge the substance theology of classical Christianity. Not having been implicated in this controversy which has grown lively only since his death, Dr. Suzuki does not address it directly, but here again I find his writings suggestive.

They bear importantly if only indirectly on the process/substance debate because of their Buddhist base.[19] The doctrine of *anicca*—impermanence, or in Whitehead's phrase, "perpetual perishing"—is fundamental in Buddhism; so fundamental in early Buddhism that it gives the flavor of process, flow, and becoming to its entire perspective. But we know that Buddhism did not stop with its earliest formulations—Theravāda may have, but not Buddhism as a whole. Whitehead's challenge to the substance thinking of mainline Western philosophy has marked parallels with Guatama's challenge to Vedantic substantialism,[20] but in the Asian instance 2500 years have afforded time for the pendulum to return closer to the mean, the Buddhist, middle-way-balance between the two extremes. Specifically, there has been time for the Mādhyamika to appear.

To this Mādhyamika I shall return almost immediately, but to conclude the present brief section the point is a simple one. As a Buddhist Dr. Suzuki harks back continuously to *anicca*, the fleeting skandhas, and the dharmas' never-ending flow. All the while, as a Mahāyāna Buddhist, he freely interposes terms that refer to things that at some level of existence have every appearance of being substances. "Dharma," "dharmakāya," "bodhisattva," "Amida," *"ki"* and *"hō"*—all these are nouns. To describe things that behave sometimes like waves and sometimes like particles, physicists have coined the wavicle." Lacking a philosophical counterpart to this word we can imagine Dr. Suzuki invoking again his "logic of *soku-hi*": "Substance is not-substance, therefore it is substance." Translated into the present context: "Only if we see substance as not set off against things other than itself—most importantly here, process—do we understand its true character as substance." And vice versa.

Conclusion

I have indicated some ways in which Dr. Suzuki's two posthumous volumes on Shin Buddhism have helped me toward kneading four theological opposites into dialectical negotiables. If I ask in conclusion why they do so, the answer that comes to me runs something like this:

Buddhism issued from the Buddha's enlightenment. That enlightenment pierced to a depth of truth so far beyond the normal that it defied verbal description and accentuated the "two levels of truth" thesis, intimated in the *Bṛhadāraṇyaka* and *Īśa Upaniṣads,* to an extent that made it pivotal for all subsequent Indian thought.[21] This thesis throws all conceptualizations into a supporting role. As *upāyas*—provisional means, instrumental devices—they can be important, even decisively important inasmuch as, skilfully employed, they can awaken enlightenment. But not being enlightenment itself, they are second-order truths and therefore always relative—for Buddhism Nāgārjuna and the Mādhyamika worked this out exhaustively and probably definitively. In Frithjof Schuon's image, these second-order truths are "celestial mirages" designed to catch as in a golden net the greatest possible number of creatures plunged in ignorance, suffering, and darkness.[22] But they are not absolute. They are negotiable.

As for first-order truth, in what is perhaps the most widely read text in modern Japan, *Tannishō,* this truth is located in the nembutsu whose "reason is where it transcends all reasonings, because it is inexpressible, indefinable and inconceivable" *(CW,* 211). If truth of this order seems to our Western minds to be slippery if not amorphous, this may be because of the degree to which our minds have been structured by Aristotle, it being, as Dr. Suzuki says, "impossible in the world of *dualistic logic* for beings to have a connection to the highest reality without the intervention of some intermediate condition," be it a conceptual representation or a symbol of some other sort. "Yet Japanese spirituality," he adds, "accomplishes this connection directly, without any difficulty" *(Japanese Spirituality,* 21, italics added). It is as if the Japanese could accept without surprise and as a matter of course that the passengers on the *Warrimoo* were cheated out of their New Year's Eve party because December 31 dropped out of their lives forever. It had vanished in the Void.

NOTES

I am indebted to Louis Nordstrom and Richard Pilgrim, my colleagues, for reading this eassy in the course of its preparation and for their helpful comments. Neither, of course, is responsible for what remains.

1. Kyoto: Shinshu Ōtani-ha, 1973.
2. Foreword to *The Kyōgyōshinshō.* Professor Nishitani served as supervising editor of the impressive project that brought these sumptuous volumes to print, a project that required seven years and a considerable staff of whom Emyō Itō and Mihoko Okamura deserve special mention.
3. Vol. VIII, no. 2 (October, 1975), pp. 163–69.
4. English translation by Norman Waddell. Japanese National Commission for UNESCO, 1972.

5. Those who knew Dr. Suzuki only through his Zen writings will be surprised to find that as early as 1949 he had written: "Of all the developments Mahāyāna Buddhism has achieved in the Far East, the most remarkable one is, according to my judgment, the Shin teaching of the Pure Land school" *(Collected Writings on Shin Buddhism,* p. 36, hereafter designated as *CW).*

6. "The winds of God's grace are always blowing, but you must lift your sail" (Vivekānanda). I once heard a New Testament scholar epitomize St. Paul's theology in language that can be excused because it makes its point vividly: "You have to work like hell because it's all been done for you."

7. *The Conception of Buddhist Nirvana* (Leningrad: Bulletin of the Academy of Sciences, U.S.S.R., 1927), p. 36.

8. Literally vow, but by extension Amida's vow not to enter enlightenment until all beings are saved, and by further extension the concept of the transfer of merit *(pariṇamāna).*

9. In the etymological sense of *arguere*: to clarify, or literally, "make silver."

10. In turning to Buddha's example rather than his words for the origin of the Pure Land emphasis, Dr. Suzuki is conceding that the basic Jōdo sūtras—*The Larger Sūtra of Eternal Life, The Sūtra of Meditation,* and *The Amida Sūtra*—cannot be ascribed to Gautama himself. Their teachings are presented as coming from his lips, but that was only to insure their status.

    Though this reading of the matter runs directly counter to Jōdo's claims, it is unchallenged by modern historians of Buddhism. Enough of me sides with these historians to bar me from challenging their reading outright, but I do think we should continue to keep in mind that the later *date* of the Pure Land texts does not close the door on the possibility of their having come from the Buddha's lips. To the Hīnayānists' citing of Śākyamuni's denial of any "closed-fistedness in the Buddha"—i.e., he held nothing back—Mahāyānists have always answered: "Granted, but did everyone understand all he taught?" Memories were good in those days and the Pāli sutras are voluminous, but need we conclude that they comprise everything, even everything of importance, that the Buddha said? Why may we *not* believe with *The Larger Sūtra of Eternal Life* that once on Vulture Peak *Śākyamuni* did indeed tell King Bimbisāra's despairing widow the story—true, whatever we think of the garb in which it was cast— of a certain Amitābha Buddha whose merit availed to save even the conspirator-in-assassin that she had been?

11. "Even a passivity which does nothing but receive has to have some active element" (D. T. Suzuki, *Japanese Spirituality,* p. 20). or

again: "A purely passive spiritual attention is quite impossible; there is always at least an incipient response on the part of man" (Hans Urs von Balthasar, *Prayer,* New York: Paulist Press, 1967, p. 98).

12. Irmgard Schloegl, *The Wisdom of the Zen Masters* (New York: New Directions, 1976), p. 25.

13. "Amida's will to help us out of the ocean of birth-and-death is no other than our faith in Amida. In Amida faith is the will to help and in us this will becomes faith; his will and our faith are consubstantial as it were, hence a perfect correspondence between the two terms of Reality" *(CW,* 69).

14. "When my life opens up very clearly, I can't help, from the depths of my heart, wanting to bow. When the mind that wants to bow to enemies and friends and demons and gods and evils and Buddhas and good friends and bad people—when this feeling comes tumbling out of my deep life, then *I am already master of the whole world, I control the entire world,* I become friends with all human and other beings" (Haya Akegarasu, *Zen Notes,* XXII, 1 January 1975, p. 3).

15. See his *Studies in Zen* (London: Rider & Co., 1955, 1957), pp. 119. ff; *The Eastern Buddhist* New Series, vol. II, no. 1, p. 80; and *Japanese Spirituality,* p. 57.

16. See Chapter Two, "Symbolism of Space," in my *Forgotten Truth: The Primordial Tradition* (New York: Harper & Row, 1976).

17. Shinran's formulation of this point is as follows: "What Buddhas teach and what Buddhas tell us to practice are as infinitely varied as the sands, or as particles of dust. Beings are... varied in disposition and mentality,... and the karmic situation in which Buddhas find them are... so varied that they are to be instructed in the most varied ways" *(K,* 98).

Dr. Suzuki applies this point to Zen and Shin in these words: "Zen is richer in intellectual elements and Shin in the affective or emotional" *(CW,* 97). Converted into Hinduism's most precise of all spiritual characterologies, this says that Zen is jñānic, Shin bhaktic. On pages 62, 64, and 73 of *Collected Writings* Dr. Suzuki explicitly correlates Shin with bhakti, but in keeping with his statement in *K,* 260, that "Zen... is... the practice of mental concentration, in which the reasoning process of the intellect is cut short," he might better have characterized Zen as meditative or concentrative, which would link it more to raja than to jñāna yoga.

18. Since writing these words I have come in quick succession upon two disparate sources that point up how aberrant this modern Western notion is. Describing the outlook of pre-civilized man, Stanley Diamond writes: "Personalism... is the most historically significant feature of primitive life and extends from the family outward to the

society at large and ultimately to nature itself. It seems to underlie all other distinctive qualities of primitive thought and behavior. Primitive people live in a personal, corporate world, a world that tends to be a 'thou' to the subject 'I' rather than an 'it' impinging upon an objectively separate and divided self. Consciousness for the primitive is the most common condition in the universe" *(The Search for the Primitive,* New Brunswick, N.J.: Transaction Books, 1974, p. 145).

Having all but forgotten that, far from being confined to primitives, this intuition informed all civilizations including our own, until a mere 200 years ago ours was the first to lose our grip on it, we will do well to read Philip Sherrard's reminder: "The Platonic hierarchy of forms is a structure of participations stretching from the highest supersensual realities down to those of the visible world. It is this structure of participations which constitutes the great golden chain of being, that unbroken connection between the highest and lowest levels of life. In this structure, there is nothing that is not animate, nothing that is mere dead matter. All is endowed with being, all—even the least particle—belongs to a living, transmuting whole, each thing is a revelation of the indwelling creative spirit. It was not until the end of the eighteenth century, with Lavoisier and his peers and followers, that the scientific intelligence in Europe became so blunted and whittled down that it lost its sense of the mysterious numinosity of all things, reduced everything either to phenomenon (fact) or to mathematical hypothesis (or, in less polite language, fiction), and conceived the physical world to be no more than so much inanimate dead matter whose chemical changes were mechanical processes based upon the so-called law of the conservation of mass" *(Sophia Perennis,* II, I, Spring 1976), pp. 42–43.

19. Process philosophy derives basically from Whitehead, and "for some years scholars have been suggesting that Whitehead and Buddhism have much in common" (John Cobb and Jay McDaniel in their introduction to the proceedings of the conference on "Mahayana Buddhism and Whitehead" that was held at the University of Hawaii in November, 1974)—a section of those proceedings appear in *Philosophy East and West,* XXV, 4 (October 1975). More recently Professor Cobb has written that "Whitehead's... creativity... is remarkably like the ancient Buddhist dependent co-origination" ("Buddhist Emptiness and the Christian God," *Journal of the American Academy of Religion,* XLV, 1, March 1977, p. 16).

20. Dr. Suzuki describes the latter challenge as follows: "The Indians... indulged too much in the static side [Their] way of thinking is to be immersed in... sameness. [Following the Buddha's lead,] the

Chinese practical mind sees [that] the 'becoming' aspect is not neglected.... The Buddha's way of thinking is that... sameness is... the infinite series of consciousness-waves" *(The Field of Zen,* London: The Buddhist Society, 1969, pp. 19, 75).

21. See Mervyn Sprung (ed.), *The Problem of Two Truths in Buddhism and Vedanta* (Holland: D. Reidel Publishing, 1973).

22. *In the Tracks of Buddhism* (London: George Allen and Unwin, 1968), p. 128.

South Asia

India and the
Infinite

Around the middle of this century Arnold Toynbee predicted that at its close the world would still be dominated by the West, but that in the twenty-first century "India will conquer her conquerors."[1] Preempting the place that is now held by technology, religion will be restored to its earlier importance and the center of world happenings will wander back from the shores of the Atlantic to the East where civilization originated five or six thousand years ago. His prediction provides an exceptionally forceful rationale, if one were needed, for reissuing the book in hand. For *The Spiritual Heritage of India* is one of the most useful summaries in print of the tradition Toynbee saw as destined to figure prominently in the long range human future.

The spiritual heritage of India is one of the world's standing miracles. It would rank among its greatest human achievements were it not that "achievement" isn't really the right word. It is more like a reception—the opening of a people to receive, through inspiration, the Breath of the Eternal. For the outbreathing of the Eternal is what India has taken truth to be.

We know that "Hinduism" is a label affixed by outsiders. Long ago, people to the west of the Indus River mispronounced its name and called those who lived on it or to its other side "Hindus," and in time "Hinduism" came to be used for their beliefs and practices. The Indians themselves knew no such word. There was no need for them to think of the truth by which they lived as other than the *sanatana*

This brief essay originally appeared as the foreword to Swami Prabhavananada, The Spiritual Heritage of India *(Hollywood, Calif.: Vedanta Press, 1979). It was then reprinted in* Vedanta for East and West *171 (1980).*

dharma, the Eternal Truth. It was Truth Itself—truth that had become incarnate in the tradition that sustained them.

How the incarnation was effected is itself an interesting point. In the West we tend to think of knowledge as cumulative: bits of information get joined into bodies of information that can grow indefinitely. India recognizes a kind of knowledge that fits this model, but she considers it "lower knowledge"—knowledge that is gained by reason and the senses playing over objective, finite particulars. Higher knowledge *(paravidya)* proceeds differently. Or rather, it doesn't proceed at all, for it enters history full-blown. It is futile to ask when this higher knowledge first appeared, for India has no notion of absolute beginnings—beginnings require time, and time for India is not absolute. The most we can say is that when a new cosmic cycle opens there are souls waiting in the wings, so to speak, with the higher wisdom already in store. Who these souls are is not a genetic accident: India has no place for chance or accident—the law of karma precludes it. The men and women who are born wise on the morning of a new creation are so because, though the world they enter is young, they themselves are not. Their *jivas* (individual psyches) having been held over from preceding cosmic cycles, they are already 'old souls'—old chronologically to be sure, but more importantly in experience. Specifically they are yogis and yoginis who used their preceding lives to cultivate what might be regarded as a kind of 'night sight'—the night vision of the spirit by which fixed stars of eternity can be seen in broad daylight. Adepts in such vision, these seers stand poised on the brink of their final liberation when the new cycle begins. Their concluding legacy to the phenomenal world is to impregnate the new cycle with reflective knowledge of the truth they have assiduously shepherded. Keeping in touch with this truth through meditation, these *rishis* (seers) transmit it orally, direct from guru to disciple, until eventually their oral tradition gets committed to writing. In India the texts that resulted were the Vedas.

If we see the Vedas in this light, as apertures through which the Infinite entered conscious human awareness in South Asia in the present cosmic cycle, what word of the Infinite do the Vedas impart?

First the warning that on this topic words are unequal to their task. They can be useful, of course, or the Vedas themselves would not have been written, but a fundamental Vedic teaching concerns the limitations of words themselves when directed towards ultimates. Sooner or later these ultimates phase beyond language entirely. *Neti, neti,* not this, not this; the map is not the terrain, the menu is not the meal—the Vedas never tire of repeating this basic point. In this kind of knowing, words do not cause understanding; at best they occasion it: from spirit to spirit communion leaps. The word "Upanishads," denoting the culminating sections of the Vedas, makes this point in its very etymology. Deriving from roots which when conjoined mean to approach *(upa)* with utter *(ni)* firmness to loosen and destroy *(sad)* spiritual ignorance, it warns the reader right off that the topics one is about to encounter call for more than book learning. For their province is that 'higher mathematics' of the human spirit where knowing merges with being. Upanishadic truth is so subtle, so abstruse, that purely objective, rational intellects are likely to miss it entirely—off such intellects it rolls like water off oil. Only when discerned in a life that is living it—a life that incarnates it in its outlook, moods, and conduct—does truth of this order become fully convincing. It is like art. There comes a time when every master musician must say to his or her pupil, "Don't bother with what I say. Just watch how I take that passage."

To be able to perform as one's teacher does, the student must become a changed person. The change begins with a change in his or her understanding—one now has some inkling of how the passage should sound—but other changes are required as well. Subtle muscular habits must be acquired and integrated, through feedback loops, with subliminal sensitivities to nuances of color and sound. The analogy helps us to see that the truths the Vedas deal with exceed language in a double sense. To the fact that the Infinite cannot be fitted into concepts which are finite by nature is joined the further fact that the knowledge in question resembles "knowing how" more than "knowing that"; it is more like knowing how to swim or ride a bicycle than like recognizing that these activities require certain movements of arms and legs. Vedantic epistemology involves yoga. To know, one must be; to deepen one's knowledge of the kind in question, one must deepen one's being.

These points must never be lost sight of, but provided they are kept in view, the mind may be given its due in the transformative process. Of the world's manifold traditions, none has held more firmly than India's to the double truth that (a) though the mind is intimately *meshed* with other components of the self, (b) it can take the lead in *changing* the self. First the student hears the truth, then he/she reasons on it. It is later, we are told, that he/she meditates on it to deepen his/her understanding and bring other components abreast of where his/her mind, as advance scout, has already proceeded.

The territory into which the mind is forever pressing is the Infinite, and if we were to look for the place where India most deserves to be credited for originality, it is perhaps here that we find it. The Chinese notion of the Tao is rich in its *sense* of the Infinite, but the Chinese were content to rest in that sense itself; they felt no compulsion to conceptualize it. The Greeks, on the other hand, tried to conceptualize everything they encountered, but this very penchant excluded them from ready access to a notion concepts could never close in on. Anaximander's Unbounded *(apeiron)* held promising possibilities, but instead of pursuing these his successors backed away from them—Greek philosophers were not about to give high marks to something that lacked determination. By the time of Aristotle, infinity had come to be associated with imperfection and lack *(Physics,* III: 6–8); it meant the capacity for never-ending increase and was always potential, never completely actual.[2] Not until the Neo-platonists did a full-blown, positive view of the Infinite emerge in the West, and then in part, perhaps, through Indian influence.[3] If we look at a map of the world, Europe looks like an appendage growing out of a central, Asian body or trunk, and in this matter of the Infinite, capitalized because affirmatively conceived, the appearance seems accurate. For not only did India give that notion its earliest explicit articulation; it made the notion central to its history. This no other civilization has quite done. To speak only of ourselves, the modern West has an infinite of sorts, but it is of a largely mathematical variety which is not infinite at all in the complete sense of the word. For though a mathematical infinite is unlimited in certain respects—with regard to extension or number, for example—it is clearly not inclusive in all respects: sounds, colors, and other things that make our world substantial and concrete have no place within it. India's infinite is otherwise. It includes everything, which gave the Indian outlook right off a striking amplitude. When we think inclusively about the West the phrase that comes to mind is "the Western world." The comparable phrase that comes to mind when we think of India is "the Indian universe."

I have labored this point about the infinite because, though it is abstract in itself, it carries concrete implications. Everyone agrees that India is different, but what is it that *makes* her different? When a newcomer sets out to locate the elusive, distinctive ingredient, the old-timers smile and wait. They wait for the moment they know well, all having encountered it in their turn. It is the moment when the visitor will throw up their hands and admit that India is indefinable, because it seems to include everything.

Which, of course, is precisely what the Infinite includes. "As above, so below"—I am suggesting that India's exceptional variety and inclusiveness derives from the fact that India saw the source of all things as Infinite in the all-inclusive and positive sense of that word: *sat,* Being in its totality, is endowed with consciousness *(chit)* and bliss *(anan-*

da). Philosophers know that to speak of such an Infinite requires paradoxes: because words and propositions are limited, every half truth they utter must be balanced by the other half they omit. The historical counterpart of this is the paradox of India—a whole host of paradoxes, actually, for wherever we turn, India confronts us with opposites so extreme they would have torn other civilizations apart but are here kept in creative tension. Bejewelled maharajas who receive as birthday presents their weight in precious stones from their starving subjects. Naked ascetics stretched on beds of nails, balanced by naked voluptuaries on temple friezes. Or the question of God: three hundred and thirty million deities sounds like polytheism gone haywire until we hear that nothing other than the sole, indivisible Brahman even exists. What are we to make of such paradoxes? How can one possibly summarize such a geography of anomolies,

> this... world of high-soaring and deep-plunging thought,... of bewildering variety and rigidity of custom and behaviour, of startling ethical purity and equally startling licence, of seemingly immovable changelessness and supple flexibility, of incredible receptivity and unalterable self-identity, a jungle of life- and thought-patterns,... this... *complexio oppositorum* (combination of opposites)?[4]

Ninian Smart probably manages as much of a summary as is possible when he writes: "The genius of Hinduism is to combine divergent practices and beliefs into one overall system."[5]

This leads into the book in hand, for one of its many virtues is the way it integrates the variety in the Indian heritage which, left to itself, can be bewildering. Even Buddhism and Jainism, technically considered by Hindus to be unorthodox, are here shown to be authentic expressions of the basic Indian vision. Or the Six Systems of Indian Philosophy; often regarded as competitors, they are here shown to complement one another. And of course philosophy and psychology are not separated from theology as if they belonged in distinct compartments. It would be too weak to say that Indian thought as it emerges in the reading of this book is interdisciplinary. It is, rather, pre-disciplinary in the rich and holistic way that Biblical, Chinese and early Greek thought are.

As for the book's author, Swami Prabhavananda, few Indians have personally reached as many Western intellectuals as he did. As my own teacher in things Indian, Swami Satprakashananda of the Vedanta Society of St. Louis, was a brother monk of his in the Ramakrishna Order and is now, at 90, that Order's senior member, this Foreword provides an opportunity for me to acknowledge my indebtedness and express my gratitude, both to these men and to the Order they served so well. In these days when the walls that separated peoples are down and the world's traditions are being lavished on one another, the Ramakrishna Order stands as a model of cross-cultural sharing at its best.

NOTES

1. Culturally, not politically. Toynbee's prediction appeared in an address he gave to The Philosophical Society of Edinburgh University in November, 1952.

2. As this difference between the Greek and Indian attitudes toward the infinite has not been sufficiently noticed, it will be well to document this last statement. In his *Thomism* (New York: Harper & Row, 1967), p. 71, Paul Grenet writes: "For the Greeks, 'finite' is complementary and synonymous with 'perfect.' (In French, *ouvrage fini* [a finished product]) 'Infinite' is pejorative and synonymous with 'imprecise,' and 'unformed.'... To-be-finite is for matter a perfection which comes to it from form." Frithjof Schuon concurs, noting that "the Greeks always have a certain fear of the Infinite, which is very visible even in their architecture: the Parthenon has real grandeur, but it expresses the religion of the finite and rational Perfect which, because it confuses the unlimited with the chaotic, the infinite with the irrational, is opposed to virgin nature" *(Islam and the Perennial Philosophy* [London: World of Islam Festival, 1976], p. 66.) Leo Sweeney summarizes the matter as follows: "From whatever angle it was approached, infinity patently clashed with the dominant Greek notion of form as equivalent to perfection" *(Infinity in the Presocratics* [The Hague: Martinus Nijhoff, 1972], p. xxvii).

3. A. L. Basham says that "the possibility of Indian influence on Neoplatonism... cannot be ruled out" *(The Wonder that Was India* [New York: Grove Press, 1959], p. 486) and Rene Guenon goes further. "Among the Neo-Platonists," he writes, "Eastern influences were... to make their appearances, and it is there... that... the Infinite [is] met with for the first time among the Greeks" *(Introduction to Hindu Doctrines* [London: Luzac & Co., 1945], pp. 51–52.)

4. Hendrik Kraemer, *Religion and the Christian Faith* (Philadelphia: Westminster Press, 1956), p. 101.

5. *Student's guide to THE LONG SEARCH* (Miami: Miami-Dade Community College, 1978), p. 243.

Vedic Religion and the
Soma Experience

I have spent so much time recently reviewing the work of others that I am growing impatient to get on with my own pursuits, but the thesis here considered is important enough to warrant another detour. Moreover, the excursion is bound to prove interesting, for it leads through one of the most colorful intellectual exploits of our century.

Having mentioned both importance and interest, let me begin with the former. Alfred North Whitehead is reported to have remarked that Vedanta is the most impressive metaphysics the human mind has conceived.[1] The extent to which it may have influenced our own western outlook after Alexander's invasion of India does not concern us here; what is at issue is origins. Etymologically and otherwise Vedanta is "the culmination of the Vedas," and the Vedas derive more than from any other single identifiable source from Soma.[2] Would it not be useful, then, to know what Soma was? Not particularly, India herself seems to have answered, judging from her scholars' lack of interest in identifying the lost plant—that characteristic Indian casualness toward history again. Western scholars, by contrast, have been curious from the first. In the two centuries since Indian studies broke upon Europe, forty-three candidates for Soma were proposed in the nineteenth century, and in the twentieth the number rose to a total of over one hundred. Any Indologist who

This essay originally appeared in the Journal of the American Academy of Religon *XL, 4 (December, 1972): 480–499 under the title "Wasson's Soma, A Review Article." It reveiwed R. Gordon Wasson,* SOMA, Divine Mushroom of Immortality. *With a section by W. D. O'Flaherty. (New York: Harcourt, Brace & World; The Hague: Mouton, 1968 [1969]. Popular edition, New York: Harcourt Brace Jovanovich, Inc., 1971, 1972.)*

settled the issue would have been assured of a permanent place in the annals not only of Indian and religious scholarship, but of historical scholarship generally. Most ranking scholars had abandoned the problem as insoluble.

This is where the story picks up drama. For when the answer arrives—and it will be the burden of my review that it has arrived—it comes not from a Sanskritist, Indologist, or academician of any stripe. It comes from outside the world of professional scholarship altogether, from an amateur—a retired banker, and a high school dropout at that. But more. Let the master clue be one of the most improbable lines in Sacred Writ: "Full-bellied the priests piss the sacred Soma;" a line which, verging on scatology, had regularly thrown hermeneutics into confusion and leveled the exegetes. Let the discovery surface in a bibliophile's dream which is a story in itself—handmade paper, limited edition, a collectors' item within a year of publication; in Salinas, California, a copy of *SOMA's* companion volumes (3) recently brought $1500. Finally, let the subject fall squarely in taboo domain—the wild, passion-charged, reason-boggling world of the psychedelics with all that word has come to mean to America in the last fifteen years—and the reader can see why I felt that my own work could wait. The immediate occasion for my review is the appearance of *SOMA* in popular editions, but it is also time for a general stock-taking, the three years since the book's initial publication having allowed time for reviews to appear in the major critical journals.

I. Where Things Stood

In the pantheon the Aryans brought with them when they swept into Afghanistan and the Indus Valley in the second millenium B.C., Soma occupied a unique position. Indra with his thunderbolt was more commanding, and Agni evoked the awe that fire so readily inspired before the invention of matches made it commonplace. But Soma was special, partly (we may assume) because one could become Soma through ingestion, but also because of what one then became: "We have drunk Soma and become immortal." The Soma hymns are vibrant with ecstasy. It appears to be virtually the only plant humankind has deified; the Mexican Indians regard mushrooms, *peyotl,* and morning glories as "god's flesh" or in other ways mediators of the divine, but the plants do not figure in their pantheons. The crucial Mandala IX consisting of 114 of the Rig Veda's 1028 hymns is dedicated exclusively to Soma, as are six other hymns, but Soma's significance extends far beyond these hymns in which Soma is invoked in isolation. "Soma saturates the Rig Veda" (7:169); the entire corpus is "shot through with Soma." "The Soma sacrifice was the focal point of the Vedic religion," writes W. D. O'Flaherty, adding

> Indeed, if one accepts the point of view that the whole of Indian mystical practice from the *Upanisads* through the more mechanical methods of yoga is merely an attempt to recapture the vision granted by the Soma plant, then the nature of that vision—and of that plant—underlies the whole of Indian religion, and everything of a mystical nature within that religion is pertinent to the identity of the plant (4:95).

Louis Renou once said that the whole of the Rig Veda is encapsulated in the themes Soma presents.

In the course of the Soma sacrifice dried plants were steeped in water and their juice pounded out with stones and wooden boards covered with bull hides. This juice was then forced through wooden filters and blended with milk, curds, barley water, ghee, and occasionally honey. To the priests who drank the holy brew it is said to have given strength, magnitude, and brilliance. "One has only to read the Soma hymns, Daniel Ingalls adds, "to grant some truth to the claim" (15:15).

Then, even as the last parts of the Vedas were being composed, Soma disappears. The Brāhmanas, codified around 800 B.C., contain no mention of it. Reverence for the god persisted; his sacrifice continues to be performed right down to today. But surrogates replaced the original plant. For nearly 3000 years, Soma retreats to the mountain fastnesses from whence it came. Like a yogin in training, deliberately isolated so his austerities won't be interrupted, Soma drops out of history—to the historians' despair as I earlier remarked.

II. Wasson Arrives

Enter Robert Gordon Wasson. In certain respects he was an unlikely candidate for the prize. He knew no Sanskrit, had no special interest in India, and years were against him; born in 1898, he was already in his sixties when he turned to Soma, and had retired from a normal career. But as he didn't just stumble on his find it goes without saying that he was equipped for the search—with wisdom of hindsight one can say, ideally so. To begin with, he was intelligent. His career bears this out from beginning to end. Without having

completed high school he was appointed to teach English at
Columbia University. Turning from that to journalism, he served as
financial reporter for the *New York Herald-Tribune* until his uncanny
sense of the business world caused J. P. Morgan and Company to
take him on and advance him, in time, to a vice-presidency. And atop
this basic intelligence Wasson had erected a specialist's repertoire.
Though he was neither scholar nor scientist by profession, there was
a field of which he was master and it was the one that proved to be
decisive: ethnomycology. Assisted by his wife, Valentina Pavlovna, a
pediatrician who died in 1959, his work in this area had led to (a)
rediscovery of *teonanactl,* the Sacred Mushroom of Mexico[3] and the
world-wide attention it subsequently received; (b) publication in 1957
of a monumental two-volume treatise, *Mushrooms Russia and History*
(3), which argued the possibility of the mushroom cult being humanity's oldest surviving religious institution; (c) reputation as founder
of a science of "ethnomycology," a name analogous to "ethnobotany;"
(d) appointment as Research Fellow (later Honorary Research
Fellow) of the Botanical Museum of Harvard University; and (e)
Honorary Research Fellow of the New York Botanical Garden and
Life Member of the Garden's Board of Managers.

These talents alone might have sufficed, but the longer one pon-
ders the Soma discovery the more facets of Gordon Wasson appear
pertinent until one has to remind oneself that he wasn't really created for this express end. Though well into his sixties when he hit the
Soma trail his health and zest for research, including field work, had
held up; ten years later he still sleeps in a sleeping bag on a screened
porch the year 'round in Connecticut temperatures that can dip to
15° below zero. His depth-exploration of the Mexican mushroom—
for ten years he and his wife spent their annual vacation in joint expe-
ditions with the great French mycologist, Roger Heim—had made
him directly, experientially knowledgeable about psychedelics and
the way they can function in a religious setting.[4] Even the careers
Wasson pursued on his way to Soma were only seeming detours:
English and journalism gave him a practice with words which was to
grace his report when it appeared,[5] and banking, being lucrative,
would put him in position to travel where field work beckoned and to
consult the authorities whose diverse pieces of expertise—Sanskrit,
history, philology, comparative mythology, folk lore, art, poetry, literature, ecology, ethnobotany, phytochemistry, and pharmacology—he
was to fit with his own mycological knowledge to produce the solution. Also, when it became apparent that the Vedic references would
be crucial, he could employ a talented Sanskritist, Wendy Doniger
O'Flaherty of the School of Oriental and African Studies of the

University of London, to translate the relevant passages. Wasson's comfortable circumstances bear, too, on *SOMA* as a *de luxe* publication, to which a later section of this review will be devoted. Its author is an aristocrat; every dimension of his life carries quality as its signature.

Finally, it was in Wasson's favor that he was not an academician. We need not go as far as Robert Graves (12) and credit his innocence of a university education with preserving his genius. It is enough to share Professor Ingall's suspicion, voiced at a testimonial dinner at the Harvard Faculty Club on the occasion of the publication of the book under review, that the specialists, each burrowing deeper and deeper down the narrowing shaft of their own specific competence, would never have discovered Soma's secret. The problem called for an amateur, a person who could approach it both afresh and across disciplinary boundaries.

The Concise Oxford Dictionary defines "amateur" as "one who is fond of; one who cultivates a thing as a pastime." The French is stronger; my dictionary renders it "lover, virtuoso." Wasson was an amateur mycologist in the French sense. His love and consequent virtuosity respecting the mushrooms rooted back into nothing less basic than his love for his wife. Newly-wed and enjoying a vacation in the Catskills, it was August of 1927 that they chanced together on a forest floor peopled with wild fungi. Their responses contrasted: he was indifferent, even distrustful, while she was seized by a wild glee. Some couples might have left the difference at that, but the Wassons were of inquiring bent. Examining their difference, they found it to be rooted in a difference between entire peoples. Dr. Wasson, a White Russian who practiced pediatrics in New York, had absorbed almost *cum lacte,* with her mother's milk, a solid body of empirical knowledge about mushrooms and a passionate regard for them; even "worthless" varieties were arranged with moss and stones into attractive centerpieces. By contrast, Gordon, of Anglo-Saxon heritage, had been shielded from the plants. Given to pejoratives like "toadstools" and exaggerated rumors of their toxicity, his people had been as mycophobic as hers had been mycophilic. In Russian literature mushrooms figured in love scenes and pastoral idylls; in English they were emblems of death. For over thirty years the Wassons devoted a part of their leisure hours to dissecting, defining, and tracing this difference until it led to the thesis—supported by comparative philology, mythology, legends, fairy tales, epochs, ballads, historical episodes, poetry, novels, and the scabrous vocabularies that escape the routine lexicographer—that at some point in the past, perhaps 5000 years ago, our European ancestors had worshipped a psychedelic mushroom, their descendants dividing according to whether they picked up on the attraction or taboo, the *facinans* or the *tremendum,* of its holy power.

Two years after the publication of *Mushrooms, Russia and History* in 1957 Mrs. Wasson died, and Gordon, forced into life-changes and with an accumulated pension sufficient for his needs, retired from banking and turned his ethnomycology from hobby into a second career. Soma was not on his docket. He wanted to look into the "mushroom madness" of New Guinea (still unsolved) and why the Maoris of New Zealand share the Eurasian association of mushrooms with lightning. Somewhere down the line he intended to examine India's largely negative attitude toward mushrooms and this led him, in 1964, to spend some weeks at the American Institute of Indian Studies at Poona where he began reading Renou's translation of the Vedas. That was the turning point. During the days that followed, on a freighter to Japan, a number of disjunct things he had learned during forty years of research fell into place. The hypothesis that Soma was a mushroom, specifically the *Amanita muscaria* or fly-agaric,[6] came to view. From then on it was a question of corroboration.

III. The Evidence

To enter all the evidence Wasson uncovered in his five ensuing years of concentrated work in the libraries and botanical centers of the United States and Europe and in the field in Asia would be to duplicate his book. Instead I shall summarize his argument under six points.

1. The references to Soma contain no mention of the leaves, flowers, fruit, seeds, and roots that pertain to chlorophyll-bearing plants. They refer repeatedly to stems and caps.

2. All the color references fit the *Amanita muscaria.* There is no mention of its being green, black, gray, dark, or blue, colors of vegetation, while the colors that are mentioned conform without exception to the mushroom's cap (bright red), the membrane, unique to the *A. muscaria* that protects it in its early stages (brilliant white) or its pressed—*sauma* = to press—juice (golden or tawny yellow). Wasson makes the affirmative point by captioning a series of stunning photographs of the fly-agaric with phrases from the Rig Veda. The color-epithet invoked most often is *hari,* which in Sanskrit

"seems to have run from red to light yellow" (4:37), always accenting its dazzling and resplendent character which the photographs, taken by Wasson himself, capture brilliantly. "The hide is of a bull [red bulls are favored in India], the dress of sheep" (IX 70⁷). This "dress of sheep," the white membrane, is invoked by a variety of analogies: "He makes from milk his robe of state" (IX 71²), or "With unfading vesture, brilliant, newly clothed, the immortal [Soma] wraps himself all around.... He has taken... to clothe himself in a spread-cloth like to a cloud" (IX 69⁵). The mushroom's rupture of this embryonic envelope, too, is noted. "He sloughs off the Asurian colour that is his. He abandons his envelope" (IX 72²). "Like a serpent he creeps out of his old skin" (IX 86⁴⁴ᵉ). The flecks of the veil that cling to the mushroom's crown after the veil bursts gives meaning to "He lets his colour sweat when he abandons his envelope" (IX 71²).

3. References to shape are equally apposite. The mushroom's head, peering through the undergrowth while still in its white skin, is "the single eye" (IX 9⁴). When its cap is fully-formed, it mirrors the vault of heaven and is "the mainstay of the sky." Or again, its curved cap can look like an udder—"The swollen stalks were milked like cows with [full] udders" (VIII 919ᵃᵇ)—and its puffy foot like a teat: "The priests milk this shoot... like the auroral milch cow" (I 137ᵃᵇ).

4. Soma altered consciousness but was not alcohol; it was a psychedelic.[7] The Aryans knew alcohol in the form of *sura,* a beer, but the time allotted for Soma's preparation in the sacrifices precluded fermentation. Moreover, whereas the Vedas generally disapprove of *sura,* noting the muddleheadedness and other bad effects it produces, Soma is not only *aduccbuna,* without evil effects; it leads to godliness:

> We have drunk the Soma, we have become immortal, we have arrived at the light, we have found the gods.
> What now can the enemy do to harm us, and what malice can mortals entertain...? Amplify, O Soma, our lives for the purpose of living.
> These splendid waters, granting much, protecting...
> Like fire produced by friction, may the waters inflame us! May they cause us to see afar and to have increasing welfare (Rig Veda, VIII 48).

5. Geography fits. *Amanita muscaria* requires, for host, the north temperate birch forest, but the Indus Valley, far to the South, lies

adjacent to lofty mountains whose altitude compensates for the southern latitude. South of the Oxus River *A. muscaria* grows only at altitudes of 8000 feet or more, and this fits with the fact that Soma was confined to mountains. Parts of Afghanistan, where the Aryans had resided before continuing their southeastward push, and the Hindu Kush through which they entered the Indian sub-continent, are *A. muscaria* country.

6. Finally, there is the line of the Rig Veda I quoted at the beginning of this article which seems to describe priests as urinating diluted Soma. The Amanita is the only psychedelic whose vision-producing properties are known to survive metabolic processing. Ritualistic urine-drinking forms a part of a number of fly-agaric ceremonies that have survived to the present. I come back to this in Section V, "Disputed Points."

IV. Critical Response

Wasson's *SOMA* appeared in 1969; this review is being written three years later. The interval has allowed time for pertinent authorities to have assessed Wasson's claim, and I list the most significant of their verdicts according to their conclusions and fields.

A. NONCOMMITTAL

F. B. J. Kuiper, Vedist, University of Leiden: "Wasson... may be perfectly right in assuming that the original Soma plant was the Amanita muscaria but... the... problem... cannot be solved beyond doubt" (18:284).

Winthrop Sargent, critic: "Wasson has given us the most persuasive hypothesis... that has yet appeared, [but] nobody really can say what Soma was" (25).

B. Confirming Sanskritists and Indologists

Daniel H. H. Ingalls, Harvard University: The "basic facts [about] the Soma plant as described in the Rigveda... cannot well be accounted for by any of the previous identifications.... They are all perfectly accounted for by the identification with the mushroom

Amanita Muscaria or fly agaric... Not all the epithets remarked on by Wasson need be taken just as he takes them.... Enough still remains to be convincing.... Wasson's... identification is a valuable discovery" (14:188).

Stella Kramrisch, Institute of Fine Arts, New York University: "Wasson proves beyond doubt... Soma was prepared from... *Amanita muscaria.* [He] has set right almost three thousand years of ignorance about the 'plant of immortality'" (17).

Wendy Doniger O'Flaherty, University of London: "For long she [O'Flaherty] was skeptical about my thesis but now... she authorizes me [Wasson] here today [at the International Congress of Orientalists, Canberra, January 1971] to say that she is a full-fledged convert" (7:169).

Ulrich Schneider, University of Freiburg. His book, *Der Somaraub des Manu,* 1971, concedes that Soma is *Amanita muscaria.*

Botanists and mycologists

A. Pilat in the Swiss bulletin of mycology: "In this interesting and magnificently produced work the noted American ethnomycologist R. Gordon Wasson proves that the religious drug known under the name of 'Soma'... is *Amanita muscaria*" (24:11).

Richard Evans Schultes, Botanical Museum, Harvard University: "The... data... fit together as tightly as pieces of an intricate jig-saw puzzle.... Wasson... provides, so far as I am concerned, incontrovertible proof of the strongest kind that Soma must have been *Amanita muscaria....* Once and for all [he has] provided [the] identification: (27:104–05).

Anthropologists

Claude Levi-Strauss, College de France: "Mr. Wasson's work establishes convincingly that, among all the possible candidates for Soma, *Amanita muscaria* is far and away the most plausible"(20).

Weston La Barre, Duke University: "The closure of linguistic, botanical, ethnographic, and ecological evidence is exhilarating. The identification of *soma* with *Amanita muscaria* is definitive, and the Sanskrit puzzle of two millennia from the *Brahmanas* to this day can now be regarded as finally solved" (19:371).

Linguists

Calvert Warkins, Harvard University: "I accept Wasson's identification of soma with *A. muscaria*. I am myself by way of being an amateur mycologist, and in my review article (in preparation for Wolfgang Meid [ed.], *Gedenkschrift für Hermann Güntert* [Innsbruck, 1973]), I hope to show that there is considerably more evidence for his hypothesis in the Rig Veda, and also in the Iranian (Avestan) data, with which he was not concerned" (from a letter, 19 June 1972, to the author of this review).

Generalists

Robert Graves, poet, mythologist, savant: "Wasson has [identified] Soma, without any possibility of scientific or scholarly doubt, as... the *Amanita muscaria,* or 'fly-agaric'.... The argument... is as lucid as unanswerable.... His book satisfies me completely.... I congratulate him on his feat" (12:109, 113).

C. REJECTING

John Brough, Professor of Sanskrit, Cambridge University: "It is...with... regret that I find myself unable to accept that [Wasson] has proved his theory that the original Vedic Soma was *Amanita muscaria*" (10: 362).

D. ROMAN JAKOBSON

Professor Emeritus at Harvard and M.I.T., he merits a category to himself, not because he is the world's greatest living linguist (which he is), but by virtue of his special relationship to the book. The fact that the *de luxe* edition is dedicated to him removes him from controversies over it, and it is unlikely that he will write about it. He permits me to report, however, that though, not being a Vedist, he feels unqualified to pronounce on Wasson's conclusion, he has been impressed from the first with the caliber of his search. Wasson is free of stereotypes and prejudices that have impeded the Soma quest, his standards of scholarship are of the highest, and he has consistently checked his findings with ranking authorities in every field he has entered.

V. DISPUTED POINTS

Though critical opinion is at this point inclining heavily in Wasson's favor, it is not unanimous. What are the points of dispute? All concern the Vedists; as the preceding section shows, no mycologist, botanist, anthropologist, or linguist has challenged Wasson's claim, and the leading ones who have expressed themselves accept it. I do not think that this discipline-specific difference need be charged to Sanskrit defensiveness—resentment at invasion of their field by an outsider, let alone one claiming victory. John Brough is clearly wrong when he says that extra-Vedic evidence is irrelevant until Soma's identity is internally established (more on this shortly), but he is right to the extent of stressing that the internal evidence is primary. Soma was a Vedic god; if the proposed referent doesn't fit the Vedic references, then we are talking about something else, not Soma. And as the Vedic evidence is notoriously meager and obscure, it is natural to find the differences of opinion clustering mainly around its interpretation.

Three Sanskritists have examined Wasson's argument in some detail. That they emerge registering the three possible votes on his thesis—Ingalls, yes; Brough, no; Kuipier; abstaining—is interesting, but our concern is with the features of Wasson's arguments that they find questionable. As the argument is complicated—not only in the number of pieces it assembles but exponentially in the arguments (subtle, diaphanous, consisting largely of associative threads) marshalled to adduce that each piece says what Wasson claims it says—it is to be expected that a sizable number of specifics come in for review. To try here to note even an appreciable sample of these would prove unmanageable; those interested in the fine print should simply read items 10, 14, and 18 in my bibliography. Fortunately, the details shape up into three broad issues, each raised centrally by one of the three prime critics.

1. What evidence pertains? Initially only Indo-Iranian evidence, says Brough.

Discussion of the use of the fly-agaric and other mushrooms in lands beyond India and Iran... have no probative value. They cannot even be adduced as confirmatory arguments for the theory that the Soma plant was *A. muscaria*. Until this theory is proved for the Rgveda, and proved beyond any possible doubt, the non-Indo-Iranian materials remain, in the strictest sense, irrelevant. Even if the proposed identification for Soma seems probable, but is not proved on the basis of internal evidence, extraneous facts are not additional evidence (10:332–33).

If Brough had meant here only that the *A. muscaria* hypothesis must be proved "for the Rgveda," his point would have been in order, but his words clearly go beyond this. The thesis must be proved virtually *by* the Rig Veda (other Indo-Iranian materials being, on the botanical point, negligible by comparison) and thus proved before looking beyond its pages: "...*until* this theory is proved...;" *"if* the Vedic case were proved, we should indeed begin to consider... widespread cultural [materials]" (10:332–33, italics mine). This is curious, not least when one thinks of the extent to which Vedic studies in the West have built from the beginning on comparative philology, mythology, phenomenology, and history in general. In a fifty-eight page rejoinder to Brough (6) to be published by the Harvard Botanical Museum, Wasson rightly labels Brough's "Berlin Wall" requirement "untenable." "Where would Biblical criticism be," he asks, "if Biblical scholars had not taken soundings in all the adjacent cultures and not least the non-Semitic ones?" The question is well put, and on this issue the decision must surely go to Wasson. Hermeneutics is one of the most subtle of sciences, and there is no predicting where useful cross-references may arise.

Not all the differences between the two men turn on the domains of evidence to be admitted. Brough says that *hari,* the most frequent color-epithet for Soma, cannot mean red, the color of the fly-agaric cap. Such an issue is indeed between Vedic philologists and to survive Wasson must have the best on his side, or where they are divided at least some of the best. He does; again as so often one is impressed by how well he did his homework. On the authority of Louis Renou he argues that *"hari* is not only a colour word: the intensity of the colour is also expressed by it. It is dazzling, brilliant, lustrous, resplendent, flaming.... I... raised this point [with Renou], being sceptical about the applicability of *hari.* It was Renou's idea that the intensity of the colour might have been the common denominator linking the fly-agaric with the sun and fire. He developed his thinking on this at some length" (6:22).

But this issue is an exception; most of the questions Brough raises root back one way or another to the basic one with which he begins: from whence shall evidence come? And, speaking as one who admittedly does not possess the competence of an Indologist, I confess that I see him as done in by his own insisted-upon insulation. Four quick examples. (a) Brough proposes that Soma was a stimulant rather than an hallucinogen. Now I know no Sanskrit, but in reading Brough on the subject I get the strong suspicion that he knows no hallucinogen, not first-hand in a hallowed context, which is the definitive knowledge of these substances in the religious sphere. My suspicion echoes Wasson's, who writes, "It is possible... that Brough does not know an hallucinogen when he describes one" (6:10). To propose as inspiration for the awe-filled Soma hymns a stimulant—"yes, a vulgar stimulant like alcohol, like the rum ration that has sometimes been given in the West to sailors and soldiers before entering a battle" (6:11)[8]—is to turn back the clock on Soma studies. I refer back to my long footnotes numbers 2 and 4 and raise the claims I registered there for their relevance to say now that the considerations they present are indispensable in assessing a Soma candidate. (b) *A propos* the "mainstay of the sky" trope, Brough finds "the idea almost comic that the Vedic poets should have seen in [a] little mushroom a model of the sky supported by a mighty pillar" (10:357). But is he oblivious, Wasson asks, of the way poets in metaphors deliberately juxtapose opposites to heighten tension and drive home their point? Had he come upon "...a sigh is the sword of an angel king" without knowing that Blake was its author, would he find the sigh/sword metaphor equally comic? Even if one insists that the model must possess isomorphically all the features of the sky's support, not only shape but strength as well, there is still the fact that strength appears in abundance in the potency of the mushroom's juice (this last is my point, not Wasson's). The unlikelihood that textual considerations require Brough's objection here is evidenced by the fact that his fellow-Vedist, Kuiper, finds

the frequent statement of the poets that Soma is the cosmic pillar which supports the sky in the world centre... the strongest argument... for Vedic evidence in support of Wasson's theory.... The general mythical notion of a central cosmic pillar hardly owes its origin to any natural phenomenon. It must be admitted, though, that the fly-agaric, if it would have occurred in the Panjab, might have been regarded as a striking manifestation of that notion (see plate XI)" (18:283).

(c) Brough thinks it counts against a candidate for a ritual drink that it should have the emetic properties of the fly-agaric (10:360). Wasson replies by pointing out that "the modern Western conventional horror of vomiting [like that of urine-drinking which will concern us shortly] is limited to our own age and culture.... In the East the attitude... is far different.... Part of the yoga discipline is to extend the range of the voluntary nervous system to include vomiting and to vomit regularly" (6:13). As the author of the present review, I can add to this my own report that in an intensive media-tional regimen my wife and I underwent in Burma in 1957, vomiting and diarrhea were favorable omens, being taken as signs of spiritual as well as alimentary purgation. (d) "Even more serious for the Soma theory," Brough writes, "is the repeated mention in the 'Exhibits' of the coma induced by the fly-agaric: see for example p. 279 ('an ecstatic stupor'); p. 315 ('transports himself into a state of unconsciousness')..." (10:360). It is difficult to see what difficulty this poses. As Wasson points out, "There are many stupors and one kind is a man in rapture. Those Europeans who observed the tribes-men in Siberia did not know what they were seeing. They contented themselves with saying 'stupor' and they were right, but they did not look far enough" (6:13). Trance regularly involves a state of dissocia-tion. The body appears disconnected because the soul is elsewhere.[9] This is such common knowledge that one wonders if Brough is thinking of a different kind of difficulty, perhaps that of conducting a sacrifice while in "stupor." But W. Caland and V. Henry in their *L'Agnistoma* note that the priest who ranked first in the sacrifice had virtually nothing to do. He remained in his place and then withdrew "to take his rest" (6:13). One thinks of the Taoist ceremonies that continue on Taiwan to this day. On the periphery, Max Kaltenmark reports, they appear as "a kind of carnival entailing ostentatious dis-play and squandering of the community's wealth. But let there be no mistake about this: for Taoists the serious business happens inside, where the gods come to dwell within the main officiant, who contem-plates them with his inner gaze.'"[10]

I may not have done justice to Brough's critique. It swayed me until I read Wasson's reply, and it is conceivable that it would do so again if he were to come back at Wasson in another round. Unless and until he does so, however, Wasson's assessment appears in order:

> In this 31-page review article Brough rakes me fore and aft with grape and ball. As the smoke slowly drifts away he finds me riding the waves pretty much as before, with a shot here and there through my rigging. The sights of his guns had suf-fered a consistent deviation from the true (6:24).

2. Do the Vedic tropes and epithets for Soma refer primarily to the plant or, alternatively, to either (a) the god, envisaged in his full, mythologized maturity, or (b) aspects of his sacrifice?—this is the basic question posed by the review of *SOMA* in the *Indo-Iranian*

Journal (18). Its author, Professor Kuiper, steeped for years in Vedic mythological and ritualistic thought, inclines toward the second, a+b, alternative, Wasson, coming to the hymns as a relatively innocent botanist, naturally thinks of plant references. Three examples will indicate the divide this creates. When Soma is apostrophized as lustrous, Wasson sees the flaming cap of a mushroom, Kuiper the radiance of the god that appears in the sacrificial heirophany. For Wasson, the Soma which "like a serpent creeps out of its old skin" is the fly-agaric bursting its embryonic membrane; for Kuiper it is the Soma-juice trickling out of the stalks in the ritual pressing. The third example concerns the line, "He sloughs off the *asuryam varnam* that is his." Even students who don't know Sanskrit are likely to recognize *asuryam* as referring to the Asuras, a class of deities, and *varnam* as denoting primarily color but by extension caste which had a color base. Wasson and Kuiper pick up on precisely this alternative *varnam* affords. For Wasson, Soma "sloughs off the Asurian colour that is his" (4:40), i.e., its original, shining membrane, for Kuiper, Soma casts off this Asuric party [i.e., group identity] that is his" (18:282). He arrives at this reading—in which he is not alone, having been anticipated by such Vedic experts as Roth, Bergaigne, and von Bradke—through knowing that Prajapati created the Asuras and Devas as representatives of two cosmic moieties, and "according to the *brahmanas* 'King Soma', when bought from the Soma vendor, is Varuna [a threatening Asura] as long as he is tied up. During this time Soma has a dangrous and inauspicious character" (18:281), and it is this, his inauspicious Asuric identity, that he sheds in the course of the sacrifice. Another way to get at the Wasson/Kuiper difference is to ask which texts apply, for Kuiper derives his readings by relying heavily on materials in the *Brahmanas* and *'Srauta-sutras* whereas Wasson discounts these on grounds that even the earliest were composed by men who either "knew not the Soma plant" or were deliberately trying to conceal its identity. Thus against Brough, Wasson would broaden Soma studies by supplementing the texts; but against Kuiper, within the texts themselves, he is a purist: within the Vedas one must rely on what was composed by the men who knew or at least knew of the Soma plant. This means sticking pretty much (though not exclusively, see 7:178–79) to the Soma hymns themselves, up to but excluding the last batch to be admitted.

The exchange works itself out to a gentleman's draw. After commenting on a certain text, Kuiper states explicitly that the conclusion to be drawn is "not... that Wasson's [alternative] comment... cannot be accepted for philological reasons" (18:282), and this is characteristic of his tone throughout. Wasson, for his part concedes to Kuiper that the Vedic "poets are often intentionally ambiguous since they refer at the same time... to two different levels: that of the ritual [with its Soma plant] and that of the myth" (18:280), but he sees in this ambiguity

> the key to a reconciliation of our two positions. Profesor Kuiper discusses the meaning of various verses in the light of post-Vedic mythological and ritualistic thought, but is he not confining his interpretation to a single level and am I not concentrating on another level of meaning (that of plant identity) (5:291)?

Even Kuiper's tendency to make more use of contexts turns out to cut both ways. The fact that "like a serpent he creeps out of his old skin" is immediately preceded by "like a big stream the juice runs through (the filter)" lends credence to Kuiper's contention, noted above, that the serpent here is the Soma-juice and its skin the stalks from which it is pressed. On the other hand, Wasson's assumption that *varnam* refers to the color of a physical object rather than a "party" gains strength from the fact that the line immediately following is "he abandons his envelope."

3. The third controversy of a general nature concerns Soma's relation to urine. All three of the Sanskrit respondees deal with it, but Professor Ingalls focuses the issue most sharply. We have noted that *Amanita muscaria* is the one known plant whose psychedelic properties withstand metabolic processing, that this fact was known and continues to be utilized by Siberian tribesmen to this day, and that a verse in the Rig Veda, IX 74[4], can be translated "The swollen men urinate the on-flowing Soma." There is, in addition, the fact that the Vedas mention a "third filter" for Soma while describing only two; Wasson thinks his third filter could have been the human organism which, there is reason to believe, reduces the nauseous properties of the fly-agaric while retaining for as many as five ingestions the chemical, musicimol, which in the dried mushroom is the psychedelic agent.

Ingalls accepts Wasson's identification of Soma as the fly-agaric but he does not think the texts report that the priests pissed Soma. He acknowledges that the chief text says that they did—"Wasson... has been sharper than most Vedic translators in seeing that the word *naro* in that verse must refer to the priests" (14:189)—but he takes the statement to be metaphorical, for in VIII 4[10] and elsewhere it is Indra who pisses the Soma. And as there is nowhere indication that in the Vedic period the gods were impersonated by priests, the priestly pissing must refer metaphorically to the point in the sacrifice where the priests, holding their pots aloft, pour the hallowed Soma into the waiting troughs.

In a review to appear in *Artibu Asiae,* Stella Kramrisch offers the obvious compromise. The texts bear out Wasson's claim that Soma-in-urine was known, and Kramrisch adds an entry of her own to the supporting list: "In the belly of Indra the most intoxicating one (Soma) is filtered" (IX 80³). It is going too far, however, to claim that the texts show priests engaged in ritual urination in the Soma sacrifice.

In the disputed aspects of *SOMA* I have considered only what I see as the three broad issues. And of course tomorrow someone may come forward with a knock-down argument that shows that Wasson's thesis can't possibly be right. But as things stand now—July 1972—I am teaching the Vedas with Soma as the fly-agaric.

VI. The Book

There remains the book as a palpable object, lying open on my desk, inviting comment in its own right as an exhibit in bookmaking.

Wasson's first book, his two-volume opus with his wife on *Mushrooms Russia and History,* appeared in limited edition of 512 numbered copies. I recall that it rated a multi-paged spread in *Life Magazine,* which may help account for the fact that, announced at $125, its sales became so brisk that the suprised publishers started raising the price and its last copies retailed at twice the original. Of *SOMA,* twelve years later, 680 copies were printed of which 250 were allotted to the United States. Being a single volume, its price was kept to $200 and again the stock was exhausted within months.

Is it known what is the most expensive book that has even been published? Whether or not it is *Soma,* the book is by all counts a sumptuous production. Wasson lavished on the bookmaking dimension of his work the same meticulous attention he devoted to the Soma search itself. The volume is in blue half-leather with dark blue spine, stamped in gold and slip-covered in fine blue linen cloth. The book was designed by Giovanni Mardersteig and set in Dante type; the text and illustrations were printed by the Stamperia Valdonega, Verona. I have already spoken of the stunning photographs: thirteen color tip-ins of the fly-agaric in its natural habitat. The paper was made by hand by Fratelli Magnani, Pescia; pages are of International Size A-4. In all it is a bibliophilic gem, as much so as the rarity it has in three years become. In the face of declining quality in botanical publications in the 1930s, Professor Oakes of Harvard used to argue that "the results of a scientist's research are jewels worthy of a proper setting." Wasson's book would have pleased him.

As I was telling the *SOMA* story in class last fall, noting that to get at the book itself students would have to get the key to the Houghton Rare Book Room at Harvard, one of them raised his hand to say that he had seen the book in the Tech Coop on his way to class. I said he must have been mistaken, so strong was my assumption that Wasson's elitism precluded in principle a popular edition. Fortunately it was I who was mistaken. Popular editions have appeared in both cloth ($15) and paperback ($7.50). They lack the jacket watercolor and generous margins of the original and their paper is not handmade, but in other respects they are faithful to the *de luxe* edition.

VII. Conclusion

Soma seems to have been rediscovered, but why was rediscovery necessary? Why did it vanish in the first place? Wasson believes that its importance, coupled with the famed mnemonic capacities of the Vedic priests, rules out its having been simply forgotten; it must have been deliberately suppressed. In *SOMA* Wasson proposed, as reason for the suppression, distribution problems. As the Aryans moved down the Gangetic plains the high-altitude mushroom became progressively less accessible. Inconsistency—now the fly-agaric, now a substitute—proved ecclesiastically unworkable; a patron discovering that rhubarb was used in his sacrifice while his neighbor got the genuine article could be difficult. A crisis developed and the governing Brahmins decided that the original had to be eliminated completely.

Recently Wasson has been inclining toward a different prospect: that the substance may have started to get out of hand. Quality declines in the last Soma hymns and some border on irreverence. Three thousand years in advance of us, India may have found herself on the brink of a psychedelic mess like the one America stepped into in the 1960s. She wasn't able to close the door on it completely; plenty of *bhang* smoking *sadhus,* in whom it is impossible to determine whether it is *sattva* or *tamas* that prevails, roam India to this day. But at a critical moment the Brahmins did everything they could to prevent such abuse. They would rather forego physical identification with their god forever than subject him to such profanation. This hypothesis, if correct, would help to explain why the Buddha felt strongly enough about drugs to list them with murder, theft, lying, and adultery as one of the Five Forbidden Things. It could also throw light on Zarathustra's angry excoriation of those who use inebriating urine in their sacrifices: "When wilt thou do away with the urine of drunkenness with which the priests delude the people" *(Avesta,* Yasna 48:10).

I will myself extend this line of thought to its conclusion. Even among the religiously responsible, sacramental psychedelics appear to have, in the parlance of atomic decay, a lifetime: half-life, three-quarters, etc., etc. They are also capricious. Opening the gates of heaven at the start, there comes a time when they begin to open either onto less and less, or onto more and more by including the demonic. It is precisely apposite that the book that introduced psychedelics to the contemporary West, Huxley's *Doors of Perception,* was followed—quickly—by his *Heaven and Hell.* It seems that if God can manifest him/herself through anything, it is equally the case that nothing can get God under its thumb, which is to say, guarantee God's countenance. It is completely consonant with the idea that the Absolute entered India by way of a mushroom to hold that at some point following, perhaps quite abruptly, it stopped doing so.

BIBLIOGRAPHY

Publications by R. Gordon Wasson Cited in the Text

1. "The Hallucinogenic Fungi of Mexico: An Inquiry into the Origins of the Religious Idea among Primitive Peoples," *Botanical Museum Leaflets* (Harvard University), XIX, 7 (1961).
2. With Roger Heim, *Les Champignons Hallucinogènes du Mexique* (Paris: Archives du Museum National d'Histoire Naturelle, Serie 7, Tome VI, 1958 [1959]).
3. With Valentina Pavlovna Wasson, *Mushrooms Russia and History,* 2 vols. (New York: Pantheon Books, 1957).
4. *SOMA, Divine Mushroom of Immortality* (New York: Harcourt, Brace & World, 1968 [1969].
5. "*SOMA*: Comments Inspired by Professor Kuiper's Review," *Indo-Iranian Journal,* XII, 4 (1970).
6. "*SOMA*: Mr. Wasson's Rejoinder to Professor Brough," in press as a monograph to be published by the Botanical Museum of Harvard University. Page numbers are those in the typescript.

7. "The Soma of the Rig Veda: What Was It?" *Journal of the American Oriental Society,* XCI, 2 (April–June 1971).

Reviews of Wasson's SOMA in English, French, and German

8. André Bareau, in *Journal Asiatique* (1969), pp. 173–76.
9. G. Becker, in *Revue de Mycologie,* XXXIV, 1 (1969), pp. 84–87.
10. John Brough, "Soma and Amanita muscaria," *Bulletin of the School of Oriental and African Studies, University of London,* XXXIV, 2 (1971).
11. P. Demiéville, in *T'oung Pao,* LVI, 4–5, pp. 298–302.
12. Robert Graves, "The Divine Rite of Mushrooms," *Atlantic Monthly* (Feb. 1970), pp. 109–13.
13. Catherine R. & Kate Hammond, "The Mystery of Soma," *Sunday Herald Traveler* (29 August 1971), Book Section, pp. 1–2.
14. Daniel H. H. Ingalls, "Remarks on Mr. Wasson's Soma," *Journal of the American Oriental Society,* XCI, 2 (April–June 1971, pp. 188–91).
15. Daniel H. H. Ingalls, in *The New York Times Book Review* (5 Sept. 1971), p. 15.
16. Jacques Kayaloff, in *The Russian Review* (April 1970), pp. 238–39.
17. Stella Kramrisch, forthcoming in *Artibus Asiae.*
18. F. B. J. Kuiper, in *Indo-Iranian Journal,* XII, 4 (1970), pp. 279–85. Rejoinder by R. Gordon Wasson, pp. 286-98.
19. Weston La Barre, in *American Anthropologist,* LXXII (March 1970), pp. 368–73.
20. Claude Lévi-Strauss, "Les Champignons dans la Culture: A propos d'un livre de M. R.-G. Wasson, *"L'Homme,* X, i (1970), pp. 5–16.
21. Portions of the above, translated by Alfred Corn, "Claude Lévi-Strauss: Mushrooms in Culture," *University Review,* 12 (1970), unpaged.
22. B. Lowy, in *Review Mycologia,* LXI, 4 (July–August 1969), pp. 849–51.
23. M. M. Payak, in *Indian Phytopathology,* XXII, 4 (December 1969), pp. 527–30.
24. A. Pilát, in *Schweizerische Zeitschrift für Pizlkunde: Bulletin Suisse de Mycologie,* XLVIII (Nov. 1970), pp. 133–43.
25. Winthrop Sargent, "Mainstay of the Sky, Foundation of the Earth," *The New Yorker* (30 May 1970), pp. 90ff.
26. Richard Evans Schultes, in *Economic Botany,* XXV, 1 (Jan–Mar. 1971), pp. 111–12.
27. Richard Evans Schultes, in *Journal of Psychedelic Drugs,* III, 2 (Sept. 1971), pp. 104–05.
28. Michael Sullivan, in *Journal of the American Oriental Society,* XCI, 2 (1971), p. 346.
29. Unsigned, "Ariadne," *New Scientist* (3 Sept. 1970), p. 491.

30. Unsigned, "Daily Closeup," *New York Post* (19 Aug. 1971).
31. Unsigned, in *Times Literary Supplement* (22 May 1969). Correspondence: 21 Aug. 1970, 11 Sept. 1970, 25 Sept. 1970.
32. S. Henry Wassén, in *Saertryk af Friesia* (Copenhagen), IX (Dec. 1970), pp. 330–32, and in *Svenska Dagbladet* (8 Aug. 1969).

NOTES

1. I have not been able to find the statement in his writings. Frithjof Schuon positions the Vedanta as follows: Its perspective finds its equivalents in the great religions, including Hinduism, but as these may be "dependent on dogmatic perspectives which restrict their immediate intelligibility or make direct expressions of them difficult of access... the Vedanta appears among explicit doctrines as one of the most direct formulations possible of that which makes the very essence of our spiritual reality" *(Spiritual Perspectives and Human Facts,* p. 95).

2. As this statement may seem excessively categorical, I give my reasons for it. Soma enjoys a special place in the Vedic pantheon. The specifics of that place will be indicated shortly, but let me acknowledge that its position warrants my allegation only when supported by recognition of the extent to which the Upanishadic metaphysics could have been facilitated by the psychedelic that Soma was, and in the Vedas was exclusively. My arguments supporting this recognition fall into three categories: personal experience, the role of the psychedelics in engendering religious perspectives generally, and the distinctive character of the Soma experience in Vedic Religion.

(a) Personal experience. I quote from the account of my own first ingestion of a psychedelic: mescalin. "Another phrase came to me: 'empirical metaphysics.' The emanation theory and elaborately delineated layers of Indian cosmology and psychology had hitherto been concepts and inferences. Now they were objects of direct, immediate perception. I saw that theories such as these were required by the experience I was having. I found myself amused, thinking how duped historians of philosophy had been in crediting those who formulated such world views with being speculative geniuses. Had they had experiences such as mine they need have been no more than hack reporters.... Beyond accounting for the origin of these philosophies, my experience supported their truth. As in Plato's myth of the cave, what I was now seeing struck me with the force of the sun in comparison with which normal experience was flickering shadows on the wall" ("Empirical Metaphysics," in Ralph Metzner (ed.), *The Ecstatic Adventure* [New York: The Macmillan Company, 1968], p. 73).

(b) On the role of psychedelics in occasioning religious purviews generally, I quote, as once before in an earlier essay, Mary Barnard. "Which," she asks, "was more likely to happen first: the spontaneously generated idea of an afterlife in which the disembodied soul, liberated from the restrictions of time and space, experiences eternal bliss, or the accidental discovery of hallucinogenic plants that give a sense of euphoria, dislocate the center of consciousness, and distort time and space, making them balloon outward in greatly expanded vistas?... The [latter] experience might have had... an almost explosive effect on the largely dormant minds of men, causing them to think of things they had never thought of before. [I interrupt to note that in reading for the present review I came across a pointed support of Ms. Barnard's conjecture, specifically the part connecting the concept of an afterlife to hallucinogens. Concerning certain Algonquin Indians in the region of Quebec, Father Charles Lallemand wrote in 1626: "They believe in the immortality of the Soul; and in troth they so assert that after death they go to Heaven, where they do eat Mushrooms" (21).] Looking at the matter coldly, unintoxicated and unentranced, I am willing to prophesy that fifty theo-botanists working for fifty years would make the current theories concerning the origins of much mythology and theology as out of date as pre-Copernican astronomy" *The Mythmakers* (Athens: Ohio University Press, 1966) pp. 21–22, 24. On the same theme by the author of the book under review: "As man emerged from his brutish past... there was a stage in the evolution of his awareness when the discovery of [an indole] with miraculous properties was a revelation to him, a veritable detonator to his soul, arousing in him sentiments of awe and reverence, and gentleness and love, to the highest pitch of which mankind is capable, all those sentiments and virtues that mankind has ever since regarded as the highest attribute of his kind. It made him see what this perishing mortal eye cannot see.... What today is resolved into a mere drug... was for him a prodigious miracle, inspiring in him poetry and philosophy and religion." (1:162). (Numbers preceding colons refer to numbered items in the bibliography, those following colons to page numbers therein.)

(c) Finally, on the specific place of the psychedelic experience in Vedic religion, these words by Daniel Ingalls, Wales Professor of Sanskrit at Harvard University, written to register a perception that came to him on reading through Book IX, the Soma Book, of the

Rig Veda after reading Wasson's book here under review. "Soma...
and... Agni... represent the two great roads between this world and
the other world.... They are the great channels of communication
between the human and the divine." But, Ingalls goes on to note,
there is a difference. "The Agni hymns... seek for a harmony
between this world and the sacred, but are always aware of the distinction.... The Soma hymns, on the other hand, concentrate on an
immediate experience. There is no myth, no past, no need for harmony. It is all here, all alive and one.... The Soma experience... was
always an extraordinary event, exciting, immediate, transcending
the logic of space and time" (14:191).

3. Recounted in his book co-authored with the greatest living mycologist, Roger Heim. See entry 2 in the bibliography.

4. Those who know my essay, "Do Drugs Have Religious Import?" *The
Journal of Philosophy,* LXI, 18 (1 October 1964), will not be surprised
when I say that I do not consider this an incidental resource. I find it
not only aetiologically natural but metaphysically apposite that
Soma's identity should have been discovered by an initiate; not, to
be sure, in the Soma cult itself, but in a Western counterpart. We
both search and find according to our sensibilities, a point which, if
I may be pardoned a personal reference, has been borne in on me
by the one discovery I myself 'chanced' to have made. Had I not
possessed, first, a musical ear which alerted me immediately to the
fact that in the Gyutu (Tibetan) chanting I was in the presence of
something subtly astonishing, and second, a musical temperament
which laid on me thereupon the need to get to the bottom of what
had so moved me, the "important landmark in the study... of music"
which *Ethnomusicology* (January 1972) credited the find as being,
would not have been forthcoming. Something comparable, I am certain, was operative in Wasson's discovery of Soma. To indicate what
it was, I quote at length from Wasson's response to the Sacred
Mushroom of Meso-America which he came upon twenty years earlier.

"When we first went down to Mexico, we felt certain, my wife and
I, that we were on the trail of an ancient and holy mystery, and we
went as pilgrims seeking the Grail. To this attitude of ours I
attribute such success as we have had. A simple layman, I am profoundly grateful to my Indian friends for having initiated me into the
tremendous Mystery of the mushroom.

"In the uplands of southern Mexico the rites take place now, in
scattered dwellings, humble, thatched, without windows, far from
the beaten track, high in the mountains of Mexico, in the stillness of
the night, broken only by the distant barking of a dog or the braying

of an ass. Or, since we are in the rainy season, perhaps the Mystery is accompanied by torrential rains and punctuated by terrifying thunderbolts.

"Then, indeed, as you lie there bemushroomed, listening to the music and seeing the visions, you know a soul-shattering experience. The orthodox Christian must accept by faith the miracle of Transubstantiation. By contrast, the mushroom of the Aztecs carries its own conviction; every communicant will testify to the miracle that he has experienced. 'He who does not imagine in stronger and better lineaments, and in stronger and better light than his perishing eye can see, does not imagine at all,' Blake writes. The mushroom puts many (if not everyone) within reach of this state. It permits you to see, more clearly than our perishing mortal eye can see, vistas beyond the horizons of this life, to travel backwards and forwards in time, to enter other planes of existence, even to know God. It is hardly surprising that your emotions are profoundly affected, and you feel that an indissoluble bond unites you with the others who have shared with you in the sacred agape. All that you see during this night has a pristine quality: the landscape, the edifices, the carvings, the animals—they look as though they had come straight from the Maker's workshop. This newness of everything— it is as though the world had just dawned—overwhelms you and melts you with its beauty. Not unnaturally, what is happening to you seems to you freighted with significance, beside which the humdrum events of everyday are trivial. All these things you see with an immediacy of vision that leads you to say to yourself, 'Now I am seeing for the first time, seeing direct, without the intervention of mortal eyes.'

"And all the time that you are seeing these things, the priestess sings, not loud, but with authority. You are lying on a *petate* or mat; perhaps, if you have been wise, on an air mattress and in a sleeping bag. It is dark, for all lights have been extinguished save a few embers among the stones on the floor and the incense in a sherd. It is still, for the thatched hut is apt to be some distance away from the village. In the darkness and stillness, that voice hovers through the hut, coming now from beyond your feet, now at your very ear, now distant, now actually underneath you, with strange, ventriloquistic effect. Your body lies in the darkness, heavy as lead, but your spirit seems to soar and leave the hut, and with the speed of thought to travel where it listeth, in time and space, accompanied by the shaman's singing. You are poised in space, a disembodied eye, invisible, incorporeal, seeing but not seen. In truth, you are the five senses disembodied, all of them keyed to the height of sensitivity and awareness, all of them blending into one another most strangely, until the person, utterly passive, becomes a pure receptor, infinitely delicate, of sensations. As your body lies there in its sleeping bag, your soul is free, loses all sense of time, alert as it never was before, living an eternity in a night, seeing infinity in a grain of sand. What you have seen and heard is cut as with a burin in your memory, never to be effaced. At last you know what the ineffable is, and what ecstasy means. Ecstasy! For the Greeks *ekstasis* meant the flight of the soul from the body. Can you find a better word than that to describe the bemushroomed state? In common parlance ecstasy is fun. But ecstasy is not fun. Your very soul is seized and shaken until it tingles. Who will choose to feel undiluted awe, or to float through that door yonder into the Divine Presence?

"A few hours later, the next morning, you are fit to go to work. But how unimportant work seems to you, by comparison with the portentous happenings of that night! If you can, you prefer to stay close to the house, and, with those who lived through the night, compare notes, and utter ejaculations of amazement." (Condensed and slightly transposed from 1:149–162.)

5. I content myself with a single example: "Often have I penetrated into a forest in the fall of the year as night gathered and seen the whiteness of the white mushrooms, as they seemed to take to themselves the last rays of the setting sun, and hold them fast as all else faded into the darkness. When fragments of the white veil of the fly-agaric still cling to the cap, though night has taken over all else, from afar you may still see Soma, silver white, resting in his well-appointed birth-place close by some birch or pine tree. Here is how three thousand years ago a priest-poet of the Indo-Aryans gave voice to this impression:

    By day he appears (color of fire), by night, silver white (IX 97[9d]).

    Soma's scarlet coat dominates by day; by night the redness sinks out of sight, and the white patches, silvery by moon and starlight, take over" (4:41–42).

6. 'Fly' from the fact that the mushroom attracts flies and sends them temporarily into a stupor (Europeans used it as a flycatcher until quite recently); 'agaric' from an error in classification. When Linnaeus came to mushrooms he found the whole domain so frustratingly complicated that he grew careless and used 'agarikon', which is actually a tree fungus, to designate the gilled, fleshy-capped mushrooms.

7. Wasson never uses this word, preferring 'hallucinogen,' but I find this unsatisfactory. With "false impression" built into the definition of 'hallucination' *(Concise Oxford Dictionary)*, the word prejudges

the ontological status of what appears. Concommitantly, it is often inaccurate if it implies that the subject presumes that what one sees is physically present before one. Even strong doses of the substances seldom produce hallucinations in this sense.

8. Wasson is picking up on Brough's stress on Soma's battle-power. He could appropriately have gone on to ask if the battles the poets had in mind were not primarily cosmic—against the ever-threatening forces of chaos and evil—rather than tribal, as Brough appears to assume. Against mythic foes stimulants would have limited utility, whereas the metaphysical triumph of righteousness is a common psychedelic assurance.

9. One day, Confucius went to visit the Taoist Holy Man.... He found him completely inert and looking like a lifeless body. Confucius had to wait for some time before he was able to address his host.

   "Did my eyes deceive me?" he said. "Or was this really so? Just now, Sir, your body was like a piece of dry wood. You seemed to have left the world...."

   "Yes," replied Lao Tan, "I had gone for a stroll at the origin of all things" *(Chuang Tzu,* Chapter 21).

10. *Lao Tzu and Taoism* ((Palo Alto: Stanford University Press, 1970), p. 146.

The Importance of
the Buddha

That Arnold Toynbee should have emerged from his twelve-volume *A Study of History* listing Gautama the Buddha as one of the dozen or so "greatest benefactors of the living generation," surprises no one, I suppose. But who was this Buddha, this "Awakened One"—one of a handful of snowflakes that deserve to be singled out from the total human snowfall for attention and gratitude? Of books on the Buddhist religion there are, as the author of the present book acknowledges, many. Odd, then, that there should be so few, and especially so few remaining in print, that focus on the founder himself.

As this book does focus on the founder there is no need for me to dwell here on the facts of his life. Instead I shall pick up on Toynbee's point and speak to its importance. What was there about the Buddha that made him important in the past and important today? Important for Westerners today, we should add, for this book is obviously addressed to readers who are spatially as well as temporally removed from the world in which the Buddha lived.

Begin with the past. The reason usually given for the Buddha's historical importance is that he founded one of the world's great religions. No one doubts that he did this, but our secular and pluralistic age has contracted the word "religion" so far in the direction of individual belief and practice—"what a man does with his own solitariness," was the way Whitehead defined it—that to peg the Buddha as the founder of a religion is to miss the full scale of his achievement.

This essay on the importance of Buddha originally appeared as the introduction to Buddha, The Quest for Serenity: *A Biography by George N. Marshall (Boston: Beacon Press, 1978).*

It would be truer to say, with Trevor Ling, that he founded a civilization—one whose soul was indeed religion, but whose body was a
body politic. As a civilization, Buddhism was a total view of the world
and humanity's place in it. It created for the community of its adherents an entire universe, one that gathered into a coherent whole levels and aspects of life that the modern world divides into economics,
politics, ethics, law, art, philosophy, and the like. E. F. Schumacher
reminded us of this by including a chapter on "Buddhist Economics"
in his *Small Is Beautiful,* but the view of Budhism as an exclusively
spiritual affair persists.

The Buddha that jumps first to mind is the one iconography so
effectively presents to us: the solitary Buddha seated motionless
beneath the Bo Tree. So strong is the hold of this other-worldly
Buddha that we forget his other side. We forget that no sooner had
he launched his ministry than he was drawn back into the royal circles he had renounced to seek his enlightenment. For Indian monarchy was in its infancy then, trying to forge a viable alternative to the
village-based Brahmanic *panchayat* (rule by five) that was fumbling
with population growth and other changes that were occurring.

The Buddha appreciated the problem and responded to it; his
message included a strong social component along with its path to
personal release. It called for a society founded like a tripod on a
three-fold base: monarchy, the *sangha* (monastic community), and
the laity. Each of these had obligations to the others while deriving
benefits from them. But this is not the place for details. What I suggest is that the reader may find it instructive to notice how often
kings, queens, and princes cross the pages of the life this book
recounts. A new civilization was in the making, and royalty no less
than commoners were drawn into the act.

The greatness of the Buddha in shaping that civilization is attested
by the greatness of the civilization itself. Geographically it spread
beyond India to bless all of Asia, while temporally it continues residu-
ally, in southern Buddhism, right down to today. Southern Buddhism
(Theravada) is usually distinguished from its northern, Mahayana
counterpart doctrinally, but the difference that underlies their doctrinal disputes is that Theravada Buddhism, standing closer to original
Buddhism, continued to cling to the ideal of Buddhism as a civilization, whereas Mahayana Buddhism never did so cling. I recognize
that this is not the usual view of the matter, but a return to the
Buddhist world last year in a visit divided between Sri Lanka in the
south and Japan to the north convinced me that it is accurate. We
have yet to see a history of Buddhism that presents the rise of
Mahayana as Buddhism revisioning itself to accommodate to civiliza-

tions other than its own—first in India when it became clear that the Vedic tradition and its *varnashrama-dharmic* social stipulations were not going to be displaced, and then in China, whose civilization never did admit of an alternative.

This divestment process—the extraction of Buddhism's spiritual essence from the total civilization in which it was originally cast—points directly to the second question I posed for this introduction, the question of Buddhism's continuing importance. For Buddhist civilization is a thing of the past; even in Burma, Thailand, Sri Lanka and Cambodia we see today only its debris. For the continuing importance of the Buddha's achievement we must look to Buddhism as a religion, capable of acommodating itself to civilizations in the plural. We have it on no less authority than that of Edward Thomas that the religious essence of Buddhism has never been definitely identified, so what follows will be an approximation only.

Consciousness feels like a passive medium, through which the world simply flows in to us as it is in itself, but this is far from the case. To begin with, we select from the world, seeing in the main what we choose to see; as the Tibetans say, when a pickpocket meets a saint, what the pickpocket sees are pockets. And even what we choose to see we structure by our thoughts and feelings: poor children asked to draw a penny will draw it larger than do rich children—it looms larger in their minds' eyes. In so many ways, what we take for the world's "facts" are actually psychological constructs, as the Latin *factum* ("that which is made") suggests. This much Buddhism shares with virtually all contemporary psychology. What it adds is that at a deeper level our thoughts and feelings are themselves vectored by what the Buddha called The Three Poisons: desire (lust, greed, and grasping), aversion (fear, hatred, and anger), and ignorance. And the greatest of these is ignorance. For it is ignorance—most pointedly, ignorance concerning our true identity, who we really are—that causes us to divide the world into what we like and dislike. Thinking that we are, in the last analysis, individuals, we seek what augments our isolated selves and shun what threatens them. What we call our "self" is the amalgam of desires and aversions that we have wrapped tightly, like the elastic of a golf ball, around the core of separate identity that is its center.

This tight, constricted, golf-ball self is inevitably in for hard knocks, which is why the Buddha prefaced his teachings with "life is suffering." For a long while Western understanding of Buddhism was arrested at this first of the Buddha's Four Noble Truths; it is from this arrested position that the charges of Buddhism as life-denying and world-negating—in a word pessimistic—have been leveled. The truth, we now almost see, is more nearly the opposite. The startling claim of the Buddha, announced in the third and fourth of his Noble Truths, is that the suffering of unregenerate life is dispensable; it can be transcended. And we can see how to transcend it. There is only one kind of person I oppose, the Buddha once observed: he who says there is no way.

This is not the place to say in detail what the Buddha saw the way to be—the book in hand presents it, at least in outline. It will be enough here to reverse the two preceding paragraphs' "archaeology of consciousness" that exposed the root of life's routine suffering and construct from bottom up a model of the alternative self the Buddha perceived. The foundation of this reconstituted self will be an enlarged self-identification. Ideally the new self will identify with everything, greeting everything that comes its way as a reflection of an aspect of its own self. But we need not be categorical. Every step in the recommended direction will be to the good. For with each step we will find our desires and aversions relaxed; more of what comes our way will feel congruent with what we sense ourselves to be. Closer to the surface of our awareness we will see that the easing of our demands on life reduces the distortions our thoughts and feelings impose upon it. The logical terminus of this line of reasoning is clear. If we could attain the limit of expanded identity—the point where we relinquished partiality toward our finite selves entirely—there would *be* no separate self and the Buddha's key insight, *anatta* (no separate self), would be directly experienced. We should not let the negative form of the Buddhist terms for this eventuality mislead us: *nirvana* is "nothing" only in the sense of "no (demarcated) thing"; *sunyata* is "void" only in being de-void of separating distinctions. The words point toward the limitlessness of the self we would become.

Needless to say, the succinctness of this formulation is no guage of the difficulties it presents. The practical agenda it sets before us is more than enough for a lifetime—in Buddhist symbolism innumerable lives are required. Still, the discovery of what life's true agenda is can arrive in an instant. And its arrival is decisive; it is hardly too much to say that to identify life's problem and set foot on the path indicated is more important than traversing the path's full length. For to set forth on the path is to turn one's back forever on the stance of victim. To pass from thinking of ourselves as *having* problems to seeing that we *are* the problem is to step from darkness into at least a glimmering light. Tears and labors may await us, but if we have truly effected the "Copernican revolution" in outlook we are already, in germ, ourselves the "Buddha"—from the root *bodhati:* he awakens; he understands. We can echo for ourselves the words with which the historical Buddha concluded his six-year quest: "I have been a fool, [but] I have found a path."

If this way of putting the Buddhist perspective seems contemporary in a way Buddhist civilization does not, I have discharged the second aim of this introduction, which is to suggest why the Buddha not only was important but continues to be important today. In doing so I suspect I have also suggested why his life and teachings are pertinent for the contemporary West and not just Asia. That I could even attempt to summarize the Buddha's message in contemporary psychological idiom is itself proof that the high walls that separated traditions in the human past are down. In part, at least, we emphatically *can* understand what the Buddha was getting at. And because our Western scientific approaches tempt us to try to explain the more in terms of the less, with the danger that in doing so we shall lose sight of the freedom that constitutes our human opportunity, we *need* to understand what the Buddha was saying. If we succeed in understanding him, a curious prediction that has been attributed to the eighth-century Tibetan saint Padmasambhava will have been strikingly confirmed:

> When the iron bird flies,
>   and horses run on wheels....
>   the Dharma will come to the land
>   of the red man.

Tibetan Chant:
Inducing the Spirit[1]

On a recent sojourn among Tibetan lamas, I stumbled on an extraordinary phenomenon that lends itself to rigorous inspection (spectroscopic analysis and computer simulation). It is the capacity of certain specially trained lamas to chant in a way that makes multiple tones audible simultaneously, the capacity of single lamas to sing—solo—chords.

I shall divide my report of this phenomenon into four parts: (1) narrative, in which I recount the circumstances under which I encountered the chanting; (2) acoustic description, which consists of a report by scientists of what, in terms of the physics of the human voice, the lamas actually do; (3) supplementing observations; and (4) hermeneutics, in which I try to assess the meaning this kind of chanting assumes in the context of Tibetan Buddhism.

Narrative

Debarred from Tibet proper because I am a United States citizen, I spent the autumn of 1964 among lamas currently in exile in north India. A chance meeting with a high lama of the Gelugpa sect on a bus to Dalhousie led to admission to Gyütü Monastery on the out-

This study originally appeared in American Anthropologist *69, 2 (April 1967): 209–212 with the title "Unique Vocal Abilities of Certain Tibetan Lamas." The technical analysis of the voiced sounds was done with the assistance of Kenneth Stevens of the Massachusetts Institute of Technology, where Huston Smith was then teaching. Huston Smith once laughingly remarked to the editor that "this was his only contribution to the empirical study of religion."*

skirts of that Punjab hill station. The original Gyutü, in Lhasa, boasted some 800 lamas; its reconstituted, exilic version houses one-tenth that number in refugee quarters that the Indian government provides as partial compensation for work on high roads in the Himalayan foothills performed by Tibetan laypersons.

It happened that I had entered the monastery on the eve of the annual four-day *puja* commemorating the arrival in Tibet of two renowned statues, one from Nepal, the other from China, important symbols of the Indian and Chinese civilizations on which Tibet has drawn and whose features it has blended uniquely. The ceremonies began at three o'clock the following morning in the "ceremonial hall," which—we were in refugee quarters—was in fact no more than a large tent. I mention this detail because the immediate impulse of the first musicologist who heard my recording of the chanting I am about to describe was to credit what he heard to resonances awakened by "the thick walls of those Tibetan fortress monasteries." In actuality, the acoustics of the "hall" contributed nothing to what he was hearing.

Some 80 lamas, richly robed, seated themselves on cushions on the dirt floor in six rows running the length of the tent, three on each side of the center, all facing the center. I was end man on one of the back rows, near the altar. For the opening hour the chanting was monotonous. A guttural, gravelly, low-pitched, unvarying drone, it reminded me of the chanting in Japanese monasteries and recalled the fact that Tibetan Vajrayana and Japanese Shingon are subbranches of the same Buddhist limb. The darkness of the early hour combined with the monotony of the drone to make me sleepy, and I was on the verge of dozing off when I was brought to my senses abruptly by what sounded like an angelic choir. The boring monotone had given way to rich, full-chorded harmony. If the accompanying bells and cymbals had begun to simulate the tones of the King's Chapel organ, I would hardly have been more astonished. My first thought was: they're singing in parts. This thought was striking enough, for I had always known harmony as a Western art form, the Orient having concentrated, by contrast, on melody and rhythm. But this jolt was nothing to the one that awaited me, for after several minutes of such chords the choir suddenly cut out, leaving everything to a single soloist or cantor. And he, seated perhaps ten feet to my right and two rows in front, was singing by himself what sounded like a threetone major chord composed of a musical first, third, and fifth. Subsequent spectroscopic analysis of the recording I eventually made shows only two of these tones—the first and third—to be distinctly audible. I believe this is due to faulty recording but cannot be certain, for it is my ear and memory against what the tape actually registers.

The balance of the story is brief. The rituals lasted for 15 hours on each of the four days, punctuated by two ten-minute toilet breaks and two meager meals served in place within the tent. Most of the time the lamas were seated, bell in the thumb-groin of the right hand, diamond scepter in that of the left. Periodically, they would wave and interweave their hands in elaborate *mudras* to accompany their chants. For about ten minutes once every hour and a half, their voices would splay out from their monotone drone into the chords of which I have spoken. It was my distinct impression that when they did this, they were all doing what the cantor did: each one of them producing all of the notes in the chord. But since the evidence I brought back affords no way of proving that the lamas were not sounding different notes of the chord, the analysis that follows confines itself to the solo portions of the chanting, not the choral portions. Richly embroidered vestments and elaborate headgear were changed periodically, and each afternoon there were ceremonial processions around the inside of the tent, culminating before the altar. The entire celebration climaxed in an elaborate outdoor fire sacrifice in the late afternoon of the final day. An anonymous benefactor (a *yon bdag*, "fee master"; or *yin bdag*, "bounty master") provided each lama with a rupee (20¢) for his 60-hour vigil; in this recompense the writer was generously included.

On the day following the puja, I located in a school near Dalhousie a tape recorder and returned to the monastery to record the effects described. On returning to M.I.T., I took the tape to my colleague, Professor Kenneth N. Stevens, who specializes in the physics of the human voice. He had not heard, or heard of, the human voice functioning in this way, and after a spectroscopic analysis of the tape, produced, with his colleague Raymond S. Tomlinson, the explanation of the solo portion of the lamas' chant that forms the next section of

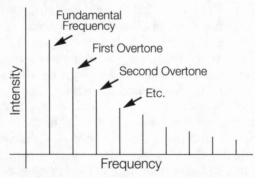

Fig. 1 Spectrum of Sound Generated at the Vocal cords.

this article. (As I watched them work, I thought of a line from C. P. Snow's *The Two Cultures and a Second Look*: "Greenwich Village talks precisely the same language as Chelsea, and both have about as much communication with M.I.T. as though the scientists spoke nothing but Tibetan." The M.I.T. scientists before me weren't speaking Tibetan, but they were working on Tibetan speech.)

The following section reproduces the report of Professor Stevens and Mr. Tomlinson.

Acoustic Description

Any voiced sound that occurs in monotone speech or in singing can be considered to be the result of the excitation of the vocal cavities by a periodic source of sound that is generated at the vocal cords. Each vibration of the vocal cords allows a brief puff of air to pass through the space between the cords (the glottis), and this pulse of air acts as the sound excitation for the vocal cavities that lie between the vocal cords and the lips. The sound that emerges from the vocal cords is relatively independent of the shape of the vocal cavities, and has a spectrum that is characterized by a fundamental frequency and a number of harmonics or overtones whose intensities decrease with increasing frequency. The spectrum of this sound generated at the vocal cords is depicted pictorially in Figure 1. In this figure, vertical lines representing the various frequency components are drawn at the fundamental frequency and at multiples of this frequency. The height of each line represents the intensity of the corresponding frequency component. During singing, the frequency of vibration of the vocal cords is controlled by adjusting the muscles in the larynx and the air pressure in the lungs. When a higher note is sung, the line in Figure 1 representing the fundamental frequency is moved up in frequency (i.e., to the right in the picture), and all other overtones are likewise shifted up so that they remain integral multiples of the fundamental frequency.

The sound that we hear, i.e., the sound that emerges from the lips, is the result of modification of the vocal-cord sound by the resonances associated with the vocal cavities. The frequencies of these resonances are dependent upon the configuration of the vocal cavities; each vowel in a given language is produced with a particular configuration of these cavities and thus is characterized by certain resonant frequencies, sometimes called "formants." The shape of the vocal cavities is adjusted by manipulating the tongue position and shape, the jaw position, and the configuration of the lips.

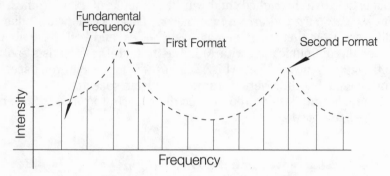

Fig. 2 Frequency Spectrum of a Typical Vowel

The spectrum of the sound that emerges from the lips for a typical sung vowel thus takes the form shown in Figure 2. In the frequency range shown in this figure, there are two resonances of the vocal cavities, manfested by two maxima in the spectrum. The dashed line joining the tops of the spectral lines is called the spectrum envelope. In general, when a vowel is sung, the pitch of the note is determined entirely by the fundamental frequency, i.e., by the frequency of vocal-cord vibration. The "quality" of the sound is dependent upon the frequency positions of the formants. Usually, a resonance of formant does not convey the auditory impression that it has a pitch that is independent of the pitch associated with the vocal-cord vibration frequency.

In the case of the specific chord-like tone that is being examined here, the fundamental frequency and the resonant frequencies of the vocal tract are adjusted by the singer to bear a very specific relation to each other. The first and second formant frequencies are adjusted so that the second is precisely two times the first; furthermore, the fundamental frequency is adjusted to be one-fifth of the frequency of the first resonance. Thus the spectrum has the form shown in Figure 3. For the particular note that was examined in detail with our instruments, the fundamental frequency was 75.5 cps, and the first and second resonant frequencies were 312.5 and 62.5 cps, respectively. Measured data on the formant frequencies of spoken vowels indicate that if a vowel with these formant frequencies were uttered at a low fundamental frequency of 62.5 cps, it would be identified as the American-English vowel "aw" (law) or "o" (low). The vowel color one hears when listening to the lama tone is in this region.

Since the fifth and tenth harmonics of the fundamental frequency are located precisely at the first and seond resonances of the vocal cavities, the intensities of these particular harmonics, which are one octave apart, are considerably higher than the intensities of the other harmonics. The relative intensities of these haronics are, apparently, sufficiently high that a musical note with a frequency of 312.5 cps can be heard, in addition to the fundamental tone of 62.5 cps. These two notes, sounded together, form a chord that consists approximately of musical note D_2 that is more than two octaves below middle C together with $E^\sharp_4$ above middle C. This, of course, constitutes a musical third.

The frequency of 62.5 cps is very low for the normal male singing voice, and cannot be reached by most singers. In their chant, the lamas sing this note by starting with a tone one octave higher and then modifying this tone (by some physiological means that is not at present understood) such that alternate pulses from the glottis are slightly different in magnitude and shifted slightly from their normal position. This procedure gives rise to a tone of one-half the fundamental frequency of the original note.

Thus a very precise simultaneous adjustment of several structures in the vocal mechanism is necessary in order to achieve the desired chordlike sound: (1) the vocal cavities must be adjusted in shape such that the second resonant frequency is exactly twice the first; (2) the fundamental frequency must be adjusted to be steady at precisely one-fifth of the frequency of the first formant.[2]

These special relations that must exist between formant frequencies and fundamental frequency are, apparently, quite difficult to achieve. The lamas seem to be able to create the combination of conditions that give rise to the chordlike sound only within a narrow range of fundamental frequencies—a range of only one semitone. [Kenneth N. Stevens, Professor of Electrical Engineering; Mr. Raymond Tomlinson, Research Assistant; M.I.T.]

Supplementing Observations

I pass from this description to several observations.

Musically, the chord effect is more than pleasing; sung solemnly in an assembly hall by an elaborately robed monastery choir with *mandala* offerings displayed on the altar, it was inspiring. As was noted, only two chords appear to be possible. The depth of the fundamental on which the basic one is founded—B, more than two octaves below middle C—makes it intrinsically impressive. When, after 20 or 30 seconds, the fundamental is raised a half tone to C the tension with the tonic is dramatic, so much so that when (after perhaps 15 seconds) the chord slides back to the tonic, the resolution is power-

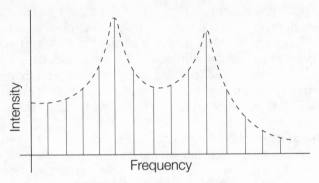

Fig. 3 Spectrum of Note Sung by Lama

ful. The prime syllables of the chords are AUM and HUM, the first and last syllables of the basic mantrum of Tibetan Buddhism: AUM MANI PADME HUM. The middle syllables mean, respectively, "jewel" and "lotus," while the first and last syllables are valued for their unique phonetic power, being defined semantically only in terms of attunement with the *Dharmakaya,* the Buddha as ultimate reality. In answer to questions posed in a variety of ways, the Gyutu lamas stated repeatedly that they could not explain the meaning of these syllables, but that while uttering them one should always make a special effort to attune heart and mind to the meaning of the holy moment.

To produce the chord effect, intensive training seems to be required. I was told that only two monasteries in all Tibet—ones that specialized in training lamas for ritual performance rather than extensive knowledge of the *sutras*—produced lamas who could chant in this fashion, and that the training began at the age of 12. *How* they train, I was unable to discover—the language barrier was too great. Whether the Tibetan physique favors such chanting is likewise unknown, but it might. Inhabitants of high altitudes, such as the Andes, tend to develop special physiques, including barrel chests, and Tibet boasts the highest average elevation in the world. This elevation is not achieved through an even plateau: Tibet is sharply mountainous, and this too has produced exceptional vocal results.

In extremely mountainous regions two high points may be separated by a relatively short distance in space, but they can be linked only, if at all, by long circuitous descent and ascent involving the expenditure of much time and strength. To overcome this environmental factor, special techniques of voice projection may have been developed to attract attention and so to identify location, to control herds and flocks, and to transmit messages. The need for voice projection is met by combining powers and tricks of breathing that have been acquired from mountain climbing with the special acoustic conditions that result from mountain-slope wind currents and echo-producing formations. The techniques of voice projection have been carried over into varieties of yodeling and distinctive styles of singing [Ekvall 1964:4].

Hermeneutics

Why do the lamas go to what is apparently great trouble to achieve the chord effect? Not, we may assume, for its esthetic yield alone, any more than medieval monks perfected Gregorian chant solely for the sake of art. Music inspires as well as delights, and as lamas are not primarily musicians, we can surmise that they developed the chord primarily for its inspirational power.

To "inspire" means, of course, to "induce spirit," or if (as Buddhists believe) the Buddha-nature is in human beings from the start, to inspire is to bring it to the fore. Sound can facilitate this process, for if through language human beings reached out and took possession of the world, through it human beings also reached inward and awakened, among other things, intimations of a higher life. India has been vividly aware of language's creative power, considering it no less than metaphysical. According to legend, Brahman himself was born from the cosmic being's mouth, a notion embedded in the fact that the root of the word "Brahman" means breath.

If the Brahmins thought sound could produce God, one is not surprised to find them believing that it could vitalize the God in human beings *(Atman)*. As prime vehicle for this power, they forged the sacred syllable (Sanskrit, *mantra;* Tibetan, *gzunis snags),* literally "tool for the mind." A mantra is not a concept, for divinity exceeds conceptualization. Nor is it a name, only designating. It might be conceived as a vocal variant of Locke's qualityless substance, around which humanity's intimations of the sacred can accumulate and adhere, but for the best mantras this image is too passive. The best mantras do not merely *accept* sacred associations, they *elicit* them. To do so, they must be natural symbols, not just conventional ones; that is, they must be ones that contain within themselves intrinsically, not just by association, features contained to greater degree in what they symbolize. AUM—the first of the two syllables on which the lamas build their chords and the paradigmatic mantra of Indian spirituality—possesses such natural symbolic qualifications in abundance. Some of these have been known since the *Mandukya Upanishad.* Compounded of the first and last syllables of the alphabet, AUM is Sanskrit's alpha and omega, the beginning and end of all that can be said. If one objects that the preceding clause should read "the beginning and end of all that can be *written,*" the Indian will not object; he or she will simply point out that orally, too, the syllable is inclusive. Correctly pronounced, it executes a glide that traverses all articulatory positions in the range of the human voice,[3] from deep in the throat (a), through the mouth's center (u), to the closing of the lips (m). The syllable compresses, therefore, speech as well as writing: "As all parts of a leaf are held together by a central rod, so all speech is held together by AUM" *(Chandogya Upanishad).* And insofar as thought rides on language, AUM contains it too in seed. It is the most compact, meaningful representation of the All, which is why the Indians hold that in it "all the positive and forward-pressing forces of the human mind are united and concentrated like an 'arrow-point'" (Govinda 1959).

What the physics of sound adds to our understanding of AUM as a natural symbol is the concept of overtones. The aural impact of that syllable need not derive exclusively from the claimed fact that it glides the full length of the vocal tract; part of that impact can derive from the fact that it is a syllable with strong overtones. For overtones awaken numinous feelings: sensed without being explicitly heard, they stand in exactly the same relation to our hearing as the sacred stands to our ordinary, mundane lives. This is why gongs appear so frequently in religious observances—they were prominent in the pujas in which the chords were set. Rich in harmonics,

> the sound of the gong extends from the lowest tone of human perception to the highest, and the tone does not cease. It stays in one's ear till its sound blends into the noise of the world. In the sound of the gong there are all sounds. It is impossible to pick out the infinitely many individual tones, and therefore it is impossible to describe the experience minutely. In the sound of the gong there is all that there is; it is one.[4]

The object of the spiritual quest is to experience life as one hears the gong, replete with overtones that tell of a "more" that can be sensed but not seen, sensed but not said, heard but not explicitly.

The lamas' chords place, as it were, a magnifying glass over the aural symbolic virtues embedded in the AUM mantra: they peak to the point of full audibility overtones that otherwise are sensed but not explicitly heard. The chords also provide a clue to why HUM, the other syllable on which the chords build, worked its way into mantric position. The human vocal cavities are such that it is impossible for them to produce vowels having separately identifiable overtones, except at low frequencies. With all their skill and effort, the lamas, to achieve their chord effects, had to begin with vowels in the region of those present in our words "boot," "good," and "law." HUM meets this requirement. It is consonant with this hypothesis, though not directly related to the lamas' chord, that the requirement is also met by *"wu"* and *"mu,"* the virtual mantras of Ch'an and Zen Buddhism as embedded in the *"wu" kung an* and *"mu" koan.*

NOTES

1. I am grateful to the Rockefeller Foundation for a travel grant that led to the findings here reported.
2. In analyzing my tape, we overlooked the fact that it was recorded on India's 50 hertz current and was being played back on 60 hertz. I have adjusted the frequencies from those in the original report to correct this mistake.
3. This is the traditional Indian view. The contemporary science of linguistics approaches sounds as discrete, not as occupying positions on continua.
4. From a student paper by Robert Blum.

REFERENCES CITED

Ekvall, Robert (1964). *Religious Observances in Tibet.* Chicago: University of Chicago Press.
Govinda, Anagarika G. (1959). *Foundations of Tibetan Mysticism.* New York: Dutton.

The West

The Western Way:
An Essay on Reason
and the Given

One who is privileged to write in tribute to Edwin Burtt fortunately does not have to give justification for choosing a cross-cultural topic. The opening pages of Burtt's chapter on "Eastern and Western Philosophy" in *In Search of Philosophic Understanding* can be paraphrased as follows: Civilizations have developed thus far in sufficient isolation from one another to permit the distinctive genius of each to unfold without premature and thereby confusing challenges from the genius of others. Thanks to this independence, each culture has developed a core of distinctive wisdom without which the world would be poorer. Today, however, we stand at a turning point, a reversal of the direction of history. Isolation has given way to interaction, bringing intense cross-fertilization of cultures. Here as in other respects history has given our century unprecedented opportunity.

All philosophers acknowledge with Burtt that today's multicultural awareness is an important new feature of our times. An appreciable number have even been prepared to agree with him in principle that this fact "opens up a more inclusive and adequate perspective in which to solve philosophy's own perennial problems."[1] But thus far very few have seen this resource as promising enough to engage their own philosophical interest. It is because Burtt has argued not just in asides but in the substance of his life's work that our new intercultural situation warrants some philosophic priority that I have drawn encouragement from him over the years.

Perhaps the best way to repay some of my debt is to pick up and carry on a little further some of the work that he has importantly

This essay orginally appeared in Philosophy East & West *22, 4 (October 1972): 441–459 which was dedicated to the lifework of Edwin A. Burtt.*

begun. I propose to attempt this by once again examining the West in world perspective. The proximate hope is that this may help us to understand ourselves better, but beyond this lie two other possibilities. First, the alternatives that come to view when we see how we differ from India and China may spark self-criticism, for to see that one's own way is not the only way leads naturally to the question: Is one's way the best way? Second, there is the possibility, noted in Burtt's own words, that the more inclusive perspective, which will hopefully emerge from the dialogue of civilizations, will provide a fresh and enriched context in which to tackle philosophy's abiding problems.

The point at which I propose to move in on the West lies somewhere in the interplay between its notions of reason and nature. In two previous essays I suggested that whereas traditional China was preoccupied with humanity's social problem and India with the psychological, the defining feature of the West has been its involvement with nature.[2] Burtt, for his part, chooses the West's confidence in reason as the point to initiate comparison with Asia.[3] That these two Western insignias—involvement with nature and confidence in reason—are not unrelated is suggested by the fact that while beginning with the first, in the course of trying to see how it eventuated in modern science, I was brought almost at once to "the Greeks'... passion for abstraction and generalization"; Burtt, though focusing on reason, does not overlook the fact that "the persistent concern of the West... has been to understand the external world."

Perhaps we need to look behind both these Western propensities to locate the point at which the tradition embarked on its distinctive tangent. A test of whether we locate it accurately would be: Does it point toward the West's distinctive discoveries; to wit, modern science, the idea of progress, the concept of the individual and human rights, and ideology? I shall apply this test at the close of the article, but first the point itself must be located.

I. The Cosmological Myth

The earliest respect in which the West showed signs of differentiating itself from the common stream of human development was in distancing itself from the given. Until it took this fateful step—stepping back, as it were, to place at arm's length and survey for the first time circumspectly and critically the milieu in which its life was set— humankind everywhere had lived under the spell of the cosmological myth. According to this myth the given was God-given. As humanity's primal matrix, it was the living womb that sustained all. It existed to nurture human beings, not to be challenged or refashioned. The way things were was the only way they could be; "given" and "possible" were identical. Norms described the way things were going. Morals were mores, right was the conventional.

On their own, India and China never seriously questioned this cosmological myth. Consequently they remained until modern times—and right down to today compared with the West—profoundly conservative, eminently natural in the sense of being rooted in strong instinctive drives. The West broke through the myth. Its dominant strands—Jewish and Greek, Hebraic and Hellenic—were opposites in many ways but alike in this crucial respect. Had it not been so they could not have survived as architectural partners of a single civilization. One or the other would have had to knuckle under.

II. Breakthrough and Distancing: The Jews

Yahweh was not a nature god.[4] After the Babylonian Exile, Yahweh was assumed to have created the natural world, but originally Yahweh was simply distinguishable from it. The competing Canaanite deities *were* nature gods: the Baals were lords of their respective fields, Astarte was a fertility goddess abetting harvests and procreation. In these deities, gods and nature fused. Not so with Yahweh; he was lord of events, of deeds, of history. Yahweh was forever commanding his people to *do* things; things, moreover, that usually differed from what was being done: "Get thee up. Go to the west to spy out the land. Go to the west, the fields are waiting."

Why was Yahweh not a nature deity? For one thing, the Hebrews were nomads so their God could not be attached to nature in the form of any fixed piece of real estate. But more important—always more important in affairs relating to the Jews—was Israel's nuclear experience, the Exodus. Yahweh had been born, in the sense of coming to life as the God of a people, in a unique historical event. This gave Yahweh a different character from other deities. Gods originally tended to be identified with maintaining the status quo: insuring that the sun rises, rains fall, and kings maintain some semblance of order. Yahweh *disrupted* appointed rounds. Yahweh was a breakthrough deity. As a transcendent God, Yahweh precluded the deification of immanence (that which is directly and immediately given). Such deification was idolatry. Through Yahweh the Jews were forced to step back. In the face of what was, Yahweh drove them to ask, always, "Is it as it should be, as I will it to be?" When a historian of the Jews of the stature of Solo Baron goes so far as to *define* Judaism as the struggle between the "ought" and the "is", "the struggle... between the ideal and the actual," one can accept that the distinction is pivotal.

III. Breakthrough and Distancing: The Greeks

If it was God's will that distanced the Jews from the given, in the case of the Greeks it was the *logos*. How did it emerge?

The closest we can come to the lost skein that issued from the remote and shadowy reaches of the Greek primitive is through Homer. His is a mind dwelling completely in the eternal world. The blind gaze of this world's greatest storyteller is robustly extroverted. Physical events and objects engage him completely. There is no subject-object dichotomy here; it is things alone that seize and impel us, not thoughts about them. That mind might *influence* (by selection, emphasis, perspective, or evaluation) what it sees is a suspicion that does not occur until much later; at this stage even the basic distinction between words and things barely obtrudes. Homer's nominalism helps hold it back. Abstractions that ignore differences, in the interests of mental efficiency, blur things which, in nature, stand out in distinct array. Homer uses few of them. He presents us with a grove of poplars or a silver birch, not simply "trees". Signals from the senses, not theories, do the reporting, outlining things exactly as they are, each in its own right. The effect is a world of vivid, concrete things and happenings, a world of bright, flashing particularity.

John Findley sees the Greek mind emerging from this original, heroic base in three distinguishable stages: the visionary (Aeschylus, Pindar, Sophocles), the theoretical (Euripides and Thucydides), and the rational (Socrates, Plato, and Aristotle). In each successive stage, thought plays a stronger, more ordering role. Whereas Homer used similes that keep things apart—"Straight through his [Simoesius the Trojan's] shoulder the bronze spear went, and he lay in the dust on the ground like a white poplar which sprang smooth in the damp of a wide lowland and its branches grew near the top"—retaining thereby a world of discrete existences, each complete and worth noting in itself, his successors used metaphors which pull things together. In "Excellent is water," the first phrase of Pindar's *First Olympian Ode,* water stands alone; but in what follows, "and gold like blazing fire shines clear at night," gold and fire interfuse to the point of sharing a single verb. The mind increasingly editorializes; it enters more opinions and sees the world increasingly through imposed meanings. Ideas rise toward the surface. In the visionary mind they do not quite break through the old reliance on sense and imagery; Aeschylus and Sophocles, though no longer content simply to report events, use—as their devices for making sense of them—myth and drama rather than theory and analysis. Ideas are clearly at work, but much of the old flash and sense-play remains. Not even the mind of the theoretical stage cuts its ties with sense completely: Euripides sticks to drama and Thucydides to the drama of history. Both, however, are obviously more excited by ideas and the prospect of understanding life by means of them than were their predecessors. Euripides comes only ten years after Sophocles; even so the mythic mold cannot contain his mind completely. His plays are a curious hybrid of situation and concept. In Thucydides the theoretical component is even more evident. Somewhere in the early stages of the war between Athens and Sparta, he was grasped by the prospect of reducing its future course to a kind of theorem and thereby writing a paradigm of wars between great states. The result was a historical account in which personal, almost visual involvement and ideas are apparent in nearly equal proportion.

If it might be said that Homer, by looking out on a world of fresh, flashing concreteness reminds us of the childhood of the eye, then Aeschylus and Sophocles may be said to recall the childhood of the mind when, no longer content simply to see, we struggled to understand, with story as our only means. By this analogy Euripides and Thucydides represent thought's youth where eye and mind are equal partners. This leaves the mind's maturity for Findley's fourth stage, the rational mind of Socrates, Plato, and Aristotle. Here sense imagery can be invoked (Plato especially resorts to it repeatedly), but it need not be. Mathematics and logic, the capacity to think without imagery whatsoever, have arrived. More, they have become reason's paradigm.

Findley's scheme can be faulted for conflating different ways of looking at the world—concrete and artistic on the one hand, abstract and philosophico-scientific on the other—with different stages of the mind's development. The Ionian philosophers antedated by a full century even the first post-Homeric period Findley describes, yet in their zeal to reduce everything to a single underlying substance (Thales' water; Anaximenes' air; and in the case of Anaximander's "indefinite" or "infinite" a substance which could not be visualized or even defined), they were as abstract as Aristotle. The objection, however, does not vitiate Findley's thesis. The artistic mind is in closer touch with the popular mind than is that of the scientist or philosopher. In drawing his examples primarily from poets and dramatists,

Findley's thesis can be assumed to describe with reasonable accuracy the general development of the Greek mind.

What interests us is whether this development differs from parallel developments elsewhere. The advancement of mind into increased self-consciousness is part of the meaning of civilization. By virtue of this advance, humanity confronts the given as if it were laid before it. An assessment is called for; some stance toward it must be adopted. In the most profound cross-cultural study that has been written to date, William Haas notes that on reaching this (logical, if not precisely chronological) choice point, civilizations have developed differently. Asia retained a deep, unquestioning confidence in nature, appreciative of it, receptive of it. Had the Chinese and Indians not risen above the natural plane they would not have spawned civilizations, but the way they transcended it was by confirming it. By contrast, the West positioned itself in opposition to nature with a stance that was reserved and critical. Western civilization receded progressively from the natural and the instinctive and set itself up against them.

I used the word "nature" in the preceding paragraph because I was paraphrasing Haas, but to many minds the word denotes, primarily if not exclusively, physical nature.[5] Thus, to avoid this possible misreading, I shall revert to my earlier word 'given.' Haas does not try to explain why East and West positioned themselves differently toward the given; he presents their opposite postures as resulting from a shocklike inburst of inspired structures on the magic world which underlay both. I am under no more illusion than he that the Eurasian divide can be explained completely, but at the same time find myself unwilling to summarily dismiss the question "why". Are there factors that at least opened Asia and the West to their respective visitations, making them differently receptive?

The earliest state of affairs the Greeks describe, and thus the state in which the given is presumed to have been least tampered with, was not one to elicit trust. In this respect the scene depicted in Homer's epics contrasts sharply with China's age of Great Harmony and the Golden Yuga from which India's history was presumed to have declined. Homer himself does not shrink from his panoply. His own values are identical with the heroic ones he portrays, which is as we should expect of a mind absorbed in its object, not distanced in critical scrutiny. *Dike,* which by the time of *The Republic* had become a distinctly moral concept (for Plato the moral concept 'justice'), was for Homer purely descriptive, meaning no more than "what is normally to be expected": when Penelope is reminding the servants what a good master Odysseus was, she notes that he never did or said anything that was cruel or overweening, nor did he have favorites, "as is the *dike* of lords," which is to say the way lords can normally be expected to behave. Homer's consonance with his scene, however, does not excuse it once the capacity to stand in judgment appears. The mythic ancestry of the Greeks that he unfolds is rife with crimes and perversities; they loom at least as large as generosity and self-sacrifice. Flagrant injustice abounds. Even the gods are party to it, impelling human beings to evil without purpose. And over all broods—not the *Tao*; and not *karma* which, inexorable though it is in linking past to present, is just and leaves the future open. Over the Greek cosmos stands fate, inexorable, master of men, women, and gods, making puppets of all. No Eden this. It is a pandemonium of instincts and passions.

If the given as recorded in the Greeks' own past was not impressive, its exemplification in the ways of their neighbors was even less attractive. The Greeks' smaller landmass caused them to be ringed more tightly, than were either the Chinese or Indians, by foreigners who were less civilized. Crude, disorderly, fantastic, violent, they were (in our derivative of the word the Greeks coined for them) "barbarians": eccentrics like the Egyptians who, though older, richer, and in ways grander, squandered their wealth in preserving dead bodies; powerful brutes like the Assyrians who debased themselves in the worship of gods that were half-animal; illiterate wandering tribes who enjoyed so little order that they needed to be constantly armed; pious ritualists like the Jews with their curious dietary habits; slavish hordes like the abject subjects of Persia. "We imagine the Greeks as cheerful, tranquil people, happily balanced," writes Gilbert Highet. "But perhaps Nietzsche was right in saying that they felt a constant and terrible pressure of barbarism, not only from around them but from within.... They must often have felt like a few sane men living in a world of maniacs and constantly endangered by the infection of madness."[6]

If barbarism constituted a fair sample of the given, there was no question of accepting it. It needed to be countered. Gilbert Murray has somewhere a nice passage on the extent to which the reliefs of the high period of Greek art dwell on the strife of humans against centaurs or of gods against giants. Our modern sympathies are apt to side with the giants and centaurs, for an age of order likes romantic violence as those safe at home like storms at sea. But to the Greeks these battles represented the life-and-death struggle of human intelligence, reason, and gentleness against the almost overwhelming powers of passion and unguided strength. It was Hellas against the brute world.

To the Ionians, who were before the rise of Athens the most advanced of the Greeks in knowledge and culture, the beachead that Hellas had secured on the world was a source of enormous pride. As an island of order and refinement in a sea of primitivism wherein one was either hammer or anvil, their civilization was far from natural. It was a creation, an achievement. Even so, it left much to be done. Hence Thales, Anaximenes, and Anaximander. The Ionian School is usually accepted as an anomaly. With its focus exclusively on the external world and powered by nothing save sheer curiosity, it seems to stand as an original vision with no roads leading to it. The Ionians look like natural scientists before the rise of science, like devotees of pure knowledge two millennia before it was to reveal its oblique utility.

Their genius is unmistakable. But that their object was exclusively scientific, "their motive simple curiosity," as Guthrie in standard fashion contends, may be questioned. Why should brilliant people spend their lives flying in the face of evidence in their determination to prove at whatever outrage to sense and sensibility that the world of manifest, proliferated variety is in truth something single? To argue seriously that cliffs and deserts are really water—or perhaps air?—calls for more than hypothesis; it requires faith, including the desperation that is often its source. Guthrie himself seems to sense this, for after asserting flatly that the Ionian motive was simple curiosity—it was the Pythagoreans on the other side of the Greek world who had practical human interests at heart—he proceeds immediately to speak of "a deep-rooted tendency in the human mind to seek... something that persists through change... an underlying identity." Wherefore? Whence comes this tendency which in the Ionians produced the "faith that beneath... apparent chaos there exists a hidden permanence and unity"?[7]

Surely Guthrie gives us the answer himself in his word 'chaos'. Who wants it? Who needs it? Permanence provides the answer to the world's precariousness, uncertainty, and erosion by time; simplicity to its welter of unmanageable multiplicity. Civilization had increased life's order and reliability impressively, but it fell short of securing these prizes completely. A residue remained for philosophy.

The device philosophy utilized was reason. That word—if we could understand the full range of its varieties and nuances, we would be at the end of our cross-cultural quest rather than at its beginning. Prominent in the Greeks' first concerted deployment of it was abstraction, the distinguishing (separating out) of features presented in experience together. If within that which is set before us (conspicuous change and multiplicity), one hopes to find their opposites (simplicity and permanence), obviously some distinctions will have to be drawn. Undesirable features must be stripped away until the prize, originally concealed, is laid bare. The Ionians launched the hunt in the direction of matter (a single, unvarying substance), the Pythagoreans in the direction of form (ultimately, numbers). But the reasoning process the two schools used was the same.

There was, however, a moment of hesitation. What if reason, the tool for the critique of the given, is without a secure base? The arts first intimate this unsettling possibility. In the visionary minds of Aeschylus and Sophocles, excitement over reason's dawning prospects is unalloyed. Euripides and Thucydides continue this excitement, but traces of shadow begin to appear. What is to be the price of the benefits reason proffers?

With fluctuating intensity this question has bedeviled the West to this day. In fifth-century Athens it swung into full consciousness with the itinerant Sophists. The word *sophistés* means 'practitioner of wisdom', but wisdom of what sort? For the Sophists it was skeptical. The genesis of their skepticism ran back to the Ionian quest for permanence, stability, and unity in a world bewilderingly mutable, precarious, and multiple. Or rather, it ran back to the breakdown of this quest. The critics who followed on the heels of the Ionians gave rough treatment to the instruments on which the Ionians had relied for their knowing, the senses. "Eyes and ears are bad witnesses," said Heraclitus in one of his plainer assertions. Parmenides' disparagement went further: all that people imagine they see and hear in the world is illusory. Relativity of the senses was an integral correlate of Democritean atomism. Bitter and sweet, hot and cold are conventional terms, he argued. Nothing real corresponds to them. What seems sweet to me might seem bitter to you, or to myself should I fall ill, for to the sick the sweet tastes bitter. The same water can seem warm to one hand or cold to another even when both hands are my own. All is a matter of the temporary arrangement of the atoms in our bodies and their reaction to the equally transient combination in the sensible object. This relativity of the senses, the skeptics pointed out, was matched by the relativity, indeed contradictoriness, of the conclusions reached by way of them. For the Ionians true reality was some variety of matter; for the Pythagoreans it was structure or form. For Heraclitus change was the *only* reality; for Parmenides change was impossible so did not exist at all.

Such were skepticism's roots. The celebrated Sophist Gorgias lost no time in carrying them to their logical conclusion. In a book dedicated to three propositions, he argued that nothing exists, if anything did exist we could not know it, and if we could know anything we could not communicate it to anyone else. But though the movement had originated with regard to the world of nature, the Sophists' practical bent *(sophistēs* meaning *practitioner* of wisdom) caused them to devote their energies primarily to working out its implications for morals and society. If hot and cold, sweet and bitter are not grounded in the world but are simply matters of how we feel at the time, must we not face the fact that right and wrong, justice and injustice are equally subjective? Nature itself contains no absolute principles governing relations between people. Nothing is right or wrong but thinking makes it so. This on good authority (Plato's) is what Protagoras' famous dictum "Man is the measure of all things," came to: the way things appear to one person is the truth for that person; the way they appear to another is the truth for that person.

A conspicuous consequence of this view was to undermine the sanction of law. Heretofore its divine origin had not been questioned; the people who originally framed the constitutions were believed to have been inspired by Apollo, and legislators continued to ask his oracle at Delphi for sanction before proceeding with their plans. This religious foundation was an easy mark for the Sophists' enthusiastic agnosticism: "Concerning the gods," observed Protagoras, "I have no means of knowing whether they exist or not." It was buffeted, too, by the Greeks' growing worldliness as traders and colonizers. Trafficking with peoples of widely divergent cultures made increasingly untenable the notion that any one mold was God-given. Finally, to observe one's friends (or worse, one's political enemies, or oneself?—Protagoras was on the 443 B.C. commission to draft a constitution for the new Athenian colony of Thurii in south Italy) instituting laws hardly shored up the notion of their divine inspiration.

From the premise that laws and moral standards are human, imperfect and relative, different consequences could be drawn. The more radical Sophists did not scruple at affirming the right of the stronger to have his/her way. All of them agreed on the total absence of absolute values and standards. Expediency, however conceived, was the only rule; each must decide on the spur of the moment what was personally most advantageous for him/her. Rules in the accepted sense of universally applicable principles were nonexistent. Right and wrong, wisdom, justice, virtue—none was more than a name, though it might have been prudent at times to pretend that it was more.

Whether skepticism and relativism, if espoused by an entire society, would lead to moral anarchy and society's collapse remains to this day an untested question. What we know is that the Greeks had risen to their fifth-century greatness through an attitude of mind that was almost skepticism's opposite: they believed; they were committed. Their way of life was a religion, for them the only operative one. Its laws had been decreed to the founding legislators by Apollo himself, acting as mouthpiece for the father of all gods, Zeus. And Athens was Athena's city: the Acropolis was her rock, it was crowned by her temple, her festival was the most important in the year's calendar. It was not a case of church and state being unseparated; they were not even distinguishable—no separate word for church existed. This fusion of religion and politics had generated a commitment that ennobled. It had inspired people to seek higher satisfactions in place of lower ones, to forego immediate gratifications for the sake of long-ranged ones, to sacrifice private for civic gains. Now the entire edifice was being threatened. With skepticism, what was to assure that these civilizing dynamics would not be thrown into reverse? "Do you think a city can go on existing and avoid being turned upside-down," asks Socrates in the *Apology,* "if its judgements are to have no force but are to be made null and void by private individuals?"

No wonder there was consternation, strong enough to blind panicky city fathers to the marked difference between Socrates' constructive questionings and the Sophists' opposite sort, and thereafter (once the confusion had been effected) to provoke the death sentence on a person as patently dedicated and civic-minded as was Socrates. Skepticism, as it broke upon the classical mind, was no academic ploy. It was not a matter of sitting behind a desk and coming up with the clever discovery that if you set up arguments in the right way it is possible to doubt everything. Classical skepticism betokened the breakdown of a meaningful world. Originally *sképsis* had meant 'observing', but under the Sophists it took on the negative sense of examining every dogma only to undercut it. Using reason as their oar, the Greeks had pushed off from the land of their given only to find the boat and the sea itself giving way from under them. They were falling off the world.

Some of the opposition to the Sophists came from die-hard conservatives who feared change of any sort, lest it topple them from their privileged stations. These men and women had their counterparts: out-and-out opportunists who were only too happy to pay a clever and worldly 'practitioner of wisdom' to supply them with justification and excuse for doing what they wanted to do. Both sides of the controversy, however, also numbered in their ranks persons who were impressive in both mind and spirit. We think immediately of Socrates, who gave his life to stem the tide of an outlook he thought precluded worthful living, and of Plato, who turned aside from a political career to take up the preliminary task of shoring up the confidences without which politics could not have had much future. These two men come to mind at once, but they too had their opposite numbers: thoughtful men and women whom the Sophists' arguments had basically convinced. If theoretical judgments are invalid, can one then act practically? Epicurus and the Cynics thought not. So they introduced the notion of *epoché*, which meant restraining, holding back, keeping down, deciding neither theoretically nor practically, concluding nothing and doing nothing. On this austere foundation they positioned themselves toward life in stoic resignation. As it was impossible to live effectively in the world, the alternative was to withdraw from it either physically, by going off to the desert like hermits to come, or emotionally, by cultivating *apátheia,* immunity to feelings generally, these being on balance painful.

The line of thought which Socrates and Plato invoked to counter the Sophist tide involved three steps: (a) knowledge is possible, (b) at best knowledge is of universals, (c) these universals are objectively real; they exist in their own right.

A. Knowledge is possible. The Sophists held two things: that knowledge is a chimera and that they could teach *areté* (effectiveness) in oratory, politics, or whatever their clients wished to perfect. By this latter claim they drew their livelihood. Socrates pointed out that these two claims are incompatible. If you want to become good at something you must know what that "thing" is about. To become a good shoemaker, for example, presupposes knowing what a shoe is and for what it is intended. If one had no idea what one was setting out to produce or the function it was to serve, how could one decide which materials to use or how to fashion them? Every effective shoemaker will know his intended product and the use to which it will be put. Generally speaking, the same holds for statesmen or generals. Thus knowledge is the *sine qua non of areté,* or in Socrates' compact dictum, "Knowledge is *areté* ." Both or none. Either the Sophists should stop claiming to be able to impart *areté* and resign the fees deriving from this claim, or they should stop preaching skepticism.

B. Knowledge is of universals. Having established to his satisfaction that knowledge is possible and indeed invoked constantly, Socrates proceeded to propose a method for improving our hold on it. Aristotle tells us that Socrates can justly claim credit for two things, inductive argument and general definition. Suppose we want to know what virtue is. The first step is to collect instances to which the word is applicable. Socrates' associates were willing to let the matter rest there, but Socrates himself insisted on pushing forward. "I only asked you for one thing, virtue," he objects in one of his dialogues, "but you have given me a whole swarm of virtues." If there are many and various examples of the thing we are trying to know, they must share some common quality, otherwise a single word could not attach to them all. From the swarm of virtues, virtue itself must be extracted. The procedure for extraction is to separate from the collected examples of virtue the properties of time and circumstance which belong to individual instances but are incidental to their being cited as examples of virtue. In this way the mind is "led on," as the Greek word for induction implies, from an assemblage of individual instances to a comprehension of their shared characteristics. Thus, a general definition emerges.

C. Universals are objectively real. Socrates rested his case with the above, but Plato, passionately concerned to defend the reality of scientific knowledge as well as moral certitude, picked up on a possible objection. Since we never encounter, say, justice in the abstract but only concrete instances of it, no two of which are exactly alike and none of which exemplifies the paradigm fully, what reason is there to think that the genuine article exists in itself? Less important than Plato's arguments on this point are his conclusions. The Socratic universals had contained both immanent and transcendent features, but Plato was the first to distinguish the two clearly and to opt emphatically for the latter. The objects of knowledge—Forms in Plato's terminology—are not just concepts in the mind. They exist in their own right. Taken together they constitute a complete world which includes a Form for every universal there is: every genus, species, element, ethical value, existent whatever. As an inclusive world, the world of Forms is also a perfect world by virtue of two related facts: individually, each Form is the perfect prototype of its kind; collectively, the Forms are arranged in perfect harmony by the reigning Form of the Good. To use the Greek word that pulls together notions of order, fitness, and beauty, it is a perfect *kósmos.* The phenomenal world in which we live imitates the Forms as best it can, and whatever reality we may attribute to it is due to its sharing, to a limited extent, in the reality of the transcendent pattern-world. To repeat, the Forms are not shadowy concepts that depend for their existence on humanity's creation and keeping them in mind. They are the only true reality, of which the sense world and clearest thoughts of people are but pale, unsteady reflections. And they are eternal; exempt from space, time, and matter's mutability. If the entire human race were to revert to barbarism, the Form of justice would not be affected in the least, though it would be even more poorly represented in the world than it is now.

I began our discussion of the Greeks by stating that what distanced them from the given was the *lógos*. All that followed was in preparation for the discussion of this concept. I shall now gloss over the differences individual philosophers, from Heraclitus to the Stoics, attached to the word (for my purposes the fact that it is somewhat protean is in its favor), and use it to designate the decisive outcome of classical reflection. To wit: the ultimate and, in final analysis, only true reality is this *lógos*. It lies behind and beneath the phenomenal world while at the same time interfusing it. It activates and directs the natural world, not fully, to be sure, but insofar as the world's recalcitrance permits. Such creativity and order as the world possesses is the *lógos'* doing. And it is rational in a double sense. It is the *object* of knowing: it is intelligible; our finite minds cannot understand it completely, but whatsoever they can understand is of it, either as experienced within the world or as conceived apart from it. And it is the *subject* of knowing: humanity's reason is a fragment of the *lógos* and resembles it more than does anything else in our mundane realm.

For purposes of this article it is unnecessary to follow any further the central highway of Western thought. When Jewish byways feed into it through Christianity, the latter at once takes on Greek coloration; before the end of the first century Christ was identified as the *Lógos* incarnate. Immense developments, of course, followed, but the foundations had been laid.

IV. The Given in the West

What interests us particularly is the position within these foundations into which the given had been maneuvered. In the sense of the milieu within which the Greeks (like other peoples) first rose to self-consciousness—a melange of matter, sense deliverances, natural drives and passions, prevailing mores—it had crumbled. But finding it impossible to live without compass points or mooring of some sort, the Greeks reconstituted the given on another shore. Or if one prefers a different image, they discovered a revised version deeper in the core of being. To them this second realm was just as much 'given' as the first had been; indeed more so, for it was less human-made and less alterable. But the two 'givens' are obviously very different; therefore, to distinguish them I shall spell the Given as *lógos* with a capital G.

A favorite way by which the Greeks themselves drew the given/Given distinction was to ask. "What is phūsei (natural in humanity) and what is *nómō* or *thései* (imposed by human beings on their natural endowment)?" And just as in the days of the cosmological myth, it was to the given that persons looked for norms, so too now, with the new Given, the *thései.* Each thing, Aristotle tells us, has its Given form which is also its teleological goal, its final cause. Its *summum bonum* is to actualize this form as fully as possible. In the Stoic versions, the human soul is a fragment or effuence of the *Lógos.* It follows that the *Lógos* is also the law of humanity's own *phūsei.* As long as one acts in accordance with one's own true nature, one complies with the Given and finds perfect freedom in its service. It is when one is false to one's Given nature that one becomes a rebel against the kingdom of God and finds oneself dragged behind the chariot wheels.

All civilizations have given/Given distinctions of some sort. The *tao* that can be spoken is not the true *Tao,* and the *dharma* our dissolute *Kali Yuga* manifests is less than a quarter of the *Dharma* in its full virility. Our task, however, is not to pursue the parallel, but rather to see precisely as we can how the specific form of the Given at which the Greeks arrived differs from its Asian counterparts.

What strikes us first is its greater remove from natural, the ordinary, the given in lower case.[8] Two concrete comparisons will help to point this up.

Barring the Incarnation, no account of truth's epiphany has played more on Western imagination than Plato's allegory of the cave. The relevant points here are, first, that to reach the truth the philosopher must not just change his or her course but make a complete about-face and get completely out of his or her normal abode. Second, when he or she returns and tries to interest his or her compatriots in the Forms that have dazzled him or her, they find these reports so threateningly foreign that they will kill the bearer. In so saying Plato, of course, was not being paranoid, that being exactly what had happened to his own teacher. Israel, too, with her comparable distancing, stoned her prophets. Opposition is the prophet's lot universally, and in Asia too, I suppose, martyrdom for principle is not unknown. It is, however, infrequent to the point that I cannot recall a clear instance until modern times. Principle is not so far removed from practice as to require it.

Our second comparison derives from the *Gītā.* On the eve of battle, Kṛṣṇa is trying to help Arjuna, who is assailed by waves of pacifism, to discern his duty. It is axiomatic that his duty must be in accord with his nature. Plato assumes the same: intellectuals should rule, the courageous should guard and defend, and those of appetitive nature should produce. But how is one's nature to be ascertained? In India the answer is embedded in the given, specifically in the caste to which the individual belongs. The possibility that an individual might be miscast does not occur. Arjuna is a *kṣatriya;* Kṛṣṇa's directive flows from that fact: "Therefore fight, O Bhārata!" With Plato things are not this simple. Children will as a rule inherit their parents' natures and hence social positions, but this cannot be assumed. In the *Gītā*, 'ought' follows from 'is'; Given (what one should do) and given (one's social position) converge. In the *Republic,* this is not necessarily so.

Both India and China hold the Given close. After the rise of self-consciousness they could no longer equate it with the given itself, but they allowed no chasm to develop between the two. Asian peoples never step out of the cosmological myth entirely. Their movements loosen its hold on them; they gain maneuverability within it. But at most, head and arms emerge, leaving trunk, legs and feet embedded. The Given's distinctiveness never grows to become inhuman; nothing foreign or essentially alien to humanity's being creeps into it. *Tat tvam asi,* the exultant discovery that crashes recurrently through the Upaniṣads like a mighty gong-beat—no more momentous words have been spoken than "That thou art." They seal identity. For East Asia, so does Mahāyāna's "All things are intrinsically Buddha-nature." Confucius' Heavenly Mandate is no transcendental substance; it infuses humanity's existence. Likewise the Tao: indefinable in itself, known only by its ways, it is translated at once into manifestations in human attitudes and behavior. Consequences of this determinedly continued kinship are extensive. Differences do not balloon into the head-on, categorical dualisms—form and matter, mind and matter, mind and sense, good and evil, God and humanity—which rip the West. Eschewing such contradictories, Asia keeps differences within the bounds of contraries: muted, complementing, dialectical polarities like *yin/yang, yab/yub, Śiva/Śakti.* Materialism with its literally infinite gulf between humanity's life of feeling and the waste of primary qualities that envelops humanity gets small footing in Asia. As the given is not alien, neither is it anagonist. Promethian defiance, Stoic resignation, Edenic exile, Sisyphian sentence, all bespeak greater distance from the Given than Asia ventured.

Push the Given far enough away and it becomes 'object'; here I am referring primarily to psychological distance, but physical distance provides an accurate and originating analogy, for things must be held more or less at arm's length before they can be recognized as objects in their own right. Haas uses 'object' to designate the far side of the divide that arises with self-consciousness in the West and 'other' for its counterpart in the East. Thus Western civilization *pro*-jects from its subject-*object* dichotomy while Asian civilizations remain relatively impacted in subject-other polarity.

The attitude that derives from taking the nonsubject to be at bottom object is, of course, objectivity. It involves, to begin with, a directionality: a mind that faces primarily outward. In alien territory or even in no-man's land one needs to be wary, on one's guard, alert for developments that might need to be parried or put to advantage. Protacted introspection could divert attention from an environment that needs monitoring. To cite objectivity as a decisive hallmark of the Western mind is to say at the outset that in contrast to the East, which focuses on the subject, the West takes greater interest in the opposite side of the division. It does so not only out of the watchfulness and prudence just mentioned but because the object, once recognized, actively invites attention.

Asia's 'other' exists only in relation to the subject and can be gotten at only through these relations. The great ninth-century Saṁkara, central figure in the Vedānta, underscores the absolute reality of *ātman,* the all-pervading Self, but accords only provisional reality to nature; as a consequence, knowledge of the latter, too, must be relative.

The object, by contrast, exists independently, which makes it interesting in its own right. Mind can visit it straightway; no subjective detours are prerequisite. Disinterested thought becomes, therefore, more natural and pertinent in the West. Earlier in speaking of the Ionians I found reason to question whether certain of their queries about nature were as disinterested as is usually assumed, but there is no doubt that the West's basically realistic epistemology, which the Judaeo-Christian doctrine of creation helped to buttress, encourages pure, not just applied, knowledge. It also encourages philosophy to develop along lines distinct from theology and psychology, both of which, being soteriological, are subject-preoccupied. In Asia the three never divide. Yet another consequence of the object's independence from the subject is the freedom of movement the subject enjoys in confronting it. Subject-correlated others cannot be shifted without the subject shifting too. Objects can be moved around and viewed from different angles while the subject stays put, or can be left stationary while the subject circumambulates them.

Objectivity originates in the mind's interaction with phenomena of the physical world, these being the object's most conspicuous representatives. Philosophically it draws impetus from the efforts of the pre-Socratics to cognize the universe and their refusal to let questions of humanity's place in it divert attention from the world at large. But once the objective bent gets going it knows no stop. Nothing looks off-limits. So what arose as a natural approach to a limited preserve became generalized into a complete mental attitude. It got built into the idea of rationality itself. The subject withdrew progressively, eventually across the entire board of what the mind has to deal with.

Modern science and the West's penchant for the physical are only the most evident examples of its urge to posit objects everywhere, to confer on everything it encounters the form and existence of external entities. So when it turns from the outer world to inner experience—the object-oriented West always gets around to the human *after* nature, whether the seminal period in question be Greek, Renaissance, or modern—the mind carries its objectivizing propensity with it. Thoughts come to be regarded as mental objects, universals as 'eternal objects,' feelings as data. This does not require that all these objects be physical in character; it is just that wherever the mind moves it casts what it encounters into the mold of objectifiable phenomena. So literature and science—psychology and psychiatry, biography and autobiography, history, drama and the novel—vie with increasing vigor to unveil the variety and intricacies of the human soul. Asia shows little interest in this kind of phenomenology, contenting itself with a limited number of archetypical examples, for the most part ones that bear on moral edification and spiritual training. In the West the disclosures are valued for themselves, for they help fill in the map of existence, which, the West, if it had its way, would unroll at its feet complete. This is the logical goal of the objectifying intellect, the final *desideratum* of its unceasing urge to confront reality as a totality of concrete, preferably picturable, objects.

Reason is deeply implicated in the objective attitude, so much so that it is impossible to say whether it is the object that pulls reason toward objectivity or reason that pushes and shapes the nonsubject into the form and substance of object. Clearly the two work together, as if each were daring the other to top its own latest inchings out onto the limb of objectivity. Intelligence is a generic human capacity spread evenly over civilizations; if Confucius or Kobo Daishi or Ramakrishna were not intelligent then no one is intelligent and the word has no meaning. But intelligence can take many forms. For the basic form it comes to assume in the West I shall reserve the word "reason," and I propose to identify six mental operations which reason lifts from the pool of generalized intelligence for attention, development, and regard.[9]

1. First and foremost, division: intelligence operating analytically to draw distinctions rather than intuitively to pull together, gestalt-wise, at a glance and partly unconsciously, the multiple factors that converge in situations and require response.

2. Clarity. Where distinctions are prized, clarity will be prized also. We are accustomed to the phrase "clear distinctions," but the words are really redundant. When the father of modern philosophy builds his methodology on clear and distinct ideas, the basic conjoint characteristic of Western reason surfaces to full consciousness.

3. Generalization. Reason's distinctions do not move toward indicating the individuality and uniqueness that each event possesses but rather in the opposite direction, toward isolating propensities that members of the same class share in common.

4. Conceptualization. This includes articulation and communicability, for language and conceptual thought proceed together.

5. Implication, entailment, the if-then propensity, the impulse to see if from truth in one area anything follows about truths in adjacent and contiguous areas.

6. Control. This presupposes division, for though the world can be accepted or rejected as a whole, it can be controlled only piecemeal. Although control requires division, division does not in itself call for control. It moves in that direction in the West because it gets implicated with the West's experience of the given as basically antipathetical and hence in need of monitoring. When philosophy conceives the essence of being as *Lógos,* it is already the *Lógos* of domination—commanding, mastering, directing reason, to which humanity and nature are to be subjected.[10]

V. Distancing and the West's Discoveries

I have proposed distancing from the given as the West's defining propensity and at the outset suggested a test for the accuracy of the proposal: Does it account for the West's four distinctive discoveries? I can only quickly register here that it does or helps to. Modern science, the idea of progress, the concept of the individual, and ideology all derive in substantial measure from distancing and the dividing/controlling propensities it awakens.

Regarding modern science, I shall content myself with two quotations. On the extent to which it derives from the division to which numbering gives ultimate, abstract expression, we have Kepler's supposition—natural for a scientist but unconvincing from any other point of view—that "as the ear is made to perceive sound, and the eye to perceive color, so the mind has been formed to understand not all sorts of things but quantities. It perceives any given thing more clearly in proportion as that thing is close to bare quantities as to its origin, but the further a thing recedes from quantities the more darkness and error inhere in it." On the way that science has been fostered by the will to control there is Bertrand Russell's report that "scientific thought is essentially power-thought—the sort of thought, that is to say, whose purpose, conscious or unconscious, is to give power to its possessor."

The extent of the gap between 'Given as ought' *(Lógos* for the Greeks, God's will for the Jews) and 'given as is' makes historical progress necessary from the start in the West. When its unremitting efforts to control begin to bear substantial fruit around the seventeenth century such progress comes to look feasible as well. Visions of heaven on earth become incentives for animating imagination.

On the individual and his or her rights, it seems obvious that the distinguishing of reason would work hand-in-glove with the dawning and accumulating of self-consciousness to drive deeper and deeper the wedge between self and society. I shall not weigh the rewards and liabilities of this division; suffice it to say that on the theoretical front the trend the partnership encourages knows no halt. Individualism proceeds to the point where the integumented self appears to be self-evidently the basic unit of human reality and social contract theories, all highly contrived, are needed to explain how groups exist at all.

Splice individualism to the hope for progress and you get ideology. If the individual *is* the basic unit of social reality individuals can be grouped at will and there is no reason why individuals should not be grouped sensibly; measures to establish more perfect unions are plausible. In Asia, ideology does not appear, since social discontent there is directed on a personal level rather than against forms and institutions. Asian society remains eminently natural in the sense of being grounded in strong instinctive drives. In politics it never seriously questioned the natural extension of the tribal chief, autocratic monarchy, while closer to home China stayed with the family, and India (facing ethnic differences) with clusters of these, or caste. All three institutions stay within natural bounds. The West does not hesitate to disrupt such instinctive groupings; institutions grounded in reason look more promising. So Plato dismantles the family while in politics, beginning with Solon in Greece and the abolition of kingship in Rome, movements are planned and executed with mounting fervor in the name of theories, principles, and basic rights.

I can think of no more instructive reading of Western civilization than with an eye to how, in detail, it conceived and delivered to the world its four stupendous discoveries.

NOTES

1. *In Search of Philosophic Understanding* (New York: Mentor, 1967), p. 274.
2. "Accents of the World's Philosophies," *Philosophy East and West,* 6, no. 1 and 2 (1957); "Valid Materialism," ed. Leroy Rouner, *Philosophy, Religion, and the Coming World Civilization* (The Hague: Martinus Nijhoff, 1966).
3. Rouner, *op. cit.,* pp. 275–287.
4. The central thought elaborated in the next several pages are paralleled to a different end in "Tao Now: An Ecological Testament," Ian Barbour, ed., *Earth Might Be Fair* (Englewood Cliffs, N.J.: Prentice-Hall, 1972).
5. *Destiny of the Mind in East and West* (New York: Macmillan, 1956), p. 64.
6. *Man's Unconquerable Mind* (New York: Columbia University Press, 1954), p. 16.
7. W. K. C. Guthrie, *The Greek Philosophers* (London: Methuen, 1967), pp. 23, 24.
8. Experts now incline to the view that agriculture originated in Southeast Asia rather than the Fertile Crescent: it was the Asian apparently who pioneered this epochal advance in human/nature interaction. Whether this bears as either cause or effect on Asia's continuing closeness to the given is an interesting question but one too speculative to do much with.
9. As I am running out of space and must bring this essay to rapid close, I shall only list these. For fuller characterizations, including how attributes 2–5 derive from reason's first and basic attribute—division—and all six differ in nuance and emphasis, if not more, from intelligence as deployed in East and South Asia, see my "Tao Now," pp. 71–93 in this volume.
10. This is the gist of the fifth chapter of Herbert Marcuse's *Eros and Civilization: A Philosophical Inquiry into Freud* (Boston: Beacon Press, 1955).

The Conceptual Crisis
in the Modern West

Let me indicate at the outset the road I propose to travel. It has four parts. As this conference focuses on the interface between science and religion, I shall begin with my reading of the problem science has created *for* religion—or, more strictly, for us in our religious lives. From there, I shall proceed to spell out the consequences this problem has occasioned. My last two sections will be brief. I shall suggest what would solve the problem that I point to, and end by asking if it is likely that the problem will be solved, or at least ameliorated.

I. The Problem

Something momentous has happened in the modern world, and the following sentence from *The Chronicle of Higher Education* (Jan. 9, 1978) puts its finger on what it is: "If anything characterizes modernity, it is a loss of faith in transcendence, in a reality that encompasses but surpasses our quotidian affairs." As this is the spiritual problem of our time, I want it to sink in, so let me recast it in two ways: in the form of an image and then by way of an anecdote.

First the image. Imagine yourself in a house in North India. You

This essay was originally given as a paper at a conference on Religion and Science in Bombay in 1985. It then appeared in a volume edited by T. D. Singh and Ravi Gomatam, Synthesis of Science and Religion: Critical Essays and Dialogues *(San Francisco and Bombay: The Bhaktivedanta Institute, 1988). The issues raised here are more systematically and extensively pursued in Huston Smith's* Beyond the Post-Modern Mind, *rev. ed. (Wheaton Ill.: Quest Books, 1989).*

are standing before a picture window that commands a spectacular view of the Himalayan Range. What the modern age has done, in effect, is to lower the shade on that window to within two inches of its sill. Angled downwards, all our eyes can now see of the outdoors is the ground on which the house is planted. In our analogy, this ground represents the material world, and let us give credit where credit is richly due: science has shown that material world— nature—to be awesome beyond belief. Still, the ground beneath our house is not Mt. Everest.

The anecdote, which makes the same point, comes from E. F. Schumacher. In his *Guide for the Perplexed* he tells of sight-seeing in Leningrad and being lost. As he was puzzling over his map, an Intourist guide approached him and pointed to where they were. "But these large churches around us," Schumacher protested "they're not on the map." "We don't show churches on our maps," the guide responded. "But that's not so," Schumacher persisted. "The church on that corner is on the map." "Oh, that," said the guide. "That used to be a church. Now it's a museum."

Precisely, Schumacher goes on to say. Most of the things that most of humankind has most believed in did not show on the map of reality his Oxford education gave him. Or if they did—and it's here that his anecdote locks into his point precisely—they appeared as museum pieces: things that people believed in during the childhood of the human race, but which we now know don't exist.

I am addressing the spiritual problem of the modern West, the loss of transcendence, and having tried to concretize the problem by way of an image and an anecdote, I proceed now to an issue it poses. There are now, in the contemporary West, two opposing views as to who we, as human beings, are. On the one hand there is the view preached in our churches and synagogues according to which we are the less who have derived from the More; we are creatures creat- ed by God, who exceeds us incomparably by every standard of worth we possess. Concommitantly, our schools teach that we are the more who have derived from the less: we are organisms that have evolved out of inert matter through the play of a mechanistic principle (natural selection) on chance mutations—from slime we have ascended to intelligence. There is no way to reconcile these opposing etiologies, yet every denizen of the modern West schizophrenically believes parts of both of them. Even those who think they have entirely outgrown theology continue to bathe in its afterglow. They too profess to believe in the sanctity of the individual and their inalienable rights, concepts which the evolutionary account cannot support. The eclipse of transcendence has placed the evolutionary account alongside our fading theological account and has confused us as to who we are. It has produced an identity crisis.

I think you see what I am doing. The central point of my lecture is that science, in the process of showering us with material benefits, has all but erased transcendence from our reality map. Having tried to bring that erasure home by way of an image and an anecdote, and having called attention to the identity crisis it has occasioned, I proceed now to *why* transcendence has been removed from our maps. What is there about science that makes it, in very principle, opposed to transcendence? I propose to address that question by way of an argument which, for the sake of clarity, I shall propositionalize in six points.

1. Science is our sacral mode of knowing. As court of ultimate appeal for what's true, it occupies today, quite isomorphically, the place Revelation enjoyed in the Middle Ages. An intellectual historian has pointed out that already a hundred years ago Westerners had come to believe more in the periodic table of chemical elements than they believed anything in the Bible.

2. The crux of science is the controlled experiment. I am speaking, of course, of modern science. Generic science (which is as old as art and religion) relies on reasoning from careful observations, but what distinguishes modern science is its introduction of the controlled experiment and its reliance on it as decisive. This explains, of course, our confidence in science (point 1 above), for it is through the controlled experiment that science achieves proof—the ability to winnow hypotheses and retire faulty ones.

Now watch this next point, for I see it, in the context of the two preceding points, as the original entry in what I have to say. At least it felt new when it occurred to me recently, for I do not recall having seen it tied explicitly to the two preceding points.

3. We can control only what is inferior to us. I mean intentionally control, for the walls of a prison cell could control my movement without being my superior. And I am also speaking of control across special lines, for within the same species variables enter that can produce exceptions to the rule; the Nazis controlled the German Jews but were not superior to them. By superior and inferior, I mean by every criterion of worth we know, and perhaps some we do not know. Many things (the moon) are greater than we are in size and many are greater in brute power (earthquakes), but neither of the cited examples are superior to us in all respects. Neither, as far as we

know, possess intelligence, or freedom, or compassion. It seems apparent that human beings control the American buffalo more than vice versa—it's that kind of correlation between power and orders of existence that this third point calls attention to.

With these three points lined up, you have probably already extrapolated this fourth:

4. Science can only reveal what is inferior to us. Ask yourself: have you ever in any science course or textbook encountered anything that exceeds us in every positive attribute we know? Carl Sagan's *Cosmos* provides us with a gauge here. Sagan defines the cosmos as everything that was or will be, but does anything superior to the human species ever show in Sagan's cosmos thus defined? The question is rhetorical; the answer is no. Those who resist that answer—who bank on science to the point that they refuse to see that its power derives precisely from the limitations of its method—will try to convert the "no" into "not yet," but the force of the preceding point, point 3, is to show logically, which is to say, forever, why the substitution won't work. Try to imagine for a moment what beings superior to ourselves might be. Disembodied souls? Angels? God? If such beings exist, science—the science that can prove its propositions through controlled experiments—will never bring them to view for the sufficient reason that if they exist, it is they who dance circles around us, not we them. They know more than we do, and will walk into our experiments if they choose to; otherwise not.

This point—the point, to repeat, that science in the tight sense in which it can prove its claims can disclose only what is inferior to us—is important, so to emphasize it, let me recast it in the form of an image. If we liken the scientific method to a flashlight, when we point it downward towards the path we are walking on, say, its beam is clear and bright. Suppose, though, we hear footsteps; someone is approaching us, and wanting to know who it is, we raise the flashlight to horizontal level. This represents turning the scientific method on our fellow human beings. And what happens? A loose connection results. The light flickers, and we can't get a clear image. Psychology and the social sciences generally can tell us *something* about people: how they behave *en masse* and how they function physiologically. The complete person, though—who s/he is as an individual, replete with idiosyncrasies, freedom, and commitments, to say nothing of soul and spirit, if these exist—science cannot reveal. To lock this in with our present point, which is again that science can disclose only what is inferior to us: it is axiomatic in the social sciences that in experiments where subjects have freedom, they must be kept in the dark about the experiment's design; they are made to occupy a tilt relation vis-à-vis the scientist who knows more about what is going on than they do. Finally (to complete our analogy), if we tilt our flashlight skyward—or toward the heavens, as we might say here—its loose connection worsens. The batteries slide to the bottom of the casing and disconnect from the bulb entirely, producing a blackout. This, of course, does not prove that there *are* things in the heavens, but it does argue that *if* there are, science will never disclose them.

The two final points in my argument belong together and follow almost routinely.

5. Because, to recapitulate, we look to science for our clues to what is real and true (point #1), and science can disclose only what is inferior to us (point #3), hence:

6. We are trying to live fulfilled (which in this context translates into superior) lives in an inferior world. Or, if we prefer, complete lives in an incomplete world. With this second wording I smuggle in my suspicion that there are things—beings—in the world that exceed us, but in the present lecture I am not arguing for that suspicion.

II. Consequences

This brings me to the second heading in my lecture's outline: the consequences that have followed from science's eclipse of transcendence. (I *say* science, but we know, of course, that science is not the agent here. It is our epoch's misreading of science that has caused the eclipse.) Social critics point repeatedly to a malaise the West has settled into; alienation, anomie, and nihilism have become recurring refrains as the Age of Reason has given way to the Age of Anxiety, and a wasteland threatens. I myself, though, feel unsure of my capacity to take the spiritual pulse of our times, so I shall defer to the social critics themselves, registering what I take to be representative statements by a social scientist, a humanist, and a natural scientist in turn.

First, a social scientist, Manfred Stanley, who speaks in this passage for Max Weber:

It is by now a Sunday Supplement truism that the modernization of the world is accompanied by a spiritual malaise that has come to be called alienation. At its most fundamental level, the diagnosis of alienation is based on the view that modernization forces upon us a world that, although baptized as real by science, is denuded of all humanly recognizable qualities: beauty and ugliness, love and hate, passion and fulfillment, salvation and damnation. It is not, of course, being claimed that such matters are not part of the existential realities of human life. It is rather that the scientific worldview makes it illegitimate to speak of them as being "objectively" part of the world, forcing us instead to define such evaluation and such emotional experience as "merely subjective" projections of people's inner lives.

The world, once an "enchanted garden," to use Max Weber's memorable phrase, has now become disenchanted, deprived of purpose and direction, bereft—in these senses—of life itself. All that which is allegedly basic to the specifically human status in nature comes to be forced back upon the precincts of the "subjective" which, in turn, is pushed by the modern scientific view ever more into the province of dreams and illusions. ("Beyond Progress," in Robert Bundy [ed.], *Images of the Future* [Buffalo: Prometheus Books, 1976], pp. 115–16).

Next, Hannah Arendt, a humanist, assesses the consequences that have followed the eclipse of transcendence:

What has come to an end is the distinction between the sensual and the supersensual, together with the notion, at least as old as Parmenides, that whatever is not given to the senses... is more real, more truthful, more meaningful than what appears; that it is not just beyond sense perception but above the world of the senses. Meanwhile, in increasingly strident voices, the few defenders of metaphysics have warned us of the danger of nihilism inherent in this development; and although they themselves seldom invoke it, they have an important argument in their favor: it is indeed true that once the suprasensual realm is discarded, its opposite, the world of appearances as understood for so many centuries, is also annihilated. The sensual, as still understood by the positivists, cannot survive the death of the supersensual. No one knew this better than Nietzsche, who, with his poetic and metaphoric description of the assassination of God in *Zarathustra,* has caused so much confusion in these matters. In a significant passage in *The Twilight of Idols,* he clarifies what the word *God* meant in *Zarathustra.* It was merely a

symbol for the suprasensual realm as understood by metaphysics; he now uses instead of God the words *true world* and
says: "We have abolished the true world. What has remained?
The apparent one perhaps? Oh, no! With the true world we
have also abolished the apparent one." (Hannah Arendt,
"Thinking and Moral Consideration," *Social Research* 38
[Autumn 1971]: 420)

The final appraisal of our situation is registered by a Nobel-prize-
winning biologist, Jacques Monod, and it is this appraisal that led me
to title this lecture "The Conceptual Crisis in the Modern West."

No society before ours was ever rent by contradictions so
agonizing. In both primitive and classical cultures the animistic
tradition saw knowledge and values stemming from the same
source. For the first time in history a civilization is trying to
shape itself while clinging desperately to the animistic tradition
to justify its values and at the same time abandoning it as the
source of knowledge.

Just as an initial "choice" in the biological evolution of a
species can be binding upon its entire future, so the choice of
scientific practice, an unconscious choice in the beginning, has
launched the evolution of culture on a one-way path: onto a
track which nineteenth-century scientism saw leading infallibly
upward to an empyrean noon hour for mankind, whereas what
we see opening before us today is an abyss of darkness.
(Chance and Necessity [New York: Vintage Books, 1972],
p. 171)

I see that I have given my entire time to the first two headings of
my lecture—the problem science has occasioned in our spiritual
lives and the consequences it is causing them—but the dispropor-
tion is not serious, for I can compress what I want to say about the
remaining matters into a brief paragraph for each.

III. Solution

The solution to the problem I have dwelt on lies in recognizing
that science concerns itself with a part of reality only, not its whole.
There is no conflict between science and religion when the rightful
domain of each is honored. Science deals with the natural world, reli-

gion with the supernatural, including its relation to the natural world. Science deals with matter and what is visible (at whatever needed degree of amplification); religion deals with spirit and the invisible, while including again the relation of these to the visible. Because religion's primary objects—God, spirit, and the like—are more remote than those of science, it must perforce take into account their relation to the natural world in which we most obviously live. The reverse does not hold, however; science does not need to take into account religion's objects. Therefore the accurate relation between science and religion is between part and whole. To repeat this important point, religion has to include the world with which science deals (not in the detail with which science deals with it, of course), whereas science need not take religion's objects into account. If we could really understand and accept this, we would be more open to potential intimations of—signals from—transcendence than we now are.

IV. Prospects

I cannot of course predict whether we *will* align science and religion in this improved way, giving religion more autonomy than the last four centuries have allowed it to explore existential realities concerning which science has no say. I do, though, sense one encouraging sign. We are, I think, coming to see that science doesn't speak for the whole of reality. The distinction between science and scientism is finally getting through.

Western Philosophy
as a Great Religion

In a striking paper titled *"Philosophia* as One of the Religious Traditions of Mankind," in J. C. Gaely (ed.) *Differences Valeurs et Hierarchy,* Wilfred Cantwell Smith argues that the Greek legacy in Western civilization deserves to be ranked as one of the world's great religions. We couldn't recognize this earlier, he says, because our notion of religion was too tightly tied to Judaism and Christianity. A century of work in comparative religion has now loosened this parochial mooring; it has enabled us to bring the entire human heritage into view, lining up its components in our mind's eye, arraying them side by side, and according reasonable justice to each. This, in turn, has given us a better understanding of what a religious tradition looks like—what it is that makes it such. Among other advantages, this new understanding doubles back to "proffer a substantial reinterpretation of Western data," including the realization that

> it is legitimate and helpful to consider... the Greek tradition in Western civilization, rationalist-idealist-humanist, within the generic context of various [other] religious traditions of mankind. It is neither absurd, nor trite, to reinterpret it as one of our planet's major religious traditions: different, of course, from each of the others yet comparable, and understood most truly when so contrasted and compared.

Like so many of Professor Smith's insights, I find this one exciting, although I propose to develop it differently from the way he pro-

This essay originally appeared in A. M. Olson and L. S. Rouner (eds.), Transcendence and the Sacred *(Notre Dame, Ind., and London: University of Notre Dame Press, 1981, pp. 19–39.)*

jected in his paper. First let me say why I think a fresh look at our Western philosophical heritage is in order.

Worldviews are shaped by their sponsoring epistemologies, which in turn are shaped by the motivations that prompt these epistemologies. We naturally want to know the kinds of things that will carry us to where we want to go.[1] Modern science has hit on an epistemology—roughly, the scientific method—that has enormously augmented our capacity to control the physical world. In catering to this particular human impulse—our will to power—with an effectiveness which epistemologies that service other human needs have not been able to equal, the scientific method has, in effect, carried the day. Tailored as much to the scientific method as common sense will allow—occasionally, as in behaviorism and positivism, somewhat more than common sense allows—modern epistemology is essentially promethean: X counts as knowledge if it holds promise of facilitating control. Like the scientific method which is its model, this epistemology is limited. It follows that the conception of the world that it sponsors is proportionately limited, for the view that appears through a restricted viewfinder is necessarily a restricted view.

This, *in nuce,* is my reason for unrolling again the scroll of our philosophical past: driven by the universal dream of knowing the way things are, I do not like settling for a partial ontology. This unrolling is my main object in the essay; but because it runs counter to the current institutionalized assumption that we have advanced philosophically more than we have wandered down a blind alley, I shall devote the first section of my essay to deepening the argument that I capsuled in the preceding paragraph.

I.

World views derive from epistemologies, which in turn derive from motivations. That the driving motivation of modern science is to control is, I take it, too obvious to need documenting. The epistemology that has fashioned our modern outlook derives from this same animus: we wove its net with the hope that the kind of knowledge it would lift from the sea of being would be the kind that would augment our effectiveness in dealing with life as a whole, *effectiveness* being defined here in its problem-solving sense. I shall limit myself to a single witness for each of the two remaining links in my propaedeutic chain: Ernest Gellner for epistemology, and Hannah Arendt for its consequent ontology or worldview.

I choose Gellner for epistemology because, being a sociologist as well as a philosopher, his perceptions carry more than private weight. I am not saying, of course, that he is infallible or even necessarily right—only that, as a philosopher-sociologist who trains his sociological equipment on philosophy as a discipline, his findings lay claim to more than private standing. Gellner focuses on the way Western philosophers have come to see things rather than on the way he himself sees them.

What is this way? Gellner admits that at first glance there seems to be no "way" in the singular; what greets us is, to use the title of the opening section of his *Legitimation of Belief,* "The Pluralist Chorus." But beneath this surface variety—even cacophony—a trend can be discerned. Most generally, it is the trend toward acceptance of epistemology as contemporary philosophy's focal task; more specifically, it is an "emerging consensus" that, to be recognized as legitimate, beliefs must now pass two tests, or "insistences" as he calls them. "There is the empiricist insistence that faiths... must stand ready to be judged by... something reasonably close to the ordinary notion of 'experience'.... Secondly, there is the 'mechanistic' insistence on impersonal... explanations."[2]

Gellner proceeds to ground these two insistences in the prometheanism I have charged with calling the tune for modern Western epistemology:

> We have of course no guarantee that the world must be such as to be amenable to such explanations; we can only show that *we* are constrained to think so. It was Kant's merit to see that this compulsion is in us, not in things. it was Weber's to see that it is historically a specific kind of mind, not human mind as such, which is subject to this compulsion. What it amounts to is in the end simple: if there is to be effective knowledge or explanation *at all,* it must have this form, for any other kind of 'explanation'... is *ipso facto* powerless.[3]

"We have become habituated to and dependent on effective knowledge, and hence have bound ourselves to this kind of genuine explanation," Gellner continues. The view of the world it produces is inevitable—I am speaking now for myself, to make the transition from Gellner to Arendt, from epistemology to ontology. Empiricism and mechanism being ill-suited to deal with transcendence and the unseen, the epistemology of prometheanism necessarily delivers a naturalistic world. "What has come to an end," Hannah Arendt wrote toward the close of her life, "is the... distinction between the sensual and the supersensual, together with the notion, at least as old as

Parmenides, that whatever is not given to the senses... is more real, more truthful, more meaningful than what appears; that it is not just beyond sense perception but *above* the world of the senses."[4]

That says it: our (promethean) motivation has elicited our (mechanistic-empiricist) epistemology, which in turn has brought forward a naturalistic metaphysics. Now the price of focusing attention on one thing is, of course, inattention to other things: when a botanist peers down his or her microscope at a leaf cell, the leaf as a whole disappears. This simple analogy alone should cause us to have second thoughts about our prevailing naturalism, so obviously is it a product of a partial epistemology. But one of the tolls that has been exacted from us on the road we have traveled is interest in truth for its own sake. Preoccupied with "effective knowledge" (Gellner's term), we have grown forgetful of Being; the self-centeredness that prompts prometheanism in the first place carries right through to the end. If motivations forge epistemologies that forge ontologies, these ontologies in turn forge anthropologies, meaning, by this last word, lives as conditioned by the worlds in which they live.

What is the feel of the life that naturalism has generated? As early as two centuries ago, Gellner points out, Kant saw "the inescapable price of this Faustian purchase of real [*sic*] knowledge. [In delivering] cognitive effectiveness [it] exacts its inherent moral, 'dehumanizing' price.... The price of real knowledge is that our identities, freedom, norms, are no longer underwritten by our vision and comprehension of things. On the contrary we are doomed to suffer from a tension between cognition and identity."[5] A hundred years later, Hannah Arendt continues, Nietzsche deepened Kant's analysis. Picking up on the point we have already cited from her, that the distinction between the sensual and the supersensual has been brought to an end, she proceeds as follows:

> Meanwhile, in increasingly strident voices, the few defenders of metaphysics have warned us of the danger of nihilism inherent in this development; and although they themselves seldom invoke it, they have an important argument in their favor: it is indeed true that once the suprasensual realm is discarded, its opposite, the world of appearances as understood for so many centuries, is also annihilated. The sensual, as still understood by the positivists, cannot survive the death of the supersensual. No one knew this better than Nietzsche who, with his poetic and metaphoric description of the assassination of God in *Zarathustra,* has caused so much confusion in these matters. In a significant passage in *The Twilight of Idols,* he clar-

ifies what the word *God* meant in *Zarathustra*. It was merely a symbol for the suprasensual realm as understood by metaphysics; he now uses instead of *God* the word *true world* and says: "We have abolished the true world. What has remained? The apparent one perhaps? Oh no! With the true world we have also abolished the apparent one."[6]

Kant for the eighteenth century, Nietzsche for the nineteenth—for the twentieth I shall choose a sociologist at my own university, Manfred Stanley:

It is by now a Sunday-supplement commonplace that the social, economic and technological modernization of the world is accompanied by a spiritual malaise that has come to be called *alienation*. At its most fundamental level, the diagnosis of alienation is based on the view that modernization forces upon us a world that, although baptized as real by science, is denuded of all humanly recognizable qualities; beauty and ugliness, love and hate, passion and fulfillment, salvation and damnation. It is not, of course, being claimed that such matters are not part of the existential realities of human life. It is rather that the scientific world view makes it illegitimate to speak of them as being "objectively" part of the world, forcing us instead to define such evaluation and such emotional experiences as "merely subjective" projections of people's inner lives.

The world, once an "enchanted garden," to use Max Weber's memorable phrase, has now become disenchanted, deprived of purpose and direction, bereft—in these senses—of life itself. All that which is allegedly basic to the specifically human status in nature comes to be forced back upon the precincts of the "subjective" which, in turn, is pushed by the modern scientific view ever more into the province of dreams and illusions.[7]

Are we ready, now, to take another look at our philosophical past?

II

Professor Smith keeps the Greek philosophical heritage intact, seeing that heritage-as-a-whole as an alternative to the Western family of religions (Judaism, Christianity, and Islam) and the religions of non-Western civilizations. Using a diagram he does not himself introduce, we might visualize his demarcation of the major historical religious alternatives as follows:

Judaism	Christianity	Islam	Philosophia: The Greek Heritage	Hinduism	Buddhism	The Chinese Religious Complex

I, on the other hand, want to take as my encompassing unit our Western religious tradition as a whole, in which the Greek component figures as one-fourth, the other three-fourths being Judaism, Christianity, and Islam. Moreover, only a fourth of Western philosophy enters the Western religious tradition: its modern half becomes too fastened to modern science to be religiously important, while half of its original, traditional half was likewise more occupied with worldly than with religious concerns.[8] Perhaps the layout on page 211 will convey my overview.

Explanations are at once required.

a. In placing Greek *gnosis* at the pinnacle of Western religion I do not mean that it is superior to Judaism, Christianity, and Islam. I mean only that when these Semitically originated communities came to conceptualize their deepest insights, a grammar for the purpose awaited them. It was, moreover, a grammar so advanced, so carefully tuned to the highest registers of the human spirit, that Christians, Muslims, and Jews alike embraced it. In Chomskian idiom, they found its grammar to be "generic"—we need think only of the equal enthusiasm with which Philo and Maimonides, Dionysius and Thomas Aquinas, Avicenna and ibn 'Arabi assimilated it. The zenith of the Western religious tradition is Greek in the sense that Greece provided its grammar and vocabulary, but the discernments this equipment was used to articulate were present in the Semitic religions from their start.

b. Analytic philosophers often point out that the novelties that have entered philosophy in our century do not token a break with its past: Aristotle, Anselm, Thomas Aquinas, and Duns Scotus, they contend, were analytic philosophers. Fair enough. But analytic philosophy's preponderantly critical attitude toward religion[9] makes me want to enter the same claim for religious philosophy. It too is solidly grounded in our philosophical past, continuing the Great Tradition.

c. Philosophers who are comparativists will see almost at once what I am up to, for it is in Vedantic idiom that my project can be stated most succinctly. This is not surprising, for the project would never have occurred to me had I not encountered India; it is from her that my controlling paradigm is lifted.[10]

I want to consider the Greek inheritance in philosophy as our

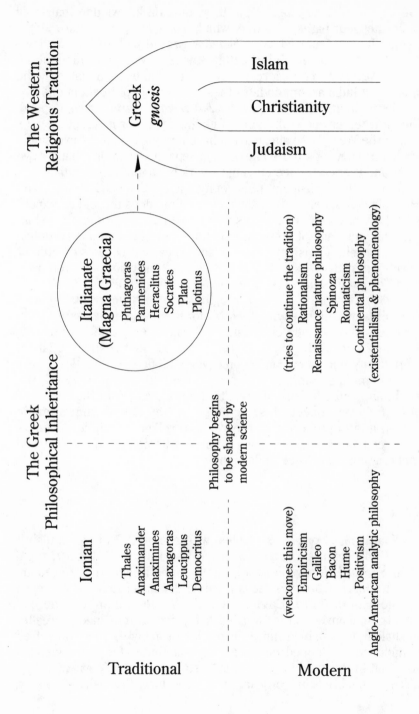

Western version of *Jñāna* yoga. It is common knowledge that India delineates four paths to God, of which *jñāna,* the path of knowledge, is one. Its chief alternative is *bhakti yoga,* the path of love or devotion, for the two remaining paths—those of work and meditation, *karma yoga* and *rāja yoga* respectively—tend to be assimilated by the first two.[11] India accommodates these two great spiritual options in a single tradition, called the *sanātana dharma* or *varṇāśrama,* depending on whether one is thinking of its theoretical or its practical side. But in the West these alternatives have not been partners in a single tradition. They look more like distinct separate traditions that for two thousand years have been trying to work out a modus vivendi.

Athens and Jerusalem, philosophy and religion, the Hebraic and Hellenic components of Western civilization: does the Indian experience have anything to say to us as we continue to work toward a harmonious marriage of these parents that have begotten us? To Indian eyes, Judaism, Christianity, and Islam appear basically as bhaktic or devotional paths which, because they don't provide much room for *jñāna* or *gnosis,* leave the latter housed with the history of philosophy. *Jñāna* visits the Western religions proper, who grant it temporary visas, we might say; but except for the duration of the medieval synthesis it isn't given citizenship.[12] We need only think of Spinoza, Eckhart, and al-Hallaj to be reminded of how restive Judaism, Christianity, and Islam can become when full-fledged gnostics appear in their midsts. Śaṅkara and Nāgārjuna had to contend with the Brahmins and Bhikkus of their traditions too, but in the end they were fully ensconced. Insofar as this essay has a programmatic thrust, it is to propose that the Western religious tradition open its gates comparably to the jnanic strand in its civilization, the strand that originated in Greek philosophy.

III

What is *jñāna* or *gnosis* (spelled with a small "g" to distinguish it from Gnosticism as a specific doctrine) as a religious category?

In *Farewell Happy Fields,* the first volume in her trilogy of memoirs, Kathleen Raine describes in some detail her father's Wesleyan Methodism in Ilford, England. On the verge of manhood he had undergone conversion to "a living faith," which remained thereafter unshaken and enabled him to live a life of many sorrows with deep confidence. He looked for no earthly happiness, for it was clear to him that in this world a human is "a stranger and sojourner." All he asked of his brief time on earth was to perform the tasks life placed before him, for task was precisely what life was—a task to be performed, sure of the reward of the faithful servant in the world to come. Ambition had no place in such a life; it was unimaginable to him, for he did not regard his life as his own but rather his Master's. What his Master willed for his life was that he spend it assisting in the titanic struggle of good against evil. This good was situated in social improvement and service rather than in nature, truth, and beauty. These latter he valued only for their "message," for moral purpose was everything—the question of salvation made it so. This relentless moralism forced a certain narrowness on his life. Still, the fineness of his moral sense infused his conduct with a beauty of its own.

A summarizing paragraph cannot do justice to Dr. Raine's account of this religious universe of her father, but that doesn't matter because it is not that universe itself that concerns us here. I have introduced it only as a foil to bring out what is of moment, namely, his wife's reaction to it. Fortunately Dr. Raine's own account is succinct enough to let her give it directly.

> My mother's evasion, after her marriage, of the religion of John Wesley was not different from her earlier evasion of John Knox; a withdrawal of attention, a failure of interest availed her more than argument and useless opposition. She had, besides, a habit of fainting in church; I never knew her to faint elsewhere, certainly not at the theatre, on the longest walk, or in the hottest greenhouse in Kew. My father I think never knew whether my mother had been "saved" or not; for she always agreed with everything he said. But at over eighty it was the *Upanishads* and the works of A. E. and G. R. S. Mead and even Israel Regardie that my mother would take down from my shelves, or travels in Tibet, or works on spiritualism; never have I seen her read any work of Christian devotion. The supernatural world was for her, as were her vivid nightly dreams, rather an escape from the moral world than, as for my father, a region of it. She confessed to me (she was in her mid-eighties then) that she was not "religious" and had always found the emotionalism of Methodism vulgar; "but I am very interested in the cosmos." Some time before this she had had a slight stroke and thought she was dying. What was it like? I asked her; and my mother's eyes flashed like those of a hawk whose hood is lifted and she said, "I was very interested."[13]

She said she was not religious, but do we believe her? Her disinterest in the kind of religion she saw around her comes through to us (in her daughter's account) categorically, but the account shows something positive at work as well—that to which she was drawn as "religion's" alternative. She was interested, we are told, in the cosmos and in her near-encounter with death. *More* than interested, actually; in these she was "very interested"—the phrase is repeated for both topics. And the question for us becomes: Do we not sense in these interests themselves something religious? Her own protestations to the contrary count for nothing here, of course, since it's precisely the meaning of the word *religion* that is at stake. In part her *religiousness* (in our enlarged definition of the word), discloses itself in the objects that interested her, for death and the cosmos are religious themes in ways that ice cream and horse racing are not. But it is in the *way* those objects drew her that the character of her religious impulse, its jnanic character, is disclosed. In contrasting her mother's interest to her father's, Dr. Raine highlights its form. Her mother's interest was disinterested in a way her father's was not; it was the "disinterested interest" that is the hallmark of jnanic religion.[14] A wife's confession that she was "not 'religious'... but" has brought us to the distinctive feature of jnanic religion or gnosis. It is religion in the presiding mode of pure interest—pure, disinterested interest, to repeat the paradoxical formulation. Hypnotized by the strangeness of a new and unfamiliar beauty, the person is fascinated, engrossed, awestruck, transfixed. The jnanic vision is so totally its own reward that the question "What's in it for me?" doesn't even intrude. In pure cases there is no "me" in the picture at all.

I am not contending that self-transcending vision is the only important thing in religion or even in jnanic religion. Questions of action (what's to be done) and the meaning of one's own individual life inevitably enter and must be dealt with—justice interested the West's paradigmatic *jñāna* yogin, Socrates, only slightly less than did wisdom. I am, though, claiming that important as these other components are, to the *jñāna* yogin they are secondary to the religious object as it transcends finally not only oneself but humanity and the entire created universe. If we cannot recognize a position that fixes on the strange, transhuman beauty of being as it passes in awe-inspiring recessions from the natural world into the infinite; or, if acknowledging that such a position exists we nevertheless refuse to grant it full religious status, I should end my essay here. For if Western philosophy is religious, it is so in the mode I have tried to describe; and if that mode is not authentically religious, Western philosophy is not a great religion.

IV

The preceding section tried to identify the heart of the jnanic position. In this final section I shall argue the religiousness of this position as it appears in the West, primarily in the gnostic strand of Greek-originated philosophy. I have already observed that the bhaktic, devotional character of Judaism, Christianity, and Islam has obscured the fully religious character of this jnanic stance. My strategy toward removing that prejudice will be to enumerate seven properties we tend spontaneously to recognize as religious and show the extent to which our philosophical tradition has housed them. There is space here only to touch on these seven themes which elsewhere I hope to expand, but perhaps their simple enumeration can help us to see why Peter Brown could note toward the beginning of his biography of Augustine of Hippo that "for centuries now, the *idea* of philosophy had been surrounded with a religious aura."[15]

1. *Philosophy's communal nature.*[16] When Whitehead defined religion as what we do with our solitariness, he was voicing at most a half-truth. More obvious is its deep involvement with our social nature; as people associate around the things they prize, their lives get woven together: synagogues, churches, and the Islamic *ummah* (community) take shape. So it was with the schools of ancient Greek philosophy. The Epicureans, Stoics, Academics, Peripatetics, and Neo-Pythagoreans were not philosophical schools in the abstract sense in which we speak of schools of thought today—positivist, idealist, pragmatic, and the like. They were also cultic communities, half ritual and half philosophy—more like colleges in the medieval, monastic sense than in the sense of even our residential colleges today. Like the *ashrams* of India and American communes today, they often sprang up around central founding figures such as Plato, Aristotle, Zeno the Stoic, Epicurus, or, later, Plotinus—individuals who were not just thinkers or professors but who were regarded as inspired. Correlatively, their students were not students in the contemporary academic sense but more like disciples. They congregated around their masters because they wanted actually to live by their doctrines. The Pythagorean communities are the extreme case here, of course. Their students were more like candidates for the priesthood than candidates for a degree at a modern university.

2. *Its cultic features.* These follow in part from the communal features just noted. Mary Douglas contends that communities become such through the conscious or unconscious rituals that knit lives together more powerfully than does conversation. But my interest

here is not in the rituals the Greek philosophers devised or adopted for their own communities. Such rituals existed; we know, to cite a single case, that "Plato's Academy was a religious association with its own divine worship, in which the cultus was of such importance that we find it explicitly laid down that one of its members should be appointed to prepare the sacrifice."[17] But the more important point, I think, is that the philosophers typically participated in the normal rituals of their communities. I see no reason to view this cynically, as if they did so for reasons of prudence or expediency. On the contrary. I take it as evidence that they saw themselves adding their insights to the religion of their people rather than using these insights to oppose that religion. (Their critique of the crass anthropomorphism and immorality of the Homeric pantheon doesn't counter that statement, for that way of imaging the divine was on its last legs for the populace as a whole.) This is not to say that the relations between priests and the philosophers were always harmonious. Being of different spiritual temperaments they at best felt somewhat awkward with one another, while at worst hostility could flame. Socrates is the classic case, having been condemned in part on the charge of teaching atheism. But the other side of that coin is his denial of the charge. I venture the generalization that whereas exoterics *(bhaktis)* often felt threatened by esoterics *(jnanins)*, not fully comprehending what the latter were up to, esoterics (the philosophers) generally saw their spirituality as continuous with that of the people, though of course they did claim to see more deeply into its meaning. The *Republic* opens with Socrates reporting, "I went down yesterday to the Picraeus with Glaucon... that I might offer up my prayers to the goddess [Bendis]," and his last words as recorded in the *Phaedo* were, "Criton, we owe a cock to Ascelepios [the god of healing]; pay it without fail."

3. *Its ultimacy.* In a well-known lecture, John Burnett argues that the core of Socrates' teaching is to be found at *Apology* 29D4 and 30A7ff., where stress is laid on the care of the soul and how to make it as good as possible:

> Men of Athens, I honour and love you; but I shall obey God rather than you, and while I have life and strength I shall never cease from the practice and teaching of philosophy....I believe that no greater good has ever happened in the state than my service to the God. For I do nothing but go about persuading you all... not to take thought for your persons or your properties, but first and chiefly to care about the greatest improvement of the soul.

Quite apart from the word *God* that appears twice in this brief statement, it is impossible to miss its author's conviction of the urgency of his mission. If religion is ultimate concern, we sense it in statements like these by Socrates or we sense it nowhere. The schools of philosophy I referred to several paragraphs back arose during a time of skepticism; the ancestral order had dissolved and men and women were looking for an alternative way to get their bearings. To say that skepticism—rootlessness, rudderlessness— didn't satisfy them is too weak; they found it intolerable and reached for truth as for a lifeline. "To Pythagoras, philosophy was not an engine of curiosity; but a way of life and death."[18] *Our* popular imaginations may picture Epicurus as a man who had good times in beautiful gardens, but his disciples called him *soter*, "savior," for he did one of the greatest things for them that a teacher can do. He freed them from anxiety.

4. *Its involvement of the total self.* Let me lead into this point through an example that may seem trivial but which points to something important. In his treatise "On Cleanliness" Epictetus writes:

By the gods, when the young man feels the first stirrings of philosophy I would rather he came to me with his hair sleek than dishevelled and dirty: for that shows a sort of reflection of the beautiful, and a longing for the comely, and where he imagines these to be, there he spends his effort. *(Discourses* 4.11)

To generalize from the case in question, Epictetus is saying that a candidate's capacity for philosophy does not turn on I.Q. alone. It roots down into regions of the person which, while they will definitely affect the mind's performance—will it be able to grow wise?—are not themselves strictly cognitive.

Few professors today could comfortably open their philosophy courses by saying, "If you hope to acquire not just knowledge but wisdom you must change your lives. You must try to tell the truth. You must cease to live in your skin-encapsulated egos with their petty wishes and try instead to identify yourself with the all-embracing Self. Seek God, pray." If on rare occasion a Western philosopher should now say something like this, it would probably be in a course on ethics or aesthetics, not metaphysics or epistemology. Yet this is the way wisdom philosophers (*jñāna* yogins) used regularly to speak. Socrates argued that if you want to keep your ability to philosophize intact it is better to suffer wrong than to do wrong. Plato taught that by using poetry and music the young should be schooled to approve what is to be approved and condemn what is to be condemned to the end that "when reason comes, he will greet her as a friend with whom his education has made him long familiar" *(Republic* 402A). Aristotle echoed that general point when he said that the young are not ready for ethical reflection, being able to understand no more than the grammar of words. In short, factual knowledge is one thing, wisdom and *gnosis* another. In the broadest sense of the word, the latter require virtue. For to borrow an image from Frithjof Schuon, light does not go through an opaque stone and barely illuminates a black wall. The knower must become like crystal or snow.

5. *Its theophanies*. Standard classifications link revelation to religion and reason to philosophy, but again the question is whether these accepted divisions cut where the joints are. For the jnanic philosophy we are dealing with does not proceed through reason alone. We have just seen that the reason it does employ ties in with deeper-lying components of the self, but the point now is that this reason is also fed by transcendent sources. In the *Meno* Plato tells us that wisdom comes to us somehow "by divine dispensation," and Parmenides clearly presents his theory "as a revelation, accorded to him by the Goddess who governs all things in person."[19] I pass over specifics like these to note three general areas where we catch sight of revelation infusing Greek philosophy.

a. The first of these places is in the mythic base out of which philosophy arose. In *The Presocratics,* Werner Jaeger points out that these thinkers capped the preceding mythic period quite as much as they launched a new beginning—Greek philosophy. And the myths they thus rounded off were held to be of nonhuman origin. It was not in merely human eulogy that Homer was called "the divine poet," for the mythic wisdom of the Greeks, like that of the Vedas, was held to be uncreated—eternal. Unlike the hypotheses of science, which come and go, it could never become obsolete, for it was believed to be not cumulative but a priori. As metaphysicians and poets alike testified, it was derived not from experiment but from inspiration. Plato said it came by *anamneses,* "recollection." It is not human but divine, belonging not to the ego but to the Self which is common to all. Today we might not speak of myths in quite these terms, but if we know our subject at all we recognize that myths are wholly different from fables deliberately fashioned by individuals to amuse or preserve a lesson learned. Myths are never intentionally made nor produced by individual authors. The least we can say is that they arise from the cumulative experience of countless generations and embody instinct and deep communal feeling.

b. If myth is collective revelation, revelations are also given to individuals. In the *Timaeus* 80B, Plato says that to our God-given vision and hearing the muses add harmony to those who can use it "intellectually... to assist the soul's interior revolution, to restore it to order and concord with itself." Etymologically, *revelation* derives from *re-velum,* 'the drawing back of a veil that conceals,' and Plato's Allegory of the Cave is as powerful an account of such disclosure as has ever been written. It is the account of the philosopher who is shown something others do not see and who is changed—and finds the universe changed—by the revelation.

c. Perhaps the most important kind of revelation is that which manifests itself in human form—an incarnation. Christ is the chief instance of this mode, of course, but he has his counterpart in Greek philosophy in the figure of Socrates. Socrates stands to Plato as Christ stands to St. Paul; we have the one through the other. It was Socrates who showed Plato the way. Plato's name barely occurs in his dialogues; for decades he effaced himself to leave the stage to his master. Compared with his fateful encounter with Socrates, everything else Plato encountered was episodic. His entire corpus is the effort to recapture the vision of Socrates and hold it up for others. How is it possible that there could have been a man of this stature? The question reaches its climax in Alcibiades" euology in the *Symposium.* Bernard Loomer once remarked that the euology makes the *Symposium* the New Testament of Greek philosophy, and establishes (almost by itself) the Platonic tradition in Western philosophy as one of the world's great religions.

6. *Its intuitive intellect.* In referring above to *jñāna*'s involvement with the total self, I noted that it links reason to human sensibilities that are not cognitive in the strict sense of that word. It follows that in isolation from these deeper sources, reason is a distinctly limited instrument. In Indian philosophy *manas* is augmented by *buddhi,* which Zimmer translates as "intuitive awareness."[20] In Western philosophy reason is supplemented by intellection.

If we watch carefully we can all sense kinds of knowledge that flow from a source in us that is different from reason. We might call this supplementing faculty *insight,* or *intuition* if we don't read that word in its Bergsonian sense. We can even call it *imagination* if we are clear that in doing so we use the word in a way almost opposite to the way Spinoza used it, siding instead with the romantic poets who elevated imagination into a capacity for apprehending realities that can be reached in no other way. For Shelley imagination was "that imperial faculty," and Blake saw the person of imagination as the person of vision, opposed by the person of reason who sees with the corporeal eye only. We are obviously involved here with the doctrine of the intuitive imagination as the distinct organ of perception in the human soul, the "eye of the soul" as Plato called it. In the full-blown medieval doctrine of *intellectus,* the object that this eye perceives is the transcendent.

What lies behind these various locutions—Hegel's distinction between *Verstand* and *Vernunft* and Spinoza's between science and intuition could be added to them—is the fact that in metaphysical matters insight is decisive. This insight cannot be produced by assembling brute data or initiating chains of formal logic, or any combination of these. For the reigning epistemologies of our time this is a scandal, for it opens the prospect of studies that require a certain level of insight as their prerequisite as well as the possibility of issues that cannot be arbitrated by additional evidence. The most each side can do is appeal to its opponent to deepen his or her powers of insight and nurture the intuitive intellect.

7. *Its ontology.* I have saved till last the ontology of the jnanic tradition in Western philosophy because I consider it decisive. Twice in these pages I have alluded to Tillich's definition of religion as "ultimate concern," but it is obvious that that phrase can be read either psychologically or ontologically. Read psychologically, religion is whatever happens to concern a person most, be it sex, ambition, or whatever. Ontologically approached, on the other hand, religion is involvement with what in fact *is* ultimate, ontologically ultimate. For the Western philosophy I have been examining, this ontological ultimate is radically transcendent, which does not keep it from being fully immanent too for those who have eyes to see. Denotatively, it is Anaximander's "boundless" or "infinite," Plato's "Idea of the Good," Plotinus's "One," and Spinoza's "Deus sive natura." It is the initial link in the Great Chain of Being that proceeds from it.

Having examined this chain at some length in my *Forgotten Truth: The Primordial Tradition,* I shall not detail it further here. I shall remark only that though reason cannot climb its links to any great height, to penetrate beyond reason into what the intuitive intellect alone can discern is the strongest drive of the gnostic's nature.

NOTES

1. "We use our criteria of rational acceptability to build up a theoretical picture of the empirical world. [Indeed] we must have criteria of rational acceptability to even have an empirical world. [As these criteria] reveal... our notion of optimal speculative intelligence... the

Western Philosophy as a Great Religion 221

'real world' depends upon our values" (Hilary Putnam, in chapter six of *Reason, Truth and History* [New York: Cambridge University Press, 1981]).

Kathleen Raine makes the same point in a way that anticipates the argument that I am commencing: "Knowledge, in any culture, is only an agreed area of the known and the knowable; 'let X equal knowledge' is premised and the proofs follow. Every X can of course yield its results. But there is always an excluded knowledge; and as the crude beginnings of science were the excluded knowledge of pre-Renaissance Christendom, so theology and all the wisdom of the spirit is the excluded knowledge of a materialistic society. As R. P. Blackmur (apropos of Eliot and Yeats) wrote in 1957, 'The supernatural is simply not part of our mental furniture.' But reality does not change its nature because we are unaware of it; a fact which the scientists themselves would not deny" ("Premises and Poetry," *Sophia Perennis* 3:2 [Autumn 1977]: 60–61).

2. Ernest Gellner, *Legitimation of Belief* (Cambridge: At the University Press, 1974), p. 206.

3. Ibid., pp. 206–207.

4. Hannah Arendt, "Thinking and Moral Considerations," *Social Research* 38 (Autumn 1971): 420.

5. Gellner, *Legitimation of Belief,* p. 207.

6. Arendt, "Thinking and Moral Considerations," p. 420

7. Manfred Stanley, "Beyond Progress: Three Post-Political Futures," in *Images of the Future,* ed. Robert Bundy (Buffalo: Prometheus Books, 1976), pp. 115–116.

8. If one defines *religion* as "ultimate concern," then of course anything can be religious; what would make it such would be the way a person relates to it. But if one defines the word ontologically rather than psychologically, objectively rather than subjectively; if one attends less to the manifold directions in which people *can* deploy their religiousness than to the kinds of things that typically *have* drawn their religious concern, a different picture emerges. Churches are then assumed to be religious in ways that marketplaces are not; and certain ontologies, due to their transcendent registers, let us say for now, again seem obviously more religious than others. This distinction does not do justice to the force and subtleties in Wilfred Smith's proposal that our philosophical heritage as a whole be viewed as religious; I merely repeat that that is not the way I am viewing it here. While owing much to Professor Smith's suggestion, my enterprise is more conventional. I wish to look at the way the strands in our philosophical heritage that lie close to common-sense notions of religion get woven into the mantle of the Western religious tradition as a whole.

9. J. J. Smart has noted that positivistic arguments that long since have been rejected as invalid in ethics and aesthetics continue to be invoked against religious assertions.

10. In Asia one normally credits one's teachers, so let me again acknowledge my debt to Swami Satprakashananda of the Vedānta Society of St. Louis, now in his nineties, for a decade of near-weekly tutorials.

11. India assumes that every spiritual aspirant will do some meditating, and one can scarcely live without doing some work as well. Whether the yogi turns work to spiritual account by discriminating between the work and the fruits that accrue from it or by offering the work as a "living sacrifice unto the Lord" depends on whether the yogi's temperament is basically jnanic or bhaktic.

12. To see what Western religion would have looked like had it paralleled India's development, we need to picture the Greeks as conquering the Semites in the way their Aryan cousins who pushed on into India conquered the Dravidians. Greek *gnosis* would then have constituted the Upanishadic capstone that would have wrestled with Judaism, Christianity, and Islam in the way the Vedic, Brahmanic, Smarta (followers of the *smritis)* tradition wrestled with India's local, indigenous, sectarian theisms; but in the end it would have been integrated with them. The Athens/Jerusalem tension is not unheard of in India; in my introduction to Frithjof Schuon's *Transcendent Unity of Religions* and my review of that book in the December 1976 *Journal of the American Academy of Religion,* I posit that it is rooted in a fundamental difference in spiritual personality types that is cross-cultural. But in India the two types are gathered in a single tradition; *jñāni* and *bhakti* get woven as warp and woof into a single fabric. This cannot (as yet?) be said of philosophy and religion in the West. "In the West... Athens [and] Jerusalem... have never set well together.... There is something indelibly plural in the very notion of the Western tradition" (Robert N. Bellah, in "Commentary and Proposed Agenda: The Normative Framework for Pluralism in America," *Soundings* 61:3 [Fall 1978]: 363).

13. Kathleen J. Raine, *Farewell Happy Fields* (New York: George Braziller, 1977), p. 73.

14. *Jñāna* is usually defined as knowledge, but as mind is the faculty that can break through our subjectivity and carry us beyond ourselves, the notion of pure or disinterested knowledge is strictly embedded in the jnanic concept. One comes to it very quickly.

15. Peter R. L. Brown, *Augustine of Hippo: A Biography* (Berkeley: University of California Press, 1967), p. 40.

16. I remind the reader that in using the word *philosophy* in this list of

characteristics it is not the whole of Western philosophy that I have in mind. I am speaking of that quadrant of it that is circled in my diagram.

17. Josef Pieper, *Leisure: The Basis of Culture,* trans. Alexander Dru (New York: Pantheon Books, 1952), p. 77.

18. F. M. Cornford, *From Religion to Philosophy* (New York: Harper Torchbook ed., 1957), p. vi.

19. Ibid., p. 214.

20. Heinrich Zimmer, *Philosophies of India,* ed. Joseph Campbell, Bollingen Series 36 (Princeton: Princeton University Press, 1951), p. 403.

PART III

CONSEQUENCES: SOCIAL, EDUCATIONAL, AND ECUMENICAL

The Relevance of the Great Religions for the Modern World

Religion can, of course, be irrelevant and often is. No human endeavor is immaculate, and one that traffics with millions is bound to emerge a mixed bag. In this respect religion is no different from other corporate enterprises—education which quickens and represses, government which orchestrates and restricts. Religion has been revolutionary and conservative, prophetic and priestly, catalytic and incubus. It creates barriers and levels them, raises church budgets and raises the oppressed, makes peace with iniquity and redeems, in part, the world. We acknowledge this mottled record right off for it would be a sad miscarriage of our Conference intent if in the act of assembling religion's delegates it were inadvertently to widen the gulf between them and their critics—between those for whom "religion" is a good word and those for whom it is not. No representatives from the Socialist nations are

---

This essay was originally delivered as the concluding address of the First Spiritual Summit Conference in Calcutta, October 1968. It then appeared as the introduction to Finley P. Dunne, Jr. (ed.), The World Religions Speak *(The Hague: W. Junk, 1970), in which it was dedicated to Thomas Merton, who died in Bangkok a month after his participation in the Calcutta conference. A revised edition appeared in Huston Smith,* Beyond the Post-Modern Mind, *revised edition (Wheaton, Ill.: Quest Books, 1989). Many of the changes made for* Beyond the Post-Modern Mind *have been incorporated into this version of the essay. Huston Smith noted in* Beyond the Post-Modern Mind *that "With the collapse of confidence in what might transcend the human, attention has gravitated in recent centuries toward the human aggregate." Nonetheless, Smith felt it important to make the point that "the importance of politics is not diminished by recognizing that it is not all-important." (184)*

here. In view of their Marxist premise that religion is opiate this is not surprising, but it is none the less a lack. So to this absent third of the world we say: whereas the ecumenical movement's first phase sounded the potential unity among Christendom and its second phase is exploring the unity latent in religions, we look to a third phase that will seek the unity latent in humankind, the unity underlying the ideologies that divide it into secularist, socialist, religious, or by "isms" whatever.

I

Religious relevance takes different forms according to the period in question. I propose to distinguish three great ages through which humanity has passed with an eye to what religious relevance has meant in each.

1. The first age, by far the longest, was the archaic. It lasted, roughly, up to the first millennium B.C. In this Archaic Period, during which humans were rousing out of their animal innocence, their chief spiritual problem was time. Lower animals are oblivious of time, for they possess neither foresight nor hindsight, neither anticipation nor memory. When human beings first acquired these time-binding faculties they found the implications terrifying: the future, they discovered, was contingent, and the past impermanent. Their recourse was to blink these terrors; insofar as possible simply to turn their back on them and deny their existence by attending to their opposite. This opposite—Great Time—was in fact timeless. It consisted of momentous originating acts which their myths told them had brought order out of chaos and established the patterns for meaningful activity: creation of the world itself, the first planting, the first mating, each act accomplished by the gods in epic proportions. For archaic peoples being *was* these timeless, paradigmatic acts which were significant, secure, and impervious to time's decay. Their religion consisted of replicating these acts through rites that were myth-ordained and myth-prescribed. Through these rites they fused their lives with Being, merging them with the meaningful and the real.

Note how little ethics entered into this first originating phase of religion. The reason is that at this stage ethics did not pose much of a problem, little more than it does for subhuman animals. People were living for the most part in small groups, in tribes or tiny villages wherein everyone knew everyone else and cooperated pretty much as do members of a normal family.

2. Following the terminology of Karl Jaspers, I shall call the second period the Axial Age, for during it human history took a marked turn, a giant swing on its axis so to speak. This is the period that witnessed the rise of the geniuses the world still honors: the great prophets of Israel, Zarathustra in Persia, Buddha and the Upanishadic seers in India, Lao Tzu and Confucius in China. This burst of religious creativity across the full arc of the civilized world, an extraordinary proliferation of prophetic genius diffused in space but condensed in time and amounting to nothing short of a mass religious mutation—this remarkable phenomenon has often been described but never satisfactorily explained. I submit that it was at root the spirit's response to a marked change in the human condition, a crisis in history's development.

By the first millennium B.C. or shortly before, agricultural improvement had advanced population and settled existence to the point where people were dealing regularly with persons outside their primary group. As a consequence, familial feelings no longer sufficed to keep society intact. Perceptive souls—we call them prophets, seers, rishis, sages, magi—saw this and summoned religion to emerge from its archaic phase to help meet the problem.

Rites and rituals are no longer enough, they said in effect.[1] You must watch how you behave toward others, for human discord can reduce life to shambles. Interpersonal relations are not the sum of religion, but religion stops in its tracks if it tries to skirt them. *Yogas* (spiritual techniques) must be prefaced by *yamas* (moral precepts), *dhyana* (meditation) and *prajna* (wisdom) by *sila* (ethical observances). "If you are offering your gift at the altar, and there remember that your brother has something against you, leave your gift there before the altar and go; first be reconciled to your brother, and then come and offer your gift" (Matthew 5:23–24). For "he who does not love his brother whom he has seen, cannot love God whom he has not seen" (I John 4:20).

Hence the Golden Rules of the great religions which we have reaffirmed this week: Christianity's "Do unto others..."; Judaism's "What doth the Lord require of thee but to do justice, love mercy..."; Jainism's *ahimsa* and *aparigraha;* Buddhism's *metta* and *karuna,* its "boundless heart toward all beings"; Hinduism's "highest [yogin] who judges pleasure or pain everywhere by the same standard as he applies to himself" (Gita, VI, 32); Islam's man who "gives his wealth... to kinsfolk and to orphans and to the needy and to the wayfarer... who sets slaves free... and payeth the poor due"; Sikhism's "humility to serve"; Confucius' human-hearted *jen.* These counsels to concern for the well-being of others have been the glory of the religions during their axial periods. They account for a good half of the resonance across credal lines that has characterized this Conference, for in the altruism of their ethics the great religions are much alike.

3. This brings us to the third great period in human history. I shall call it simply the Modern Age and mark it as having been inaugurated by the rise of modern science in the Seventeenth Century and the Enlightenment in the eighteenth. The Modern Age differs from its predecessors in seeing social structures as malleable. In previous ages, institutions—family systems, caste and class, feudalism, kingship, chief and emperor—were regarded in much the way we regard the laws of nature; they were ingrained in the nature of things. Now they are recognized as contingent, and by the same token fallible. The corollary is immense. For if society *can* be changed, it often *should* be changed, in which case its members are responsible for seeing to it that it is changed.

Obviously this new perspective enlarges the scope of ethics enormously. Whereas religion's ethical dimension was minimal in the Archaic Period and personal in the Axial Period, today it has become both personal and social, both individual and collective. For to repeat: if social structures can be good or evil and are subject to human volition, people are responsible for their quality.

II.

Against the backdrop of these three stages of human history the question of religious relevance becomes more manageable. What makes religion relevant depends on the age in question. Archaic religion was relevant without containing much in the way of ethics at all, for ethics was not then a pressing problem. But if religion had idled ethically in the Axial Period when ethics had become a problem, it would have lost step with relevance and disappeared.

Similarly today, social ethics having emerged as a new human responsibility, if religion defaults on this responsibility it will lose the relevance it has thus far enjoyed. Personal kindness is no longer enough. Institutions affect human well-being no less than do interpersonal relations. This being so, enlightened compassion calls for social responsibility as much as for face-to-face good will.

Item: It is now an established fact that if a child does not get a certain minimum of protein before the age of six he or she will be mentally deficient for the rest of life. Our Conference is meeting in a city in which 100,000 inhabitants have no homes but the streets, where gutters serve as bathrooms and sidewalk corners are at once bedrooms for human beings and stables for beasts. Here in this Calcutta where "Above the packed and pestilent town/Death looks down" no amount of personal kindness is going to insure that all children will receive the protein they need if for no other reason than that most of the persons who are in a position to see to it that they do live geographically removed. Direct, face-to-face kindness (the "cup of water given in my name") won't solve the problem, but indirect, organized institutional kindness (UNICEF, or Save the Children Federation, or more equitable trade agreements) might.

Item: It took all of human history up to the middle of this century to develop an economy—that of the United States—capable of growing at the rate of 2½% per annum. Such a growth rate, if sustained, would enable children to be roughly twice as wealthy as their parents. Less than twenty years separate us from 1950 and already two economies (the West German and the Japanese) are pushing 10% per annum growth. If economies sustain this order of growth, children stand to be roughly six times richer than their parents and thirty-six times richer than their grandparents. These figures point up the fact that after capital accumulation reaches take-off momentum it increases exponentially. This places nations that take off early at an enormous advantage; they leave other nations not just behind but increasingly behind. The gap between them and less developed nations widens. The consequence is that if events proceed on present course, the world is going to become in the remainder of our century even more unbalanced in wealth and power than it is already. As the population explosion is centering in the "have not" nations, the "have" nations will represent a decreasing proportion of the world's population while possessing an increasing proportion of the world's wealth and power. Pointing as this does towards a world composed of islands of affluence off a mainland of misery, the situation is neither just nor healthy.

Item: Ten years ago it came clearly to view that for the first time in human history enough metabolic and mechanical energy is available to provide high standards of living for everyone in North America almost immediately and everyone in the world within forty years despite the population explosion. All that stands between us and such universal affluence is invention of the social institutions needed to effect the requisite distribution.

In a way nothing is new here for human well-being has always been affected by its social matrix. The novelty is that, brought to the realization that social institutions are to an appreciable extent humanly contrived. We now acknowledge our partial responsibility for them. We have reached the point in history where we see that to be indifferent to social institutions is to be indifferent to human life.

Not that religion should be converted into social action. Religion must be socially responsible without equating itself with such responsibility. Moreover, it should engage society in a specific way. These qualifications are subtle, but they are important—sufficiently so as to occupy us for the balance of this statement.

III

Let me recast in slightly different terms the three dimensions of religion which historically have appeared successively. Archaic Religion did not focus on humanity, individually or collectively, at all. It looked beyond the human, to divine metaphysical realities from which humanity derived and in which it remained grounded. Religion anchored the current generation in those timeless realities through rituals which (as was noted) linked finite, ephemeral human acts to heroic paradigms that gave them enduring substance and meaning. It was as if its rituals and their attendant myths plugged human doings into timeless templates that charged them with significance and exempted them from time's decay. In subsequent ages, religion articulated this eternal tie explicitly; it spoke (and continues to speak) of immortality, and of anchoring life in the divine presence and the Eternal Now. The move, though, is the same. It counters time's vicissitudes by binding us to the eternal.

Axial Religion added interpersonal concerns to religion's original Archaic agenda, and nurtured conscience, compassion, self-knowledge, and forgiveness. In adding social responsibility to these two preceding agendas, Modern Religion effects a third extension. But it must be an extension, not a replacement—everything turns on this difference. If in the Axial Period religion had relinquished its eternal concerns when it picked up on love of neighbor, it would have cashed in religion for ethics. It did not, of course, do this; statements like "We love, because he first loved us" (I John 4:19) and "It is not for the love of creatures that creatures are dear, but for the love of the Soul in creatures that creatures are dear" (Bhidad-Aranyaka Upanishad, II, 4) make clear that the ethics of Axial Religion was in direct touch with its religious source. Whether the social thrust of Modern Religion is genuinely religious or only seemingly so, being in actuality indistinguishable from secular social action, depends on whether it represents an extension of religion's prior, transcendent-and-interpersonal concerns—love of God and love of neighbor, respectively—or has cut these lifelines.

Tracing our steps backwards through these three concerns, religion would no longer be religion if it attended only to society, for to do so would contradict its conception of the human self. A perfect society (if that notion makes sense) would not produce perfect selves, for the sufficient reason that human worth cannot be bestowed: it must be achieved, because our inner, self-creating, volitional pole is too much a part of our nature to allow us to be manipulated: we are not automata. Given our vulnerability, external circumstances can crush us, which is why organized religions must do what they can to prevent this from happening; but the opposite does not pertain. Circumstances, however well contrived, cannot fulfill us because (to repeat) fulfillment cannot be conferred. By providing food, controlling temperature, and introducing anodynes if need be, comfort can be bestowed, but not nobility, or even happiness; these must be won individually. Being aware of this fact, religion can never rest its case with doing things for other people. Working on oneself—the cleansing of the inward parts—is always part of its agenda. (We have the dictum that it is never possible to do as much for others as one can do for oneself, namely save one's own soul. The Zen version is earthier: everyone must perform one's own toilet.) Neither the agents of social action nor its beneficiaries are exempt from this stricture.

This is the point of Whitehead's definition of religion as what one does with one's own solitariness, and why Kierkegaard gave such attention to human subjectivity. Because this inner, Archimedean point provides the springboard for both of religion's subsequent extensions—into Axial Religion's interpersonal *karuna* (compassion) and *caritas* as defined by St. Paul in First Corinthians 13, and into Modern Religion's further extension into social ethics—we can turn to this springboard directly. Thus far I have described it as focused on time and eternity, but other issues get drawn in; they are elusive, but terribly real. In earlier times we could (in the West) have named the transcendent or eternal focus of religion which we encounter in the depths of our own inwardness "God," but in our century the contours of that word have blurred, beyond which stands the complicating fact that it has no exact equivalent in Afro-Asian faiths. Archaic, eternal religion is obsessed with "why" questions, beginning with why something exists rather than nothing. It deals with the individual's stance toward the world, whether s/he feels at home in it or alienated from it—the ways s/he belongs to it and does not belong to it but is separate from and stands over against it, pointing thereby to an ultimate beyond it. Eternal religion grapples with the failure that in one form or another visits everyone—how we can live with ourselves and feel acceptable when in so many ways we know that we are not. Its root concern is (as I have said) in some way with time: how everything can matter, as we feel in some sense it does, when in the long run it would appear that nothing matters. Running throughout is the question of meaning; how life can be meaningful when so much of it reads like an idiot's tale. Eternal religion knows that there are no discursive answers to these questions. It ranges time and space for insight—*prajna,* vision, a revelation which, by-passing words, will disclose directly why we exist and why the world is the way it is, in much the same way that loving explains why we are male and female.

IV

Even Marxists now concede that "faith for the Christian (and by implications for Buddhists, Hindus, and the rest) can be a stimulus for social commitment,"[2] a marked qualification of their original perception of religion as the opiate of the people. It would be pleasant to think that religion's transcendent and interpersonal dimensions protect it against the special dangers to which social programs are heir—fanaticism, projection, means-ends casuistry, and discouragement—but nothing turns on this. With such safeguards or without them, religion must now address the world.

Its social efforts differ from those of secularists primarily in their interpersonal, transcendent roots, but there is another difference: religion's guiding social goal must be general. Images of a new heaven and a new earth, of lions lying down with lambs, of messiahs and *maitreyas* and swords beaten into plowshares are vague, but in this case savingly vague. For sharpened much further they become ideologies. Ideologies have their uses, but sooner or later all are surprised by history. One or another may merit qualified support at a given moment, but to become tied to any would be to lose the freedom and flexibility religion needs if its social voice is to be timelessly contemporary. Probably no social goal more specific than that every human being—child of God in theistic idiom—have an equal change at life's opportunities deserves unqualified religious endorsement.

Though I have argued that religion must now include all three of the components enumerated, it would be foolish to contend that everyone should attend to them equally. People are irreducibly different; in religion this makes for priests and prophets, for hermits and householders. It is even appropriate that there be sects that highlight the components differently, as did Confucianism, Taoism, and Buddhism in traditional China. But in a tradition or culture as a whole the three should be reasonably balanced.

V

I have argued two theses: to remain relevant, religion must become socially involved; to remain religious, such involvement must retain ties with religion's earlier concerns. It happens that with respect to these theses, East and West have, today, complementing strengths and weaknesses. When in May, 1968, the "Ceylon Daily News" quoted the eminent Buddhist authority Dr. Walpola Rahula as asserting that development of a sustaining economy for all of the people is as much a religious duty as any other, and that "cultivating a farm properly is better than building many temples," it showed that Asian religions are not unmindful of the need to involve themselves deeply in their adherents' struggle to pull themselves out of the straightjacket of hunger, underemployment, and indebtedness. Throughout Asia swamis, monks, and lay people are changing the image of Hinduism and Buddhism. Religious leaders of many stripes write tracts on problems of modernization, encouraging lay people and fellow leaders alike to participate in economic and social development. In much of Asia we seem to be witnessing something like a Protestant Reformation in its Weberian sense. If Max Weber were living today, he would have to revise his judgment of the Asian religions; he would find "worldly asceticism" beginning to operate in them too to break barriers to economic, social, and political modernization. But the qualifying phrase "beginning to operate" is important. By virtue of their strong prophetic heritage and even more because industrialization has shown them how much society *can* be changed, Western religions can still help Afro-Asian faiths to see the necessity of social participation. Meanwhile Asian religions can alert those of the West to the danger that threatens *them*, the danger of focusing exclusively on society, neglecting religion's interpersonal, transcendent roots, and becoming in consequence unrelievedly secular. In "Up to Our Steeple in Politics," two ministers chide their fellow Christians for swallowing the prevailing American assumption that "the political order... is the *only* source and authority to which we can and ought to repair for relief from what ails us.... Politics has become *the* end. We have been gulled into believing that whatever ails us... can be cured exclusively by political and social nostrums."[3]

"If there be East and West/It is not wisdom," sang that delightful Tibetan saint Milarepa. In view of what East has to learn from West today about religious *relevance,* and West from East about *religious* relevance, his words acquire new meaning.

Historical Update

In the two decades since this essay was written, the fate of our planet has emerged as yet another human responsibility, its newest frontier. Consequently, the picture that was sketched above should now be emended to read as follows: Religion began in the individual's direct relationship with the transhistorical and ultimate—God by whatsoever name. From this inviolate starting point and continuing center, it has proceeded to shoulder, successively, concern for interpersonal relations and society's institutions and structures. To live up to its calling, it must now add to these agendas, concern for other species and life's sustaining environment.

NOTES

1. "I hate, I despise your feasts, and I take no delight in your solemn assemblies" (Amos 5:21). *"Lower...* knowledge (is) of... ceremonials" (Mandaka Upanishad; italics added).
2. Heinz Kloppenburg in: "The Civilization of the Dialogue," an Occasional Paper published by the Center for the Study of Democratic Institutions, Santa Barbara, California, p. 21.
3. Will D. Campbell & James Y. Holloway, *Christianity and Crisis,* XXIX, 3 (March 3, 1969), p. 36.

Another World to Live in, or How I Teach the Introductory Course

All of us who heard Ninian Smart's lecture on this topic last week sensed, I am sure, that his is an eminently viable way to teach the Introductory Course. At the same time it provides me with an ideal foil, for our two apologias, juxtaposed, highlight how differently the course can be approached. Smart wants to apprize students of religion's power—it's truth is a secondary issue. He wants his students to see that it is impossible to understand social movements and history generally if religion is left out of account. I naturally agree,[1] but my priority is the opposite—for me religion's truth is uppermost. The difference between us is in part personal, but it is also disciplinary. Ninian approaches religion from the angle of phenomenology and the social sciences, whereas I, a philosopher, find phenomenology confining. Ontology is too central to be bracketed.

Of the three questions Ninian proposed that we ask about the

This essay was originally presented as part of the series of lectures on "Teaching the Introductory Course" at the University of California at Berkeley in 1987. These lectures were part of a larger project funded by the National Endowment for the Humanities (NEH). The grant was given to Berkeley/Chicago/Harvard to explore A Global Approach to the Study of Religion. Several well-known teachers of religion were invited to give lectures on their approaches to the introductory course in the study of religion. The week prior to Huston Smith's lecture, Ninian Smart of the University of California at Santa Barbara and the University of Lancaster in the United Kingdom had offered his approach to the introductory course. Earlier Frank Reynolds of the University of Chicago had offered his approach to the introductory course. Huston Smith's lecture then appeared in Religious Studies and Theology, 7; (1987) 54–63, *before appearing in Mark Juergensmeyer (ed.)* Teaching the Introductory Course in Religious Studies *(Atlanta, GA: Scholars Press, 1990), pp. 209-220.*

Introductory Course—What is our subject? What is our objective? Who are our students?—I find the second most important and I shall devote almost half of my statement to it. After indicating the goal I set for myself, I shall say how I try to reach it.

I. My Objective

More clearly in retrospect than while I was regularly teaching the Introductory Course I see that my central object was to offer my students another world to live in. Offer it to them, not herd them into it, but I shall defer that point—for now the other world itself is at issue. T. S. Eliot's admission that good poets borrow while great poets steal encourages me to confess that I lifted the phrase "another world to live in" from Evelyn Underhill. Once before I used it in something I wrote, and I shall quote the passage because it points to the aspect of religion I most want my students to notice.

> The Lord appearing high and lifted up to Isaiah; the heavens opening to Christ at his baptism; the universe turning into a bouquet of flowers for Buddha beneath the Bo tree. John reporting, "I was on an island called Patmos, and I was in a trance." Saul struck blind on the Damascus road. For Augustine it was the voice of a child saying, "Take, read"; for Saint Francis a voice which seemed to come from the crucifix. It was while Saint Ignatius sat by a stream and watched the running water, and that curious old cobbler Jacob Boehme was looking at a pewter dish that there came to each that news of another world which it is always religion's business to convey.[2]

What is this "other world" that religion announces?—invariably announces, I would say, when it is alive. We can call it the Transcendent World if we keep in mind that it is also fully (though hiddenly) immanent, and I see nothing in education more important than making it available to students who want it.

They do not have a fair chance at that world today, for almost everything in their culture, their education emphatically included,[3] works to throw it into into doubt."If anything characterizes 'modernity,'" *The Chronicle of Higher Education* tells us, "it is a loss of faith in transcendence, in a reality that encompasses but surpasses our quotidian affairs."[4] Our students inherit that loss. I consider the loss to be serious, and also (ironically) unnecessary, for it results from a conceptual mistake. Because that mistake encroaches on my subject—religion—I take it as part of my responsibility to correct it, which is why I set reclamation-of-the-lost as my foremost course objective.

I mentioned in passing that a good part of this statement will be devoted to that objective, which means that I shall not get to course content until my last section. This may seem disproportionate, but I think the priority is justified. Peter Drucker says the most common mistake corporations make is to pour time and energy into devising brilliant answers to the wrong question, and his point applies here as well. If we select a second-rate objective for our course, its most brilliant execution will not redeem it from being less than it might have been. What justifies an objective is the precision with which it identifies the foremost need of our students in the area of our responsibility. It is because that is not a simple task that I give it major billing in what I have to say.

I said that our loss of the Transcendent World has resulted from a mistake, and the mistake is this: We assume that the modern world has discovered something that throws the transcendent world into question, but that is not the case. It is not that we have discovered something. Rather, we have lost sight of something. For reasons that are completely understandable but nonetheless regrettable, we have unwittingly allowed ourselves to be drawn into an enveloping epistemology that cannot handle transcendence.

In various ways perceptive observers have been saying this for a century or so, but with something of the rush of discovery I recently hit on a way to strip the mistake to its bare bones, reducing it to virtually a syllogism as follows.

1. *Science has become our sacral mode of knowing.* As court of ultimate appeal for what is true, it occupies today almost exactly the place that Revelation enjoyed in the Middle Ages. An intellectual historian has pointed out that already a hundred years ago Westerners had come to have more confidence in the periodic table of chemical elements than in anything the Bible asserts.

2. *The crux of science is the controlled experiment.* I am speaking of course of modern science. Generic science (old as art and religion) relies on reasoning from careful observations, but what distinguishes modern science is its introduction of the controlled experiment and reliance on it as decisive. It is this addition that has caused modern science to take off from generic science and remake our material and conceptual worlds. It explains our confidence in science as well, for the controlled experiment delivers proof, winnowing hypotheses and retiring those that fail its test.

3. *We can control only what is inferior to us.* Intentionally control,

that is, for chains can fetter my movement without being my superior. Also, this principle holds only between orders of existence, for within the same species variables can skew the picture: the Nazis controlled the Jews without being superior to them. By superior/inferior I mean by every criterion of worth we know and probably some we know not. Many things are superior to us in size (the moon) and brute power (an earthquake), but neither are superior to us in all respects, including intelligence and freedom. Human beings controlled the American buffalo more than vice versa—it's that kind of correlation between intended power and orders of existence that this third point flags.

4. The conclusion follows inexorably. *Science can disclose only what is inferior to us.* Have we ever in any science course or textbook encountered anything that exceeds us in every positive attribute we possess? The question is rhetorical—the answer is no. What might beings that are superior to us be? Discarnates? Angels? God? The point is, *if* such beings exist, science will never disclose them for the sufficient reason that it is they who dance circles around us, not we they. Because they possess perimeters we are not even aware of, let alone able to control, it is impossible for us to reduce the variables that pertain to them to the point where experiments could produce on/off, clear-cut proofs.

Nothing in this "syllogism" proves that there *is* anything superior to us, but it does prove that *if* there is, science cannot bring it to light. It proves that conclusively, I would think, save to those whose enthusiasm for science leads them to associate that word with truth in its entirety rather than with truths that are discovered by a particular method. This confuses things to no end. It also does science the disservice of rendering it amorphous and forcing it into the impossible position of trying to be all things to all people, eventually where it falls short of that goal now.

Absence of evidence is not evidence of absence—it might help students break through the metaphysical muddle of our time if we taught them to chant this as a modern mantrum. Because the science of acoustics has nothing to say about beauty, it doesn't follow that Brahms isn't beautiful. It's easy to see this in restricted domains, but expanding the point to worldviews is difficult, hence J. C. Smart's report that positivism is dead except in religion. So to drive home the exposé of our modern mistake which I have been circling, I want to return to my syllogism and run through it again by way of an analogy.

If we liken the scientific method to a flashlight, when we point it downward, towards the path we are walking on say, its beam is clear and bright. Suppose, though, we hear footsteps. Someone is approaching, and to see who it is we raise the beam to horizontal level. (This represents the social sciences and the light they cast on our species.) What happens? The light starts to flicker; a loose connection has developed. The social sciences can tell us some things about ourselves—the physiological substrates of experience and how people behave on average. The complete person as an individual, though, eludes its clutches. Replete with idiosyncrasies, freedom, and commitments, to say nothing of soul and spirit if such components exist, she/he slips through the meshes of science as sea slips through the nets of fishermen. To tie this directly to our syllogism's conclusion—that science can disclose only what is inferior to us—it is axiomatic in the social sciences that in investigating areas where freedom figures, subjects must be kept in the dark about experimental design. This places them in a tilt relation to scientists who know more about what is going on than they do. Finally (to complete the analogy), if we tilt our flashlight skywards—towards the heavens may we say in present context—its light gives out completely. Its batteries drop to the bottom of the casing leaving us completely in the dark. Once again this does not prove that the heavens are populated. It argues that if it is, science cannot apprize us of that fact, much less introduce their denizens.

And science is what now provides us with our sense of reality—we are back to where our syllogism took off. And back to why I want to offer my students an other-than-flashlight world to live in, to bring to full circle this section on course objective. Unaware of what has happened—blind to the way method has vectored metaphysics and epistemology constricted worldview—modernity with a stroke of its methodological pen has all but written off the region of reality that religion up to the last century or so has been riveted to. As E. F. Schumacher reflected toward the close of his life: most of the things that most of humanity has most believed in did not appear on the map of reality his Oxford education handed him as it launched him on life's adventure.

Are we to think that this is a minor thing that has happened—one which we and oncoming generations, powered by the gusto of new-burgeoning life, can take in stride? I think not. Take it perhaps we can, but I do not think our species can take it in stride. We were meant for better things: complete worlds, not the half-world of modernity. And since the shrinkage is unnecessary, resulting as I have noted from a mistake, who is to spring students from their metaphysical cage if not we? I do not see other departments of the university rushing forward, arms outstretched and waving, to volunteer, which is not surprising, given that the university is itself "rooted in the scientific method" as Steven Muller, President of The Johns Hopkins University, points out.[5] For the way that method cramps the social sciences one can consult Robert Bellah's essay in the *National Institute of Campus Ministries Journal,* Summer 1981; for the way it has skewed philosophy in our century, we have Richard Rorty's address to the Eleventh Inter-American Congress of Philosophy;[6] and I have, myself, taken a run at its effects on the humanities at large in the essay "Excluded Knowledge," in my *Beyond the Post-Modern Mind.*

But enough of polemics. I am not saying that enlarging our students' ontology should be the only aim of religious studies. I am, though, arguing that that object should be one of our aims, and as I do not see it mentioned elsewhere in this series, let me say why the other course objectives I find presented need to be supplemented.

II. Alternative Objectives

We all know that Robert Bellah isn't Ninian Smart, and that neither of them is Wilfred Cantwell Smith. Still, as sociologist, phenomenologist, and historian respectively, all three represent "the human sciences," as the social sciences are now frequently called. So with apologies for seeming to make clones of them, I shall lump them together as representing the social/phenomenological approach which holds that teaching should center on the features of religion that can be grasped objectively.

Having already endorsed this as a legitimate approach if it is supplemented, I shall let John Updike note what happens if the supplement is dropped. In his novel, *Roger's Version,* a young computer hack who is also a Jesus freak, corners a professor at the Harvard Divinity school to solicit his help in getting a grant to prove God's existence via the New Physics. In the course of his pitch he lets drop what he thinks of the Divinity School's approach to religion.

> "What you call religion around here is what other people would call sociology. That's how you teach it, right? Everything from the Gospels to *The Golden Bough,* Martin Luther to Martin Luther King, it all happened, it's historical fact, it's anthropology, it's ancient texts, it's humanly *interesting,* right? But that's so safe. How can you go wrong? Not even the worst atheist in the world denies that people have been religious. They built these temples, followed these taboos, created these

traditions, et cetera. So what? Your average normal cheerful nonbeliever says it was all poetic, pathetic foolishness, like a lot of other aspects of human history. I looked over your catalogue before I came, and studying all that stuff doesn't say *anything,* doesn't *commit* you to anything, except some perfectly harmless, humane cultural history. What I'm coming to talk to you about is God as a *fact,* a fact about to burst upon us, right up out of Nature" (p. 19).

Updike burlesques, of course, but his point about what happens when religion is relentlessly objectivized is valid.

The alternative to social science objectivity that gets billing in this Institute is the Chicago school's hermeneutical approach. Frank Reynolds admits that religious studies has a normative agenda, but simply "one that it shares with all other interpretative enterprises that are fostered within the academy." Reynolds wants above all to make students aware of the different ways religion can figure linguistically. He wants them to see the aims and strategies the various ways employ, together with their underlying motives and assumptions. Somewhere in this religious wordplay, philosophical/theological claims enter the picture, but no more than Smart is Reynolds concerned to grapple with those claims, wrestling sinuously to assess their truth. His focus is on providing students "with critical strategies for unearthing motives and assumptions, laying them bare to criticism."

Here again I agree that teaching these critical strategies should be part of the agenda of religious studies, but only if it doesn't sidetrack (by deferring indefinitely) the issue of truth claims. For the dark truth *here* is that if the strategies Reynolds teaches were turned reflexively on the hermeneutic emphasis in religious studies itself— used to excavate *its* motives and assumptions—the exaggerated attention hermeneutics now enjoys would recede, restoring the endeavor to its normal, unbloated place. For there are not neutral methods. Every method stipulates what it will accept as evidence and stakes out a domain within which acceptable answers must fall (see again my "Excluded Knowledge" referred to above). Consequently, to privilege method—in this case hermeneutic strategies—over truth is to conceal rather than disclose what's going on. This is a heavy charge, but something fundamental, not just to religious studies but to the dynamics of our whole current intellectual scene, is at work here. It's too big to go into here, but something that Wilfred Smith, that most useful of living historians, picked up while he was at Harvard can be taken as its telltale trace. In the report on liberal education that was hammered out while Smith was there, the word "truth" doesn't even appear.

I am growing concerned about the way I keep putting off the content of my course, but one more preliminary must be touched on. There are teachers who grant that ontological objectives are *logically* appropriate for religious studies but are not sure that they belong in the academy.

III. Academic Propriety

We are a skittish lot, we teachers of religion. Newcomers to the academy, we see bugbears and bogeymen where colleagues in more established departments do not. Because we teach about people who can get so possessed by something—so *en-theos-iastic,* to use what is etymologically the exactly right word here—that they preach, and proselytize, and yes (as the shadow side of all this) go on at times to persecute, we fear that we may be tarred with those self-same traits. If the law doesn't come at us with "separation of church and state" clauses, an academic review board may, charging that we have hidden theological agendas and are not objective. So best to teach religion social scientifically, as sociology, psychology, anthropology, and history. Or phenomenologically, bracketing the truth-issues of theology and metaphysics. Distance ourselves from our subject. Think critically, but not religiously. Teach *about* religion, but not religion per se.

These distinctions have never seemed quite real to me, perhaps because I have somehow been exempt from the nervousness that attends them. For as long as I have been teaching, this whole matter of academic propriety has been for me one big non-issue. One can, of course, manufacture an issue by imagining egregious cases, but I have never encountered a case that was real. Not once have I felt, or sensed that my students or colleagues have felt, the slightest discomfort with my pedagogical style. (Content, vis à vis my colleagues, is another matter.) And the reason seems clear. I don't *want* to strong-arm anyone. It's the pedagogical instantiation of Augustine's "love God and do what you please." Because pedagogically my heart is pure, I can relax and teach spontaneously. A key component of this spontaneity is, of course, witnessing to the truth as I see it and giving it every assist I can manage, but that lies on a different continuum from strong-arming and indoctrination. If as teachers we are debarred from witnessings to the truth that we see—and giving thereby an ounce of direction to our time, are we allowed to hope—what are we up to? As for review boards, I would *love* to have one come my way charging that I load the dice in favor of transcendence. It would give me a "bloody pulpit" for pointing out a thing or two to the university about the way its prevailing assumptions and procedures condition student's minds in the opposite direction.

Mention of pulpits, though, does lead me to make one retraction. I said that academic propriety has not been an issue for me, but I do wonder from time to time if I sound preachy or like a public scold. I think of something Charles Lamb once said to Charles Kingsley. Kingsley asked Lamb if he would like to hear him preach sometime, to which lamb responded, "I don't think I have ever heard you do anything else."

The tone in which I teach is not different from the tone of this present statement. Am I preaching?

IV. Course Content

I have spent more than half of my paper arguing the objective for my course because it seems to differ in kind from the others in this series. In outline and content, on the other hand, the course is only routinely distinctive.

I begin with the big picture, which again betrays my metaphysical bent. I find meaning descending from the whole to the part as much as it rises from part to whole—I like to know where I am in the world at large before I start poking around in my backyard. So I begin my Introductory Course with a gimmick which I call "Slicing the Religious Pie." A pie serves well, not only because it (like the world) is round, but also because we slice pies in the way we draw distinctions in thought.

I begin with the pie uncut. This represents (to invoke the title of a bygone book) "our believing world"—human history in its entirety as it testifies to woman/man as *homo religiosus*. What are we to say of religion as this generic component of human nature? In short, how should religion be defined? There is no single way, of course, so I propose a working definition of the course. Religion is the human outreach for—its tropism toward—the one, the more, and the mystery.

The one. The dream of unity, of wholeness, of integrity and integration draws us irresistibly. Split personalities are tragic, and we all need to get our acts together. Moreover, this drive for unity reaches beyond ourselves. We seek at-one-ment with the ground of our existence, or whatever we label the final context in which we live and move and have our being.

The more. We are transitional creatures. We live always on the verge—on the threshold of something that exceeds all that we have thus far laid hold of or experienced. In Nietzsche's aphorism, the human is a bridge, not a destination.

The mystery. Detective stories have debased this luminous word. In its traditional, numinous sense, a mystery differs from both a puzzle and a problem. A puzzle has a trick to it. With a problem there's no trick, but it does have a solution. A mystery is that distinctive kind of problem where the more we understand, the more acutely we perceive how much we do not understand. Understanding and discernment-of-ignorance proceed concomitantly. The larger the island of knowledge, the longer the shoreline of wonder.

Wherever religion surfaces authentically, we find it powered by these three lures. That's the pie uncut. (Unauthentic religion is religion pressed into the service of worldly ends—the desires of the unregenerate ego. Folk religion contains a lot of it, and of course to some extent it creeps in everywhere. I come down hard on this distinction between authentic and inauthentic religion, but then I pretty much drop it, mine not being a course on religious pathology or even anthropology.)

As, now, we ready ourselves to cut the pie, where should we begin? It's a way of asking, What is the most important initial distinction to draw in cutting a pie in half, so I draw a horizontal line through my blackboard circle and write above the line "historical" and below it "tribal." Historical religions have sacred texts and a cumulative tradition; they are also more differentiated in the sense the Robert Bellah effectively elucidates in his essay "Religious Evolution."[7] By contrast, tribal religions are typically oral. Eliade called them archaic, and "primitive" is another acceptable designation if the word is not used pejoratively; civilization and writing bring gains, but losses as well. I use the Native Americans as my opportunity to speak well of tribal religion before leaving it to attend for the rest of the course to the historical ones.

Dividing those religions into their Eastern and Western families produces the second cut in the pie. The Western families include Judaism, Christianity, and Islam, and the Eastern one Hinduism, Buddhism, Confucianism, and Taoism. (I point out that this overview uses broad strokes and omits smaller religions such as Jainism and Shinto.) Naming the religions on each side of the divide produces ostensive definitions, but that is only my starting point; I go on to suggest theoretical points on which Eastern and Western religions differ. The differences are of emphasis only; each feature that one family highlights turns up in the other family as well, but subdued. On the subject of God, the Western religions stress God's personal nature while the Eastern ones pay more due (than has the West) to his/her/its transpersonal reaches. Regarding the soul, Western religions emphasizes the individual soul while Eastern religions introduce the universal soul (Atman, anatta, Buddha-nature, and the like). In faith, the West emphasizes what Tillich called prophetic faith (the holiness of the ought) while the East highlights ontological faith (the holiness of the is).

This is rich terrain. The distinction between the personal and transpersonal regions of the divine comes as a revelation to most students. It suggests something that had never before occurred to them; namely, that if the personal God that has been pressed on them seems unbelievably and uninspiringly anthropomorphic, this need not be the end of the religious road. Beyond that personal God, even in the West, stands Eckhart's Godhead and Tillich's "God above God," muted counterparts of nirvana, nirguna Brahman, and the Tao that cannot be spoken. The entire apophatic, mystical, negative theology lies in wait. The notion of a universal soul—what the New England Transcendentalists called the Oversoul—is equally liberating to many. Emerging as they are from adolescence, college students have begun to sense the limitations of "the skin-encapsulated ego," as Alan Watts called it, and are ready for an alternative. As for the two kinds of faith, with the near collapse of modernity's hopes for historical progress, students are ready to think seriously about alternatives or complements.

A semester allows time for one more cut. From a distance the East can look like one homogeneous mass, but as we draw closer to it—come to understand it better—we find it dividing into South Asia (India for short, but including Sri Lanka, Tibet, and aspects of Southeast Asia); and East Asia (China for short, but including Japan, Korea, and again aspects of Southeast Asia). India and China are as different from each other as either is from the West. Nothing in China is as "Indian" as our Middle Ages, while the Chinese have a practicality and down-to-earthness that modern Westerners resonate to more readily that do Indians.

Having geographically separated the East Asian, South Asian, and Western families of religions, I again plunge for substantive issues— issues that have import for students' lives—by proposing that the groupings present interesting and important philosophical differences. To be human is to interface on three fronts: with nature, with other people, and with ourselves. These confrontations present us with natural, social, and psychological problems. In their great formative periods, the three families of religions have deployed their energies differently on these problems. Specifically, the West has attended more to nature than have the other two traditions. China, for her part, specialized in the social problem, while India concentrated on psychology.[8] Each made discoveries in its area of specialization that continue to be important, while by the same token each can usefully learn from the other two if it has wit and will to do so.

Having opened my course with the embracing framework of my religious pie, I devote its remainder to filling it with content. Throughout, my intent is to carry students as far as possible into the existential outlook of the religious subjects whose tradition is on deck. To sign off with the point with which I opened this statement, my indirect intent (but foremost hope) in all this is to use these empathetic, quasi-shamanic journeys to enlarge my students' sense of reality—the ontological options they perceive as available to them. I invoke a bit of history to get a tradition on stage, and I gesture towards its rituals and art. Its embracing view of the self and its world, though, is always stage center. This reflects my personal interests as well as the fact that my courses have always been listed or cross-listed in philosophy.

NOTES

1. See my "Does Spirit Matter? The Worldwide Impact of Religion on Contemporary Politics," Introduction to Richard Rubenstein (ed.), *Spirit Matters* (New York: Paragon House, 1987).
2. "The Incredible Assumption," in *Beyond the Post-Modern Mind*, p. 190.
3. "While 94 percent of Americans believe in a supreme being only 73 percent of Harvard and Stanford alumni so believe. Whereas 63 percent of Americans generally hold that religion is a very important part of their lives, only 24 percent of the Harvard and Stanford alumni responded affirmatively" (Harold Lindsell, *The New Paganism* [New York: Harper Row, 1987], p. 137).
4. January 9, 1978, p. 18.
5. *U.S. News and World Report,* November 10, 1980.
6. *Proceedings of the American Philosophical Association,* Vol. 59 (July 1986).
7. Chapter 2 in his *Beyond Belief* (New York: Harper Row, 1970).

8. See my "Accents of the World's Philosophies," and its companion piece, "The Accents of the World's Religions," the first two essays in this volume.

This Ecumenical Moment:
What Are We Seeking?

Gathered as we are from the ends of the earth, poised on the brink of a week that is sure to be interesting and holds promise of being more than that: What are we seeking? What have we come hoping to find?

I think of four possible areas of gain: social, academic, theological or doctrinal, and personal.

Let's begin with the social.

1. SOCIAL

We live in a world that is scourged with animosity—factions, fratricide, hatred, and war. Governments, profligate in death, are spending over $2 billion a day on war or preparations for war. Religion becomes implicated in these conflicts. Pogroms, crusades, wars of religion—Cardinal Newman's anguished cry still rings in our ears: "Oh how we hate one another for the love of God!"

In their relations with each other, though, Buddhism and Christianity seem to have been spared on this score. Currently at peace with one another, they don't even have much of a history of conflict. This happy absence of friction between our two faiths gives us the opportunity to join ranks in considering how we might work together to temper the nationalism, power struggles, and injustices that plague our world. Three of our five evening sessions will deal

This essay was originally a plenary address in 1987 at a major international conference in Berkeley entitled "Buddhism and Christianity: Toward the Human Future." It then appeared in Japanese Religions 15, 1 (January 1988).

with peace, the rights of women, and ethics, successively. And two of our working groups are likewise concerned with the sociopolitical implications of our traditions, addressing as they do Religion and Violence and Liberation Theology.

As we look toward these socially oriented portions of our program, it will be well to rid ourselves of any notions that may still be around to the effect that Buddhism and Christianity are religions of the spirit only—inward, private occupations that seek the salvation or enlightenment of individuals without concern for the workings of society. This reading is so flawed that I want to hold it up for inspection as it relates to both Buddhism and Christianity.

First Christianity.

Marcus Borg's *Jesus: A New Vision*[1] argues that everything in Jesus' life flowed from his relation with God; he would spend entire nights soaking himself in God's presence, refueling or recharging himself, we might say, with divinity. And what issued from this empowerment? Mighty acts, to be sure, of healing and the like, and exemplary personal comportment. But more. It issued in a social program so explosive that it led almost immediately—within a year—to Jesus' death. For he was calling his people to stand their social program on its head—to replace their "politics of holiness" with a "politics of compassion." The deliverance of the Jews from their oppression, Jesus taught, turned not on meticulous observance of religious laws, but on compassionate attention to human needs.

And the Buddha's message was not different in this underlying, basic respect. Jesus, born to a carpenter of subject people, was in no position to challenge the reigning order of his day directly: Not Rome but his people's response to Rome was his political focus. But the Buddha's case was different. Iconography has so effectively presented us with an otherworldly Buddha, seated motionless beneath the Bo Tree, that it has obscured the other side of his mission. We forget that as soon as he began to teach he was drawn back into the royal circles he had renounced to seek release. For Indian monarchy was in its infancy then, trying to forge a viable alternative to the village-based Brahmanic *panchayat* (rule of five) that was fumbling with population growth and other changes that were occurring. The Buddha saw the problem and responded to it; his message included a strong social agenda along with its path of personal release. That he broke caste we remember, and I feel sure that our Thursday evening lectures on Women in Christianity and Buddhism will bring out that both Jesus and Buddha related differently to women than their mores dictated.

But the Buddha had a larger program, that supported those

actions. Its details, which called for a society founded like a tripod on three legs—monarchy, the *sangha,* and the laity—do not need to be rehearsed here, any more than does the question of whether those details would fit our world today. The point is a general but important one. The branch of Buddhism that grew to be the largest, the Mahayana, was the one that achieved its eminence by penetrating and adapting itself to China, an empire that was open to metaphysical and spiritual enrichment but hadn't the slightest intent to change its political structure. The consequence is that we have come to think of Buddhism as an *adjunct* to civilizations—which in China, Korea, Japan, and Southeast Asia it has been. What we forget is that Buddhism as an artery within civilizations that were otherwise constituted, important as this artery has been and still is, is a fraction of the teaching the Buddha originally proposed. It presents us with a Buddhism that is a religion only, not the civilization that Guatama proposed as an alternative to the Brahmic civilization that had become so corrupt that it needed to be challenged more or less in its entirety.

The difference between a civilization and a religion is that the former orders an entire way of life—economics, education, art, mores—not just its spiritual enclaves. It has been a personal thesis of mine that the standard ways of distinguishing Theravada from Mahayana Buddhism (via the Arhant/Boddhistattva contrast, and the like) are less illuminating than the one that regards Theravada as the branch of Buddhism that sought to perpetuate Gautama's vision of Buddhism as a civilization—this as against the Mahayana's settling (as in East Asia it had to) for Buddhism as a religion only.

Whether or not this definitional thesis is correct, the underlying point seems solid. Those of us who want to explore the social implications of Buddhism (as E. F. Schumacher did in his "Buddhist Economics") can draw inspiration from the founder of Buddhism himself.[2] Both Jesus *and* the Buddha proclaimed visions that have strong social implications.

I turn now to the academic objectives of this conference.

2. ACADEMIC

The two Honolulu conferences that preceded this one were exclusively for academics, and academics have taken the lead in organizing this one. I don't know the breakdown, but clearly many of us in this hall are teachers. As such, it is our vocation to understand as accurately and profoundly as we can—in the present case to understand Buddhism and Christianity to the end of spreading this understanding to the world at large.

If we look back over the road that has been traveled, we can draw courage from the progress that has been made. Throughout this second section of my talk I will speak only of the West's understanding of Buddhism, that being the side of the ledger I am familiar with.

Our first major advance was to get rid of the West's initial impression that Buddhism was a religion of pessimism and life-negation. Of all the Buddhist scriptures, *The Dhammapada* is probably the one best known to the world; it may still be the only Buddhist text that has been translated into all of the world's major languages. The key refrain in this text is *sabbe sankhara annica, sabbe sankhara dukkha, sabbe dhamma anatta.* And how was this thesis originally rendered for the West? The English translation read "All is transient, all is sorrow, all is unreal." It took some time for Western scholars to see that the Pali words *sabbe sankhara* do not refer to existence as a whole. They refer to something quite specific: the latent tendencies that we have deposited in our subconscious minds by our past thoughts, desires, and actions. It is those accumulated tendencies, those conditionings, that are *dukkha,* which is to say predominantly painful and pain-producing. Fortunately, though, as the Pali text makes clear, those tendencies are also *anicca* or transient, which means that we are not stuck with them forever. As for their being unreal, the Pali word that "unreal" was used to translate is *annata,* which even beginners in Buddhism now know does not mean possessing no reality whatsoever. It means lacking a permanent, substantial essence which would lock us in. By such mistranslations a call to hope and endeavor was turned into a pronouncement of bleak resignation. Lama Govinda was not the first to call attention to the extent to which nineteenth-century Buddhologists were influenced by Schopenhauer's interest in the religion. What got through to Europe in that early wave was as much Schopenhauer's pessimism as the Buddha's actual teachings.

My second example of progress concerns the words *nirvana* or *nibbana,* and *sunyata.* The negative in the first syllable of *nirvana* and the connotations of "emptiness" and "void" in *sunyata* left early students of Buddhism perplexed. Could it be that the Buddhist path, with the strict, arduous discipline it often entailed, was no more than "a grand stairway that leads nowhere," as one scholar couched his puzzlement?

Something has happened in the West over the past half-century that has helped to relieve, if not entirely resolve, this second misunderstanding. The West has rediscovered its own mystical, apophatic tradition. Between the infinite and the finite there is (in a very real sense) no commensurability whatever; God's being in its fullness and totality outstrips our finite intellects so radically that there comes a point where anything we try to say about it must seem more false than true. This is the point that mystics make with their *via negativa* and cloud of unknowing. Our recovery of their point here has (to repeat) opened the West to the prospect that Buddhism's negatively couched concepts, too, might have their rationale. Someone has suggested that one of the signs that a new idea has gotten through to at least the literary public is that it surfaces in a *New Yorker* cartoon. By that index, the West has caught on to the affirmation that negation can harbor. The cartoon I am thinking of showed the usual two bums in a seedy bar resolving life's mysteries. One was explaining to the other: "I don't mean nothing that's *nothing*! I mean nothing that's something." Professor Masao Abe and Steve Odin's Dialogue Group on Sunyata and Kenosis have a week to get clear on what that skid-row pundit had in mind, but it's a sign of progress that we are, in effect, taking his point seriously.

The third area in which we have clearly progressed is the God controversy. We still have a way to go, but Christianity's unqualified theism and Buddhism's nominal atheism no longer look like the flat disjunction it once seemed. As this topic is closely linked to the preceding one, it is enough here to put the matter simply. The variety of schools of Buddhism, which stretch all the way from Theravada on the one hand to Jodo Shinshu on the other—this variety of *schools* on the Buddhist side, together with the multiplicity of meanings the word *God* carries in Christendom (an assortment that ranges all the way from the God of Abraham, Isaac, and Jacob to the Godhead of mystics and philosophers)—this diversity in both our traditions makes it highly improbable that the God issue must freeze us permanently into polarized opposition.

So: Buddhism isn't pessimistic. Nirvana isn't absolutely nothing. And God is a subject about which Christians and Buddhists can talk earnestly, not stop talking. These are real gains. I am not sure, though, that they add up to our being over the hump in Buddhist–Christian understanding. We wouldn't be here if we didn't know that there's more to be done, but I want to add something that is less obvious. New obstacles to understanding may be appearing on the horizon to replace the old obstacles that have been surmounted. I shall mention two.

Thanks to the labors of linguists and historians, information about

Buddhism and Christianity is increasing in leaps and bounds. This tempts us to assume that our knowledge of our two traditions is increasing as well, but I'm not sure that this is so. "Where is the knowledge that is lost in information?" T. S. Eliot once asked, adding, "Where is the wisdom that is lost in knowledge?"

To come to the point, two movements are afoot in the academy today that I fear may offset the progress the West has thus far made in Buddhist understanding.

The first is in anthropology. In a presentation that Lee Yearley of Stanford made to the NEH Institute on the Study of Religion here in Berkeley last month, he voiced concern that our entire understanding of the non-Western world may fall under the influence of an anthropological program that has been in the making for a couple of decades. Its premise is couched with such sophistication that you feel rather flat-footed and naive if you don't buy into it, but it comes down to this: though language has objective constraints when we speak for the physical world, when we turn to other matters the only constraints we can lay hold of are internal ones. They derive from worlds of discourse that generate our minds in the first place and then lay down the rules by which we think. By this reading of the matter, anthropology ceases to be a study that tries to depict who human beings are and how they live, for we can't get out of our linguistic horizons (our linguistic cocoons or cages, I'm tempted to say) to contact peoples' ways of life. Instead, anthropology becomes an essay in rhetorical style—a form of literature. Clifford Geertz's 1986 California lectures (still unpublished as far as I can discover) dealt with this issue, as does Robin Horton's essay "Tradition and Modernity Revisited."[3] Using African versus Western science as his test case, Horton reviews anthropologists' twenty-year effort to separate science from truth, or—in more general terms—the claims of rhetoric from the claims of reference. If their scission succeeds, Christians' very attempt to gain an accurate understanding of Buddhism will be thrown into question, for accuracy presupposes reference.

The second hazard to our understanding of Buddhism I sense brewing is this: typically, Buddhologists are a minority (if they are not loners) in departments of philosophy and religious studies wherein they teach. To stay in the swim of things and get a hearing they feel compelled, almost, to relate their work to the problems and thinkers that are dominant in philosophy and religion at the moment. Invariably, of course, those problems and thinkers are Western ones, but that's just the start of the problem. The Buddhologist likewise gets swept up in the prevailing methodologies in philosophy and religion, and starts looking for resonances between Buddhism and the reigning philosophies of our time. So we come out learning that Zen masters were really Heidegger in his previous incarnations, that Nagarjuna was a proto-William James, that Chuang Tzu was a linguistic analyst, or that *sunyata* closely resembles Derrida's notion of *differance*. I am exaggerating, of course, and I certainly don't want to say that comparisons of this sort are misguided in principle. What I am calling for is more recognition than I hear voiced of the following fact. Because, in comparisons of this sort, it is the Western terms that are in favor—Heidegger, William James, language philosophy, or Derrida, as the case may be—there is a strong pull to tailor traditional Buddhist frames of reference to modern Western ones, whereas I suspect that we get closer to the truth if we tailor Heidegger to the Roshis, Wittgenstein to Chuang Tzu, William James to Nagarjuna, and Derrida to *sunyata*. This, though, is only a personal opinion which obviously could be mistaken.

As a personal opinion, that preceding point marks a turning point in this address. Up to now I feel that I have been speaking for us all in articulating the social and academic objectives of this conference; that seemed appropriate for a conference kick-off. But as I turn to the second half of my statement I find it impossible to continue in that mode. Here my opinions—they feel like convictions to me, but let's call them opinions—may be atypical, to the point (perhaps) of being in this context idiosyncratic. Of course I could hide them, but that would be not to take this week seriously. So I shall state them as clearly and succinctly as I can, asking you to hear them as "lobs from left field," if you will—possibilities to be thrown into the Waring blender of this week's discussions. They are items to take into account, if anyone feels inclined to do so.

3. Doctrinal

In Christian parlance, this third section is theological, but *theos* doesn't fit smoothly with Buddhism, so I replace theology with doctrine. Some will protest even the word *doctrine*, arguing that the Buddha's "noble silence" excludes beliefs, but I disagree, so here is the first of the opinions that the doctrinal section will be woven of.

What do we hope to gain, theologically or doctrinally, from this week?

My answer may surprise you. I don't think we should expect *any* theological gains—that is to say, none of substance. Here and there a doctrinal point in the other tradition may highlight or remind us of its counterpart in our own, but additions or revisions, no. This may sound deflating, like a council to lower our sights and accept our limitations, but I intend the opposite: It is a strong affirmation. For the reason we needn't tinker with the doctrinal structure of our respective traditions is that each of them contains within itself "truth sufficient unto salvation," to invoke the Christian expression. In consequence, neither tradition needs any "organ transplants" from the other, if I may put the matter so. To look for doctrinal change through dialogue would presume that individually or in committee we either have the wisdom to remake our creeds, or will be provided with that wisdom by the Holy Spirit or Buddhist inspiration. I am not confident of either alternative.

Which leads me to say a word about the people who are not here—not those who would have loved to be here but didn't hear of the conference or haven't the time or the money to attend. We are a privileged group, and should *gassho* with gratitude to the *prattitya-samutpada* that has made possible our being here.

The people I am thinking of are the ones who are absent for reasons of principle: the people who wouldn't be caught near a gathering of this sort. Our inclination is to assume that they boycott ecumenical functions because they are intolerant—narrow-minded, bigoted, and prejudiced. If we do so characterize them, though, it shows that we too are intolerant. We are intolerant of them, just as they are intolerant of us.

What I find myself wanting to say is that they have a point, and that it is an important one. There are dangers in what we are doing here, and not to perceive them is to mistake the nature of the spiritual quest. (I am picking up here on what Edmund Perry last evening reported Gustav Weigel as saying to the effect that interfaith dialogue isn't for everybody.)

What I find underrecognized in most ecumenical discussions is this: when religion is serious, it comes to us as a summons from the Absolute. And as such, it asks of us an absolute response—a response of all that we are and to absolute extent. But we can respond absolutely only to what we believe is absolutely true.

The plurality of religions challenges their absoluteness—the absolute truth of any of them. For in their doctrines and rites the religions contradict one another. And in doing so, they relativize one another, for truth is that which cannot be contradicted.

For most persons religious truth is identical with the forms in which it comes clothed: its incarnations, its scriptures, its doctrines and creeds, its rituals and rites, its art and other enveloping, sustaining symbols. To repeat this crucial point (it being the point I find ecumenical gatherings least prepared to face), many persons are unable to distinguish between truth and the forms in which it is couched. The cause of their inability needn't concern us. Perhaps they are of a different spiritual temperament. Or they haven't had as much time as we have had to think about the matter. As I say, we don't have to decide the reason, but the fact remains: many persons are unable to distinguish between truth and the forms in which it is couched. So those persons are faced with a choice. Either they retain their Absolute, which means absolutizing the forms in which absolute truth comes to them: extra *ecclesiam nulla salus.* Or they admit the relativity of the forms in which their truth comes packaged (if we may put the matter thus crudely) and in so admitting relativize their entire faith.

If the logic of such people is correct, and I think it is, they confront us with a choice. Would we prefer to have them with us, having their religious faith relativized by the relativizing of religious forms (Christian and Buddhist alike) that I foresee going on here all week? Or do we respect the distance they prefer to keep, agreeing with them that faith is more important than tolerance?*

There is, I think, a way to retain the religious Absolute (which life, I believe, seeks and at its best finds) while freely admitting the relativity of relgious forms—even, ultimately, the relativity of the great religious traditions which are providential assemblages of forms. It requires, however, that we locate the Absolute outside the realm of forms altogether, in the divine stratosphere, if I may put the matter thus while immediately retracting the metaphor because the Absolute is also absolutely imminent—it is always exactly here. How the Absolute can lie beyond forms altogether and yet be apprehended is too long a story for this hour, so I shall say only two things:

First, I believe that it can be positioned beyond forms.

---

*It is more important, first, because faith is positive—it is *in* something—whereas tolerance (with all its importance) is negative, a withholding of judgment. And second, tolerance requires limits. (It is decisively important what faith is *in,* but directed toward the right object—God, or Amida Buddha's saving power, say—it is ideally unlimited.) We should probably always be working to increase our tolerance of persons, but with ideas and behavior the case is different. As the old adage has it, in the end morality comes down to drawing the line somewhere, as does truth as well. In both truth and morals, there comes a point where we must ask ourselves: If there isn't anything that we are against (i.e., intolerant of), is there anything that we are really for?

And second, for those who cannot so position it, it may be better on the whole for them to keep theologically to themselves. It is expedient for them to cooperate with others in good works, which includes reducing misunderstandings, but theological dialogue is for them highly problematic.

Philip Hwang is one of our number and I recall his pointing out to me in Seoul the distinctiveness of the religious situations in Korea—its population is evenly divided between five religions and they get along quite amicably. "How do they manage to do so?" I wondered. "They don't talk to one another," he replied.

Karl Barth would not have objected to this modus operandi. He never denied that the *kerygma* (divine message) may have occurred outside Christendom. What he said was that that possibility was of no interest to the Christian theologian.

4. PERSONAL

Though I see no need for the doctrinal structures of our traditions to change, there is always the possibility of positioning ourselves more creatively within their frameworks. My point will be clearer if I give examples, so I shall cite three from my own experience.

I can remember as if it were yesterday the inrush of energy that followed my discovery of India's four yogas. I had learned from the gospel of Luke that we should love God with our whole heart, soul, strength, and mind, but the way Hinduism picked up on these four components of ourselves and delineated distinct spiritual practices for each—*bhakti* as the yoga of the heart, *jnana* as the mind's yoga, *karma* as yoga for our strength or energy, and *raja* yoga for our souls—was exhilarating. As was the revelation in my Vedantic teacher's characterization of Christinity as "one blazing path of bhakti yoga" On the heart front, he went on to say, the West has nothing to learn from Asia, but those whose spirituality extends in other directions find themselves less supported. Applied to my own case, this helped me to see, first, that by temperament I was a *jnana yogin*—one whose primary approach to God was through understanding—and, second, that as such I had every right to pursue Christian Platonism as the neglected (and to some biblical theologians suspect) stream in my tradition that spoke most meaningfully to me.

Coming to Buddhism, I felt a comparable inrush of energy on discovering that its Three Poisons—greed, hatred, and delusion—are the chief obstacles to the Christian virtues of humility, charity, and veracity. To find these two great religions pointing ethically in the same direction was itself invigorating—it was like the scientists' resort to independent verification to check the truth of a hypothesis—but that was only the beginning of my gain. I had had difficulty trying to cultivate the Christian virtues directly: How, for example, does one go about trying to be more humble? Buddhism's back-door approach was more concrete, for once I started watching for the poisons, greed (to mention only the first one, including greed for self-aggrandizement) began to surface at every turn. Because poison is in the system *now,* one can deal more tangibly with it than with the health that lies somewhere in the distance.

A third transfusion of spiritual energy came from the Buddhist (as also Hindu and Taoist) unblinking recognition that there comes a time in our understanding of the Ultimate when not only personal categories but all categories must be set aside.

At a certain point in my odyssey the Christian emphasis on God's personal nature appeared excessive and confining: It made God seem cloyingly anthropomorphic. When I later discovered the mystics' distinction between God and the Godhead, I saw that the apophatic, transpersonal abysses of God's nature are honored in Christendom too. But it was Asia that introduced me to the distinction and pointed me to its buried presence at home.

CONCLUSION

It seems clear that most of the impetus for dialogue today is coming from Christians, and this is understandable. Christianity has been so bruised by modern secular and scientific styles of thought that it needs help from its Eastern, more traditional, allies. For only by looking East (or West if we are in California) to the more readily apparent and integral metaphysical truths and contemplative methods of Hindu, Buddhist, and Muslim teachings can the Western believer begin to discover the spiritual resources that have been more deeply hidden at the center of their own religion. Meanwhile, if Asians are more reluctant to enter into dialogue, they have reason. There is danger that our scientistic, secular accretions may rub off onto them.

But let me close with the spirit to which we might aspire in this week's conversations. Walpola Rahula and Edmund Perry covered that point so well last evening that a salutation that comes down to us from Tibet is all that I feel I need add. Marco Pallis tells us that on meeting a stranger from abroad Tibetans used to ask "To which sublime tradition, revered sir, do you belong?"

NOTES

1. Marcus Borg, *Jesus: New Vision* (San Francisco: Harper & Row, 1987).
2. The reference is to "Buddhist Economics" in E. F. Schumacher, *Small Is Beautiful* (New York: Harper & Row, 1989, ed.), pp. 56–66.
3. In Martin Holls and Steven Lukes (eds.), *Rationality and Relativism* (Cambridge, Mass.: MIT Press, 1982).

Postmodernism's Impact
on the Study of Religion

Postmodernism has not displaced modernism; the two outlooks jostle one another as they compete for the current western mind.[1] So my subject is actually the impact of modernism and postmodernism on religious studies. Chronologically, I define modernism as the outlook that dominated the West from the seventeenth to (and into) the twentieth century, but which has had to share the stage increasingly with postmodernism as the decades of our century have unfolded. Substantively, modernism is the outlook that accepted the scientific worldview as definitive, while postmodernism is that scientistic worldview adjourned but not replaced. While the modern mind was flat because science cannot get its hands on values and the vertical dimension that betokens their worth, the postmodern mind is amorphous. Doubting that a deep structure exists, it settles for the constantly-shifting configurations of the phenomenal world. That my definitions focus on worldviews signals that I am approaching my subject metaphysically. I think we get farther that way than if we approach modernity via Hobbes, Locke, and the French Revolution.

With modernism and postmodernism thus defined, what is religion?

Religion's Central Posit: A Hierarchical Universe

It has not been easy for us to maintain our bearings in this tumultuous century, so I propose to roll back the decades to its opening

This essay was originally given as a plenary address at the annual meeting of the American Academy of Religion, Nov. 19, 1989, in Anaheim, California, and was published in the Journal of the American Academy of Religion *LVIII/4 (1990): 653–670.*

and ask William James to remind us what religion is. In his 1901–02 Gifford Lectures, *The Varieties of Religious Experience,* he tells us that "religion says that the best things are the more eternal things, the things in the universe that throw the last stone, so to speak, and say the final word."

Note at once that by this report religion talks about things—the "best [and] eternal things"—which warns us right off that it is headed for trouble with postmodernism, for "things" sound suspiciously like "essences," and talk about them sounds suspiciously "referential"—words postmodernism is not fond of. But let's stay with James.

The things that religion focuses on, he tells us, are of a special sort. They are the best things, which positions them above their inferiors on value's vertical dimension. Moreover, those "best things" are superior to other things not only in their worth but in their power as well.

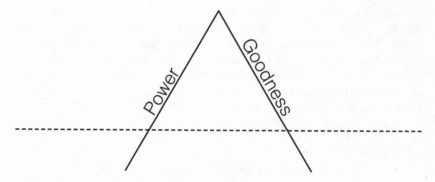

If we diagram the claim, it looks like this

The simplest way I know to characterize this religious view of things is to say that it is an "ontological hierarchy." Ontology here refers to nothing more complicated than things that exist (Greek: *on* = being), while hierarchy recognizes that among the things that exist, some are better than others. These better things naturally present themselves imagistically as being above the rest, given the laws of spatial symbolism, which are not arbitrary but are drawn from the structure of the human body. Our heads are more important than our feet, as proven by the fact that if we had to amputate one or the other, we would not debate.

This seems straightforward, but I belabor it because one problem postmodernism has created for the study of religion is to deprive us of the language we need to say what needs to be said. Here at the very outset we have a case in point. Postmoderns continue to validate the word "ontology" while decisively changing its meaning, but metaphysics—which ontology converts into as soon as the things denoted are positioned in relation to one another—is immediately suspect. And hierarchy even more so. I am banking in this statement on our having advanced to the point where we can winnow that suspicion and stop equating hierarchies with masculine thinking and oppression, for in point of fact it is impossible to think—not just think masculinely but to think at all—without acknowledging not only the existence of hierarchies but their appropriateness in certain contexts. Like it or not, we live in a hierarchical world, wherein gradations not only in size, strength, and complexity, but also in intelligence, skills, and compassion confront us at every turn. So we speak of higher education, higher mathematics, the higher things of life, and our superiors. We needed to go through a period of reproaching hierarchies indiscriminately in order to see how destructive they can be and have been, but I am assuming that we are ready to move beyond that stage in order to target the enemy more accurately. The enemy is oppressive, destructive hiearchies, not hierarchies *per se.* A loving family with small children is a benevolent hierarchy, as is a well-ordered classroom.[2] To revert to James—who got us into hierarchies right off because religion turns on their existence—God (in whom superlative power and goodness converge) provides us with the paradigm of beneficent hierarchy.

What did modernity do to that hierarchy?

Modernity: The Hierarchy Collapsed

The answer is obvious. Modernity collapsed it to its this-worldly base. We used to refer to this as the rejection of supernaturalism, but now phrases like "the death of God" and the collapse of the vertical dimension are more common. "If anything characterizes 'modernity,'" *The Chronicle of Higher Education* reported several years back, "it is a loss of faith in transcendence in a reality that encompasses but surpasses our quotidian affairs" (9 January 1978:18).

The earthquake that effected that ontic collapse was modern science. Prior to its rise, people looked to Revelation for their disclosures of reality, which disclosures typically registered heavens above, hells below, and the earth between. In less pictorial language, the Revelations testified to some version of what Lovejoy called the Great Chain of Being, stretching from the least existent to the *ens perfectissimum,* which (as he tells us) "the greater number of subtler speculative minds and great religious teachers [everywhere], through the Middle Ages and down to the late eighteenth century [accepted] without question..." (26, 59). Ernst Cassirer bears him out. "The most important legacy of ancient speculation," he writes, was "the concept and general picture of a graduated cosmos" (9). The successes of modern science, however, persuaded people that science's reports about reality were more reliable than those of Holy Writ. An intellectual historian has estimated that already by the nineteenth century Westerners were more confident that chemical elements exist than that any of the distinctive things the Bible speaks of exist. And science cannot register transcendence, or the vertical dimension.

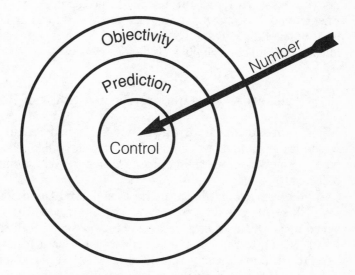

This is what science—modern science—is.

Science monitors observables, especially as quantifiable. It cannot handle values, meanings, purposes, qualities, invisibles, and our superiors.[3] As all of these six things lie on the vertical dimension, which science cannot touch, it is not surprising that that dimension collapsed when science displaced revelation as reality's arbiter. If you confine your gaze to a horizontally fixed telescope, things that are at right angles to that telescope are not going to divulge themselves.

I hurry over this point because we are reasonably on top of it (though on the conscious level only, instinctively it remains one of those things we know but never learn). We do, however, need to notice the way philosophy conformed itself to science's ontological reduction by reducing its epistemology concomitantly. Kant oversaw that project. His insistence that the categories of human understanding mesh only with impressions that have an impact on us through our physical senses debarred those categories from service elsewhere, and (by Kant's explicit claim) turned metaphysics into "the science of the boundaries of human reason." Kant's uncharacteristic emotionally charged descent from reason into sarcasm in dealing with Swedenborg stemmed from his clear realization that "should the philosopher make room in his philosophy for even one [of Swedenborg's reports] of spiritual, manifestations... what astonishing consequences would follow!" (112–113). Astonishing indeed; nothing short of the collapse of the entire epistemological machinery he was working out to meet modernity's requirements.[4] Phenomenology followed in Kant's wake, and reformulated his cutoff into "bracketing" questions of existence. But it is time to turn to the impact of all this on religious studies.

Modernity's Consequences for the Study of Religion

The most conspicuous effect modernity had on our profession was to cause us to distance ourselves from our subject. For the most part, we now project religion onto other people whom we study objectively.

A little satire won't harm us here, and John Updike is up to the job. Those of us who have read *Roger's Version,* Updike's thinly veiled spoof of the Harvard Divinity School, will recall the moment when Dale, a young computer hack who is also a Jesus freak, corners Roger in his Divinity School office to solicit his help in getting a grant to prove God's existence via computers and the new physics. In the course of his pitch he drops his guard and lets Roger know what he, Dale, thinks the Divinity School is doing by way of contrast.

What you call religion around here is what other people would call sociology. That's how you teach it, right? Everything from the Gospels to *The Golden Bough,* Martin Luther to Martin Luther King, it all happened, it's historical fact, it's anthropology, it's ancient texts, it's humanly *interesting,* right? But that's so safe. How can you go wrong? Not even the worst atheist in the world denies people have been religious. They built these temples, followed these taboos, created these traditions, et cetera. So what? Your average normal cheerful nonbeliever says it was all poetic, pathetic foolishness, like a lot of other aspects of human history. I looked over your catalogue before I came, and

studying all that stuff doesn't say *anything,* doesn't *commit* you
to anything, except some perfectly harmless, humane cultural
history. What I'm coming to talk to you about is God as a *fact,* a
fact about to burst upon us, right up out of Nature. (19)

Updike is satirizing of course, but, as we all recognize, only in
part. Departments of Bible have become departments of religion
which have become departments of religious studies, for though religion is a touchy subject for both government and the university,[5] it is
not easy to fault *study.* So we pour our departmental energies into
features of religion that have objective, empirical grounding—philology, archaeology, historical influences and textual parallels—and
bracket the question of whether the beliefs that generated those fall-
outs were mistaken or true. Theology pursued systematically rather
than historically seems a breach of academic protocol, and philosophy of religion backs away from talk that seeks to penetrate directly
into God's nature, to talk about God-talk. God-talk is talk that is useful for religious purposes whatever we think of those purposes, as
distinct from talk that is useful for other purposes.

The phenomenological *epoche* that was earlier mentioned has
abetted this distancing act. As phenomenologists of religion we neither affirm nor deny; we merely table the question of whether the
gods our students study exist. Our rationale for this move is that
bracketing our beliefs enables us to enter more fully into their
beliefs, but I am not confident that it works that way. Darrol Bryant
has written that "when the injunction not to enforce [our] frame of
reference in studying other peoples and religions... is transformed
into an ontology of ignorance concerning that towards which the
believer walks, we refuse to walk the crucial second mile where real
compassion and new dimensions of understanding might arise," and
it does strike me as curious that when it is a work of art that we propose to access, we counsel "voluntary suspension of disbelief,"
whereas in accessing a religious standpoint we counsel the opposite.
If I may enter a personal note on this point, I have (over the years)
been "charged" with belonging to all seven of the traditions I
describe in *The Religions of Man*[6]—charged with belonging formally
to four, and at heart to the other three—but it never occurred to me
to doubt that the objects of their devotion exist. I do not understand
how agnosticism could have augmented my empathy.

When we turn from studying other peoples to our own traditions,
biblical studies provide perhaps the best index as to how we have
been affected. The New Testament scholar Marcus Borg speaks so
pointedly to the issue that I shall quote him at length.

To a large extent, the defining characteristic of biblical scholarship in the modern period is the attempt to understand
Scripture without reference to another world. Born in the
Enlightenment, modern biblical scholarship has sought to
understand its subject matter in accord with the... image of
reality that dominates the modern mind.

In the battle between supernaturalism and rationalism which
reached its peak in the early 1800's, the reality of the other
world... was essentially denied... Explanations... within the
framework of a one-dimensional understanding of reality were
offered for texts which spoke of "supernatural" phenomena....
Texts reporting miracles were either understood psychosomati-
cally or as mistaken perceptions of quite "natural" events...

In our century, the aggressive denial of the twofoldness of
reality has largely been replaced by a "bracketing" or ignoring
of the question. The major sub-disciplines which have emerged
in the past several decades are those which can be done without reference to other levels of reality: studies of the way the
biblical writers redacted the tradition which they received, the
form and functions of various literary and oral genres, the
rhetorical structure of texts, social factors shaping or reflected
in texts, the development of early Christian tradition expressed
in the texts, etc. All share in common the fact that they focus on
the "this worldly" aspects of the texts: their sources, forms,
functions, social and historical "rootedness," etc. They treat the
kinds of questions and claims that are intelligible within the
framework of the modern worldview.

Borg grants that biblical texts *as texts* are completely this-worldly,
but they often speak about another reality which "in modern scholarship... is seldom the subject of study." Hermeneutical approaches to
both the Old and New Testaments have stressed their historical and
this-worldly import. Interpretation of the Hebrew Bible has been
dominated by the "covenant-historical" model which holds that what
is important is "not what the Old Testament might say about another
world, but its concern with historical existence in this world." This
emphasis flows partly from the fact that the Hebrew Bible is organized around a historical narrative, but it "is also because... in the
modern period... the visible world of space and time... is the world
we think of as 'real'."

New Testament scholarship exhibits the same dynamic. Here the
influential figure has been Rudolf Bultmann, whose classic essay on

the Bible's "three-story universe" was taken as a call to read the Bible existentially rather than ontologically. This meshes with Karl Barth's confessional theology, which intentionally withdraws from the empirical domain and makes no metaphysical claims.

Having veered (via Bultmann) from biblical studies into theology, I shall let short comments on Paul Tillich and Process Theology conclude this section.

Tillich gave us a way to finesse ontology by redefining our subject as "ultimate concern." He was himself seriously invested in the objective pole of that concern, but the times have been against him and its subjective pole has all but preempted his definition. Religion is whatever concerns a person or a people most. This can, of course, be the Living God, but equally it can be nationalism or financial success. Politically, Tillich's move was adroit; it keeps us in business, for almost everyone has something their lives prioritize. But shifting religion's ballast from James' objective claim to a subjective stance has opened the door to what Joseph Kitagawa describes as "the trivialization of religion to such an extent that almost anything seems to fit under its rubric" (13). And some people feel co-opted. Because religion is for them a bad word rather than a good one, they resent being tarred as religious simply because they give their lives to something. We have the anecdote of Norman O. Brown jumping to his feet and shaking his fist at Tillich following his lecture at Wesleyan University as he shouted, "Your definition deprives me of my God-given right to be an atheist!"

As for Process Theology, it adheres to ontology, and to hierarchy as well, for it positions God almost infinitely above other occasions in power and worth. But it insists that the line between God and the world be drawn within nature so that we can be naturalistic theists (see Smith 1989). To posit a reality that is categorically unlike nature would reopen, the door to miracles, which modernity will not countenance. So God must not be an exception to the metaphysical categories that describe the empirical world. God is their chief exemplification.

As a transition to postmodernism, let me summarize the impact of modernism on religious studies through the worlds, again, of Darrol Bryant:

> The problem with the modern study of religion is that it unfolds with a *modern* view of reality that is, in principle, hostile to the truth known in religion. For in the modern view, reality is wholly explicable from within, there is no Beyond that must be appealed to understand what is. Nor is there any Beyond that is

mediated in the religious life of humankind. How then, can we understand religion when the implicit ontology or view of things that we bring to the study of religion rules out *a priori* the ontologies of the religious traditions within which religion unfolds?

Postmodernism's Rejection of Worldviews in Principle

If modernity rejected the traditional multi-storied worldview, postmodernism rejects all worldviews. It rejects the scientific, one-dimensional worldview into which modernity slipped because it recognizes it to be not scientific but scientistic. And it rejects world-views generally, largely for political reasons. For if a worldview is taken to be an objective report of the way the world is, it will be privileged over the way the world looks from other angles of vision. It will marginalize alternative perspectives and the people who subscribe to them.

So postmodernity differs from modernity, but it does nothing to reinstate the ontological transcendence that James cited as religion's generic posit. Instead, it offers us reality as kaleidoscopic. With every turn of the wheel of time and place, the kaleidoscope revolves and its pieces gestalt anew. Beyond these endlessly shifting gestalts there is no appeal, and as far as we can tell, nothing.

Call it historicism, call it constructivism, call it socio-linguistic holism, call it neo-pragmatism, this is what postmodernity comes down to. It is ambiguity elevated to the level of apotheosis. And thereby rendered self-contradictory, I remark in passing, but of what use is consistency when another turn of the kaleidoscope relativizes the original take. I mentioned politics as postmodernism's catalyst, and this is certainly what gives it its appeal. Who wants to challenge a position that purports to champion the oppressed, and in fact does champion them? But pluralism gives postmodernism stature also. When people lived in tribes and cloistered civilizations, they were not aware of having views of reality; there was, for them, simply the way the world was. Worldviews did not come to attention until global shoulder-rubbing confronted people with alternative versions thereof. But if human history opened with only the *world* (views of it having not yet come to light), and if for an interval both sides of the polarity were acknowledged (the *world* and *views* thereof), with postmodernism, the world vanishes. Only *views* remain. No world. You will forgive me if I insert a quote from Mirabai, India's greatest medieval saint, a woman: "I have felt the swaying of the elephant's shoulders, and now you want me to climb on a jackass? Try to be serious."

The epistemology that banishes the world is commonly called holism. Theoretical holism argues for the organic character of thought: concepts cannot be understood in isolation; their meaning derives from the theoretical systems in which they are embedded. Practical holism goes on from there to argue that, because thinking invariably proceeds in social contexts and against a backdrop of social practices, meaning derives from—roots down into and draws its life from—those backgrounds and contexts. In considering an idea, not only must we take into account the conceptual gestalt of which it is a part; we must also consider Wittgenstein's "forms of life," and Heidegger's historical horizons and ways of being-in-the-world, whose "micro-practices" (Foucault) give those gestalts their final meaning.

I referred to this holistic epistemology during a conference in Malaysia last summer, and when I assumed my place in the audience to listen to the next speaker, I found myself staring at a visual metaphor for what I had been talking about. Kuala Lumpur is in the tropics, and the stage was a veritable garden, not of potted flowers, but of flowering trees set in huge clay urns. I saw the visible parts of those trees as representing theoretical holism whose components are in explicit view, while their invisible roots represented practical holism's subliminal micropractices on which theoretical holism feeds. There remained the clay tubs in which the trees were set— clear index of holism's deficiency, for potted soil is quickly exhausted. Insulated from a viable ecosystem, it dies. Gazing on that metaphor for an artificial and unviable epistemology, I found myself wishing for Nietzsche's hammer. I wanted to smash those pots that draw hermeneutic circles around historical horizons and forms-of-life, as if they were isolated and self-enclosed—shut off from other forms of life, and from the trans-human worlds as well. The central conclusion of Wittgenstein's later years, David Pears tells us, was that "there is no way of getting between language and the world and finding out whether there is a general fit between them"(39), and Richard Rorty says that twentieth-century philosophy in general is ending with "the sense of humanity as... an historical being... whose activities in all spheres is to be judged *not by its relation to non-human reality* but by comparison and contrast with its earlier achievements and with utopian futures" (748).[7] I repeat: I wanted to break open those pots which left to themselves would stifle and kill their trees. I wanted to restore those trees to the "entangled banks" that Darwin so loved—ecosystems without restriction that extend, ultimately, to include everything.

> Ah, not to be cut off,
>   not through the slightest partition
>   shut out from the law of the stars.
> The inner—what is it?
> If not intensified sky,
>   hurled through with birds and deep
>   with winds of homecoming. (Rilke:43)

Postmodernism's Consequences for the Study of Religion

If modernism led us to play down religion's transcendent referent where we did not deny it outright, postmodernism is doing something equally disturbing. It is reshaping language in ways that make it difficult to consider the *possibility* of ontological transcendence without being charged with speaking ineptly. If we wish to ask—open-endedly but seriously—whether a reality answering to James' power-worth splice exists, we are blocked from the question by being told that we are off on the wrong foot in framing the issue as we have. Our wording betrays "metaphysical tendencies," metaphysics here being tagged to repression. It is trapped in a this-world/other-world binary bind. It slopes toward "realism," which "reifies" its referents and turns God into a "being among beings," which would lead us to seek its "essence" through "referential language" that purports to "correspond." As all those words and phrases are dismissive epithets for postmoderns, a language is being woven that places theism in double jeopardy. Theists are made to feel that before they get to the substance of their claim, they violate language in the way they propose to state it. The charge is not identical with the positivists' contention a generation ago that religious assertions, are meaningless, but there is a disconcerting resemblance.

Wittgenstein and Heidegger were the chief architects of postmodern philosophy, and attempts to provide foundations for science initiated their moves. Wittgenstein moved to his forms-of-life after concluding that science could not be grounded in the Vienna Circle's indubitable certainties of logic and sense data because such certainties do not exist. And the same search for foundations for science drove Heidegger's teacher, Husserl, to phenomenology. Heidegger himself, though, concluded that Husserl's transcendental ego was artificially aloof, so he seized that ego and plunged it into the lived world, converting it into *dasein*. Despite their different routes, Heidegger and Wittgenstein intersect on the common ground of holism. The strength of their convergent moves is their break with subjectivism, modernity's enthronement of the Cartesian ego. In making that ego its epistemological starting point, modernity handed individuals hunting licenses to use the things they encountered for their own ends. Heidegger is at his very best in reversing this approach. In contrast to Leibniz's monads which lack windows, *dasein* is little else but windows.[8] And the things those windows open onto are not to be exploited, but tended, cared for, nurtured, and shepherded. Having enabled those things to be, *dasein*'s stance toward them should be one of reverential solicitude.

This is magnificent counsel, infinitely relevant for reversing the course of modernity's rapacious pillaging that endangers our planet. No wonder so many of us claim Heidegger as a religious ally. But as Charles Taylor pointed out at the Applied Heidegger Conference in Berkeley in September 1989, Heidegger's reverential stance toward the things of our world is logically separable from other features of his philosophy, and the question for religious thinkers is whether those other features favor or occlude ontological transcendence. It depends on which Heidegger you read, and what you make of his entire corpus. The early Heidegger does not work in our favor. The closest thing to God that emerges in that totally holistic Heidegger is social practices, it being they that make us, not we ourselves. In that context, Being is no more than the region in which theology works ontically, which makes relativism theology's last world.[9] In the late Heidegger, however, Being assumes an identify of its own, and gives itself to be known by *dasein* in the poetic names through which we address it. Heidegger himself holds back from some of the names religious texts propose, but as this Heidegger allows for a referent our terms can approximate, he opens the door to discussions as to which terms fit best. If I am right in characterizing Heidegger in this way, he helped to turn modernism into postmodernism, but held back from the latter's unqualified holism.

As for Deconstructionism's part in postmodernism, there is nothing wrong with its project in principle. This essay is itself deconstructionist in seeking to identify the conceptual decisions from which modernism and postmodernism were constructed to the end of asking if we want to remain under their aegis. But Derrida's disinterest in *re*constructing (after deconstructing has done its job) pulls against the wholeness that religion—and life itself, for that matter—

reaches out for. His strength lies in his reminder that there is a surd in every woodpile, no socio-lingustic construct can pull everything together. This sounds promising in suggesting that there is *something* beyond constructs that stands judgment on them. But if we pick up on that point and try to ask seriously what that something is, we are advised that every answer will be a (deconstructable) construct, which sucks us back into holism's Black Hole. To an archer who remains thus under cover, there is no reply.

This Auspicious Moment: The Convergence of Science and the Wisdom Traditions

My take on what has happened in and to our discipline has not been a cheerful one. The Autumn 1989 issue of *The American Scholar* reports that "much of modern theology is a deep embarrassment to anyone committed to the life of the mind," adding that "thologians themselves... speak of professional meetings at the American Academy of Religion as a place where one [has] to rummage around in the garbage cans in search of food" (557). Given this bleak assessment, it may come as a surprise to find me saying that I consider this an auspicious moment for the study of religion. The reason is the way science is conspiring with the wisdom traditions to restore the hierarchical universe—which is also the hierophanous universe—to its rightful place as the generic religious posit. I say "science and the wisdom traditions" rather than "science and religion" because the word "religion" includes its institutional expressions, and institutions are invariably ambiguous. Ramakrishna likened religion to a cow that kicks, but gives milk too. If people think they can winnow religion's institutional record more precisely than that, they are welcome to the project. For now, I focus on the way the winnowed wisdom of the human race, as impounded in the "data banks" of the world's enduring sacred texts, has seen reality.

James epitomized its vision as hierarchical, and this is the way science too sees things. Nature presents us with a hierarchy of size: the mega-world of the astronomers, the macro-world of everyday experience, the micro-world of classical physics, and the quantum world that is smaller yet. And there are levels of complexity: Aristotle's mineral, plant, animal, and rational names them in one way, while the disciplines of physics, chemistry, biology, and psychology refine his list.

Two things define a level: (1) Each has its distinctive population; physicists deal with particles, but not with chemical compounds or biological cells; (2) each population is governed by its own distinctive laws; Newton's laws of motion do not hold for Brownian movements. In addition, two principles apply to levels: (a) where complexity is the measure, causation is both ways: from the higher to the lower, and *vice versa*; (b) higher populations cannot be wholly accounted for in terms of lower ones. Reductionism doesn't work.

At some point the levels of science stop. Psychosomatic medicine provides a useful case study as to where the cutoff lies, for it shows science now acknowledging a level of reality—mind—that it formerly ignored. The influences of mind and emotions on the body's immune system can be partially tracked, for thought and feelings are within our purview. The religious question is whether there are additional echelons on the scale of being whose measure is complexity and intrinsic worth. Should they exist, we would be able to sense them only dimly, though momentously, for they would exceed us in the way our minds exceed the minds of dogs.

Scientists who are also thoughtful human beings are open to the prospect of additional orders. "We know there's more," Victor Weisskopf once exclaimed to me at M.I.T.; "we just don't know how to get at it." The geniuses of the wisdom traditions developed ways of getting at it, but this is not the place to go into their prayer-and-fastings, their mediational techniques, and their transcendental dialectics. What we want to know is the "more" those spiritual exercises disclosed. Universally it has consisted of registers of being that exceed us by every criterion of worth we know, and doubtless some we know not. Or possibly a single register. When I asked my Syracuse colleague Bill Alston whether he subscribed to a hierarchical ontology, he countered shrewdly, "How many levels?" God and the world he was prepared to grant; additional levels met with his reserve. I have myself found three ontological levels—four if we include the everyday world—surfacing so regularly cross-culturally that they look as if they reflect underlying structures of some sort.

Spiritual Personality Types	*Realities They Focus On*	*Institutional Expression*
Mystic	Godhead	Initiatic Orders
Monotheist	God	The Great Traditions
Polytheist	The Spirit Realm	Folk Religion
Atheist	Everyday World	Unorganized

For now, I settle for Alston's two levels and table the others. The domain that exceeds us is invisible, and this emerges in the second, complementing definition of religion that William James offers in his *Varieties:* "In its broadcast terms, religion says that there is an unseen order, and that our supreme good lies in rightful relations to it" (59). Modern science, materialistic to the core, rejected invisibles out of hand, and we are still so under its sway that it remains almost impossible for us to take seriously the prospect that there are things that do not need physical underpinnings. But postmodern science is moving closer to the traditional view on this score. Ninety percent of the "matter" in our universe is now judged to be "invisible"; some say ninety-nine percent. By invisible, scientists mean that it does not impact any of their instruments. By "matter," which they place in quotation marks here, they mean that it attracts conventional matter. The only kind of attraction they know at that level of magnitude is gravitational, but for all they know the agent could be Aristotle's Unmoved Mover.

The invisible can be scientifically tracked by another route. On the micro-level, the strength of forces relates inversely to size. For example, "the amount of energy associated with light corpuscles increases *as the size is reduced...* The energy necessary to create a proton is contained in a light pulse only about 10^{-13} centimeter in diameter. And the energy of a million protons would be contained in a light pulse a millions times smaller" (Young: 2). One of the tributes the Qur'ān pays to Muhammad is that "he did not begrudge the unseen" (53:11). Now that science, too, has stopped begrudging it, perhaps it will not be long before we academic religionists stop begrudging it as well. But we should be aware of what that means. It means that (a) there is an invisible order, (b) with its own population and ways of behaving, (c) which has the capacity to intervene in orders that are below it in ways that are comparable to the way anxiety can influence the functioning of a digestive track to cause ulcers. In plain words, it means reinstating the supernatural. I was taught that supernaturalism is the ultimate "no-no" in our profession, for it would ostracize us from the academy. Science, though, which now seems to point beyond itself at every turn, has rehabilitated the word for me. Science flings open, not just windows in *aggorniamento,* but skylights onto orders of transcendence that are objectively there, while being infinitely awesome in outstripping everything else in both power and goodness.

Of course, nothing I have said proves the existence of superior orders excelling us in intrinsic worth. But have we forgotten our Kierkegaard, who points out that though we think we would like proofs, they would dehumanize us by removing our prerogative to decide? Because the last two centuries have worked to decide for us that supernaturalism is *outré,* I enter four problems that currently baffle scientists completely, and I suspect will continue to do so because their answers lie on levels of reality that science cannot access.

One concerns the nature of matter, which invades our material realm disguised as either wave or particle, but which refuses (on our level) to remove those guises to disclose its actual identity.

The second is the nature of life, for as R. C. Lewontin points out, "despite [our] knowledge of the structure of protein molecules down to the very placement of their atoms in exact three-dimensional space, we do not have the faintest idea of what the rules are for folding them up into their natural [living] form" (18).

The third is morphology; what causes the cells of an organism, all endowed with the same DNA, to multiply in ways that produce different kinds of cells for brain, bone, muscles, and hair? This is the issue Rupert Sheldrake's morphogenetic fields addresses.

Finally, how do biological species arise? Darwin thought he answered that question, and most of us have been schooled to agree that (give or take a few adjustments like punctuational equilibrium) he succeeded. I think that we are mistaken in so assuming. Evidence from all of the seven fields that Darwinians appeal to—the fossil record, population breeding, natural selection, embryology and vestigial remains, biochemistry, biogenesis, and mathematical probability—is turning against their claim (Smith 1989: ch. 8). Arthur Koestler was no creationist, but already a decade ago he was calling Darwinism a citadel in ruins.

What I most want to urge is a return to the ontological truth claims of our field as impounded in the world's great religious traditons, a return in which we do not underestimate their enduring validity. At minimum, this would give our students the opportunity to choose which world they want to live in—modern, postmodern, or religious—for as things now stand, the university does not offer them the third of these options. How much the alternative can mean to some of them I shall let one of my recent students attest through a note he appended to his final examination:

> Well, that's about it. I'd like to say, though, that this class has been absolutely incredible. I learned a lot but I also had fun. You took something usually relegated to conversations at 4 A.M. with a friend over a steaming pizza and dove headfirst into it, and in the process taught us how to swim through life a bit. Thanks for teaching us. It wasn't a class. It was an adventure.

NOTES

1. I am grateful to Robert Scharlemann for rescuing me from several mistakes as I was writing this address. He should not be held responsible for any that may remain.
2. For the consequences of 1960s experiments in freeing education of hierarchies, see Swidler.
3. Strictly speaking, this statement needs to be qualified somewhat. The necessary qualifications, which do not affect my general point here, can be found in the opening chapter of Smith 1976 and 1989.
4. For full discussion of Kant's struggle with the paranormal generally and Swedenborg in particular, see Kriven.
5. For the university because "the university is rooted in the scientific method," as Steven Muller noted on being inaugurated President of The Johns Hopkins University.
6. See my revised edition, with inclusive gender, *The World's Religions* (San Francisco: HarperSanFrancisco, 1991).
7. In another formulation he tells us that we have "replaced the distinction between appearance and reality with the distinction between ways of describing the world which we find useful for certain purposes and those which we find useful for other purposes." From an unpublished paper on "Heidegger and the American Cultural Left."
8. I am indebted to Hubert Dreyfus for this comparison.
9. Cf. Heidegger's 1927–1928 lecture on "Phenomenology and Theology." Heinrich Ott unwisely bought into that lecture.

References

Borg, Marcus (1991). "Root Images and the Way We See the Primordial Traditions and the Biblical Tradition." In *Fragments of Eternity*. Ed. by Arvind Sharma. Dorset, UK: Prism Press.

Bryant M. Darrol (1991). "To Hear the Stars Speak: Ontology in the Study of Religion(s)." In *Fragments of Eternity*. Ed. by Arvind Sharma. Dorset, UK: Prism Press.

Bultmann, Rudolf (1941–1961). "New Testament and Mythology." *In Kerygma and Myth*. Ed. by H. W. Bartsch. New York: Harper & Row.

Cassirer, Ernst (1963). *The Individual and the Cosmos in Renaissance Philosophy*. Trans. by Mario Domandi. New York: Harper & Row.

James, William (1901/1961). *The Varieties of Religious Experience*. New York: The Macmillan Company.

Kant, Immanuel (1915). *Dreams of a Spirit-Seer*. Trans. by Emanuel Goerwitz. London: New Church Press Limited.

Kirven, Robert (1988). "Swedenborg and Kant Revisited," In *Swedenborg and His Influence*. Ed. by Erland J. Brock. Bryn Athyn, Pa.: Academy of the New Church. pp. 103–120.

Kitagawa, Joseph (1980). "The Theological School as a Community of Scholarship." *Criterion* 19/2:9–14.

Koestler, Arthur (1979). *Janus: A Summing Up*. New York: Vintage Books.

Lewontin, R. C. (1989). *New York Review of Books* April 27.

Lovejoy, Arthur (1936/1964). *The Great Chain of Being*. Cambridge Mass.: Harvard University Press.

Muller, Steven (1980). Interview in *U.S. News and World Report* November 10.

Pears, David (1986). In *The New Republic* May 19:38–43.

Rilke, Rainer Maria (1989). *Last Poems*. Oakland, Calif.: Okeanos Press.

Rorty, Richard (1986). "xxx." *Proceedings of the American Philosophical Association* 59:747–753.

Smith, Huston (1976). *Forgotten Truth*. New York: Harper & Row.

Smith, Huston (1989. *Beyond the Post-Modern Mind,* 2d. ed. Wheaton, Ill.: Quest Books.

Smith, Huston, and David Ray Griffin (1989). *Primordial Truth and Postmodern Theology*. Albany: State University of New York Press.

Swidler, Ann (1980). *Organization Without Authority: Dilemmas of Social Control in Free Schools*. Cambridge, Mass.: Harvard University Press.

Updike, John (1986). *Roger's Version*. New York: Alfred A. Knopf.

Young, Arthur, (1980). *Which Way Out?* Berkeley: Robert Briggs Associates.

Bibliography

BOOKS BY HUSTON SMITH

The Purposes of Higher Education (New York: Harper & Bros., 1955).
Republished Greenwood Press, 1972. Danish translation, 1983.
Chapter VI reprinted in Chas. Merrifield (ed.), *Leadership in
Voluntary Enterprise* (Oceana, 1961). Chapter III reprinted in L.
Averill & W. Jellema (eds.), *Colleges and Commitments* (Philadelphia:
Westminster Press, 1971).

The Religions of Man (New York: Harper & Row, 1958; Mentor, 1959;
Harper Colophon, 1964; Harper Perennial Library, 1964). Swedish
edition, *Mansklighetens Religioner* (Raben & Sjogren, 1966). Korean
edition, 1973. Pakistani edition (Lahore: Suhail Academy, 1984),
Danish edition, *Religioner: Ost og Vest,* 2 vols. (Borgens Forlag, 1984).
Indonesian edition, *Agama-Agama Manusia* (Jakarta: Yayasan Obor
Indonesia, 1985). Japanese edition, forthcoming. Chapter VIII, Sec. 8,
reprinted in Donald Walhout (ed.), *Interpreting Religion* (Englewood
Cliffs, N.J.: Prentice-Hall, 1963); Chapter V reprinted in R. Eastman
(ed.), *Coming of Age in Philosophy* (San Francisco: Canfield Press,
1973); Chapter IX reprinted in Titus, Hepp, and Smith, *The Range of
Philosophy* (New York: D. Van Nostrand, 1975).

The World's Religions, a revised and expanded edition of *The Religions of
Man,* (San Francisco: HarperSanFrancisco, 1991).

The Search for America, edited and co-authored (Englewood Cliffs, N.J.:
Prentice-Hall, 1959).

Condemned to Meaning (New York: Harper & Row, 1965).

Forgotten Truth: The Primordial Tradition (New York: Harper & Row,
1976; Colophon edition, 1977; Torchbook edition, 1986). Chapter One
reprinted in D. Goleman and R. Davidson, *Consciousness* (New York:
Harper & Row, 1979). Pakistani edition (Lahore: Suhail Academy,
1981).

Beyond the Post-Modern Mind (New York: Crossroad Press, 1982).
   Paperback edition, Quest Books (Wheaton, Ill.: Theosophical
   Publishing House, 1984, revised 1989). Chapter Three reprinted in
   Philosophy Today, Spring 1982, and *The International Philosophical
   Quarterly 22,2* (July 1982).
With David Ray Griffin, *Primordial Truth and Postmodern Theology*
   (Albany, N.Y.: SUNY Press, 1989).

Articles (Selected)

"The Operational View of God: A Study in the Impact of Metaphysics on
   Religious Thought," *Journal of Religion* XXXI, 2 (1951).
"Accents of the World's Philosophies," *Philosophy East and West,* VII, 1
   and 2 (1957).
"Values: Academic and Human," Chapter 1 in M. Carpenter (ed.), *The
   Larger Learning* (Dubuque, Ia.: Wm. C. Brown Co., 1960). Reprinted
   in *The Christian Scholar* XLIII (Winter 1960).
"The Revolution in Western Thought," *The Saturday Evening Post*
   Adventures of the Mind Series (26 August 1961). Reprinted in Wm.
   Cozart (ed.), *Dialogue on Science* (Indianapolis: Bobbs-Merrill, 1967),
   and in *Iqbal Review,* XXV, 1 (April 1984).
"The Accents of the World's Religions," *The Australian Bulletin of
   Comparative Religions,* I (1961). Reprinted in John Bowman (ed.)
   Comparative Religion (Leiden: Brill, 1972).
"Twenty Years of the Atom," *The Nation* 195, 20 (15 December 1962).
   Reprinted as "The New Age" in Donovan Smucher (ed.), *Rockefeller
   Chapel Sermons,* University of Chicago Press (1967), and in *The
   University of Chicago Magazine* LXI, 8 (May 1967).
"Between Syncretism and the Ghetto," *Theology Today* XX, 1 (April
   1963).
"Empiricism Revisited," in Charles Brettal (ed.), *The Empirical Theology
   of Henry Nelson Wieman* (New York: Macmillan, 1963).
"The Death and Rebirth of Metaphysics," in Wm. Reese and E.
   Freeman, *Process and Divinity: The Hartshore Festschrift* (La Salle, Ill.:
   Open Court, 1964).
"The Humanities and Man's New Condition," *Liberal Education* L, 2
   (May 1964).
"Do Drugs Have Religious Import?" *The Journal of Philosophy* LXI, 18
   (October 1964). Reprinted in David Solomon (ed.), *LSD: The
   Consciousness Expanding Drug* (New York: Putnam, 1964); Joel
   Feinberg (ed.), *Reason and Responsibility* (Belmont, Calif.:
   Dickenson, 1965); Tillman (eds.), *Introductory Philosophy* (Harper &
   Row, 1967); Charles L. Reid, *Basic Philosophical Analysis* (Encino,

Calif.: Dickenson, 1971); Robert Wolff, *Philosophy: A Modern Encounter* (Englewood Cliffs, N.J.: Prentice-Hall, 1971); Hanscarl Leuner (ed.), *Religiose Erfahrung und die Droge* (Stuttgart: W. Kohlhammer, 1972); Joseph Faulkner (ed.), *Religion's Influence in Contemporary Society* (Columbus, Oh.: Charles Merrill, 1972); Row and Wainwright, *Philosophy of Religion* (New York: Harcourt, Brace, Jovanich, 1973); F. Streng, C. Lloyd, J. Allen, *Ways of Being Religious* (Englewood, Cliffs, N.J.: Prentice-Hall, 1973); J. Rachels and F. Tillman, *Philosophical Issues* (New York: Harper & Row, 1972); in part in John J. Heaney (ed.), *Psyche and Spirit* (New York: Paulist Press, 1973); William Alston and Richard Brandt, *The Problems of Philosophy* (Boston: Allyn and Bacon, 1974); W. L. Fogg and P. E. Richter (eds.), *Philosophy Looks to the Future* (Boston: Holbrook Press, 1974); William Bruening, *Self, Society and the Search for Transcendence* (Palo Alto, Calif.: National Press Books, 1974).

"Valid Materialism: A Western Offering to Hocking's 'Civilization in the Singular'," in Leroy Rouner (ed.), *Philosophy, Religion, and the Coming World Civilization* (The Hauge: Martinus Nijhoff, 1966).

"The Irenic Potential of Religions," *Theology Today* XXIII, 3 (October 1966). Reprinted in Edward Jurji, *Religious Pluralism and World Community* (Leiden: E. J. Brill, 1969).

"Transcendence in Traditional China," *Religious Studies* II (1967). Reprinted in James Liu and Wei-Ming Tu (eds.), *Traditional China* (Englewood Cliffs, N.J.: Prentice-Hall, 1970).

With K. Stevens, "Unique Vocal Ability of Certain Tibetan Lamas," *American Anthropologist* 69, 2 (April 1967).

With K. Stevens and R. Tomlinson, "On an Unusual Mode of Chanting by Certain Tibetan Lamas," *Journal of the Accoustical Society of America* 41, 5 (May 1967).

"Psychedelic Theophanies and the Religious Life," *Christianity and Crisis* XXVII, 11 (26 June 1967). Reprinted in *Journal of Psychedelic Drugs* III, 1 (September 1970).

"Technology and Human Values," in Cameron Hall (ed.), *Human Values and Advancing Technology* (New York: Friendship Press, 1967).

"Human Versus Artificial Intelligence," in John Roslansky (ed.), *The Human Mind* (Amsterdam: North Holland Publishing Co., 1967). Reprinted in *Renew* (Winter 1970).

"Secularization and the Scared," in Donald Cutler (ed.), *The Religion Situation* (Boston: Beacon Press, 1968).

"Empirical Metaphysics," Chap. 5 in Ralph Metzner (ed.), *The Ecstatic Adventure* (New York: Macmillan, 1968).

"Like It Is: The University Today," *The Key Reporter* XXXIV, 2 (Winter 1968–1969). Reprinted in *The Wall Street Journal,* March 20, 1969.

"Empiricism: Scientific and Religious," Chap. 4 in Bernard Meland (ed.),

The Future of Empirical Theology (Chicago: University of Chicago Press, 1969).

"The Reach and the Grasp: Transcendence Today," Chap. 1 in H. Richardson and D. Cutler (eds.), *Transcendence* (Boston: Beacon Press, 1969). Reprinted in Norbert Schedler (ed.), *The Philosophy of Religion* (New York: Macmillan, 1974).

"Tao Now: An Ecological Testament," in Ian Barbour (ed.), *Earth Might Be Fair* (Englewood Cliffs N.J.: Prentice-Hall, 1972).

"Man's Western Way: An Essay on Reason and the Given," *Philosophy East and West* XXII, 4 (October 1972).

"Wasson's SOMA: A Review Article," *Journal of the American Academy of Religion* XL, 4 (December 1972).

"The Well of Awareness: A Review Article," *The Eastern Buddhist* V, 1 (May 1972).

"The Jesus Prayer," *The Christian Century* XC, 13 (28 March 1973).

"The Relation Between Religions," *Main Currents in Modern Thought* XXX, 2 (November–December 1973). Reprinted in Yusuf Ibish and Peter Wilson (eds.), *Traditional Modes of Contemplation and Action* (Tehran: Imperial Iranian Academy of Philosophy, 1977).

"The Point of Death," with Samuel Todes, in Stanley Troup and William Greene (eds.), *The Patient, Death, and the Family* (New York: Scribner, 1974).

"Two Kinds of Teaching," in Thomas Buxton and Keith Prichard (eds.), *Excellence in University Teaching* (Columbia University of South Carolina Press, 1975). Reprinted in *The Key Reporter* of Phi Beta Kappa XXXVIII, 4 (Summer 1973); in *The Journal of Humanistic Psychology* XV, 4 (Fall 1975); in H. Chiang and A. Maslow, *The Healthy Personality* (New York: D. Van Nostrand, 1977), and in. T. W. Bynum and S. Reisberg, *Teaching Philosophy Today* (Bowling Green University: Philosophy Documentation Center, 1977).

"The Meaning of Tradition: A Conversation with Huston Smith," *Parabola* 1, 1 (Winter 1976).

"Frithjof Schuon's *The Transcendent Unity of Religions:* Pro," *Journal of the American Academy of Religion* XLIV, 4 (December 1976).

"Four Theological Negotiables," *The Eastern Buddhist* X, 2 (October 1977).

"Excluded Knowledge: A Critique of the Modern Western Mind Set," *Teachers College Record* LXXX, 3 (February 1979). Reprinted in Douglas Sloan (ed.), *Education and Values* (New York: Teachers College Press, 1980).

"Features Review Article: Coomaraswamy, Selected Papers and Biography," *Philosophy East and West* XXIX, 3 (July 1979).

"The Sacred Unconscious," in *Re-Vision* II, 2 (Summer/Fall 1979). Reprinted in R. Walsh and D. H. Shapiro (eds.), *Beyond Health and Normality* (New York: Van Nostrand Reinhold, 1983); in John White (ed.), *What Is Enlightenment?* (Los Angeles: J. Tarcher, 1985); and, expanded, in *The Journal of Humanistic Psychology* 25, 3 (Summer 1985).

"Western Philosophy as a Great Religion," in Alan Olson and Leroy Rouner, *Transcendence and the Sacred* (Notre Dame, Ind.: University of Notre Dame Press, 1981).

"Beyond the Modern Western Mindset," *Teachers College Record* 32,3 (Spring 1981).

"What Wilfred Smith's Against, and For," *Religious Studies Review* 7, 4 (October 1981).

"Science and Theology: The Unstable Detente," *The Anglican Theological Review* 63, 4 (October 1981).

"Scientism in Sole Command," in *Christianity and Crisis* 42,11 (21 January 1982).

"Evolution and Evolutionism," in *The Christian Century* 99,23 (7–14 July 1982). Reprinted in *National Forum* LXIII,2 (Spring 1983).

"Spiritual Discipline in Zen and Comparative Perspective," *The Eastern Buddhist* XVI, 2 (Autumn 1983). Revised for inclusion in James Duerlinger (ed.), *Ultimate Reality and Spiritual Discipline* (New York: Paragon House, 1984).

"Two Evolutions," in Leroy Rouner (ed.), *On Nature* (Notre Dame, Ind.: University of Notre Dame Press, 1984).

With Daniel Goleman and Ram Das, "Truth and Transformation in Psychological and Spiritual Paths," *The Journal of Transpersonal Psychology* 17, 2 (1985).

"Spiritual Personality Types," *The Hamline Review* X (Spring 1986).

"Can Religion Endure the Death of Metaphysics?" *Religion and Intellectual Life* III, 3 (Spring 1986).

"Is There a Perennial Philosophy?" *Journal of the American Academy of Religion* LV, 3 (Fall 1987).

"Another World to Live In, or How I Teach the Introductory Course," *Religious Studies and Theology* 7, 1 (January 1987).

"Can Modernity Accommodate Transcendence?," in William Nicholls (ed.), *Modernity and Religion* (Waterloo, Ont.: Wilfrid Laurier University Press, 1988).

"This Ecumenical Moment: What Are We Seeking?" *Japanese Religions* 15,1 (January 1988).

"The Crisis in Philosophy," *Behaviourism,* 16, 1 (Spring 1988).

"The Conceptual Crisis in the Modern West," in D. T. Singh and Ravi

Gomatam (eds.), *Synthesis of Science and Religion* (San Francisco and Bombay: The Bhaktivedanta Institute, 1988).

"Philosophy, Theology, and the Primordial Claim," *Cross Currents* XXXVIII, 3 (Fall 1988). Reprinted in Robert Carter (ed.), *God, the Self, and Nothingness* (New York: Paragon House, 1990).

"Has Process Theology Dismantled Classical Theism?" The 1988 Bellarmine Lecture, St. Louis University. *Theology Digest* 35,4 (Winter 1988).

"Remembering Aldous Huxley," *Los Angeles Times Book Review*, 20 November 88. Reprinted in *Journal of Humanistic Psychology* 29,3 (Summer 1989).

The View from Everywhere: Ontotheology and the Post-Neitzschean Deconstruction of Metaphysics," in Henry Ruf, ed., *Religion, Ontotheology and Deconstruction* (New York: Paragon House, 1989).

"Feature Book Review of *The Essential Writings of Frithjof Schuon,*" *Philosophy East and West* XXXIX, 4 (October 1989).

"Encountering God," in Benjamin Shield and Richard Carlson (eds.), *For the Love of God* (San Rafael, Calif.: New World Library, 1990).

"The Central Curricular Issue of Our Age," in Mary Clark and Sandra Wawrytko, *Rethinking the Curriculum* (New York: Greenwood Press, 1990).

"Chinese Religion in World Perspective," *Dialogue and Alliance* IV,2 (Summer 1990).

"Postmodernism's Impact on the Study of Religion," *Journal of the American Academy of Religion* LVIII, 4 (Winter 1990). Reprinted in *Contemporary Philosophy,* XIII, 8 (March–April 1991) under the title "Hierarchy Essential to Religion."

"Turning *The Religions of Man* into *The World's Religions:* Reflections on the New Edition," *Anima,* Summer 1991.

"Two Traditions—and Philosophy," in S. H. Nasr and W. Stoddart (eds.), *Religion of the Heart: Essays in Honour of Frithjof Schuon* (Washington, D.C.: Foundation for Traditional Studies, 1991).

"Dignity in Difference: Organic Realism and the Search for Community," in Leroy Rouner (ed.), *On Community* (Notre Dame, IN: Notre Dame University Press, 1991).

FOREWORDS, PREFACES, AND INTRODUCTIONS

1. Foreword to *The Three Pillars of Zen* by Philip Kapleau (Boston: Beacon Press, 1967).
2. Introduction to *A Buddhist Bible,* edited by Dwight Goddard (Boston: Beacon Press, 1970).